THE
NOOM
MINDSET

THE
NOOM
MINDSET

Learn
the Science,
Lose *the* Weight

First published in the USA in 2022 by Simon Element,
An imprint of Simon & Schuster, Inc.

First published in Great Britain in 2022

by HEADLINE HOME
an imprint of HEADLINE PUBLISHING GROUP

1

Cataloguing in Publication Data is available from the British Library

Hardback ISBN 978 1 4722 9797 6
Trade Paperback ISBN 978 1 4722 9862 1
eISBN 978 1 4722 9800 3

Interior design by Laura Levatino

Printed and bound in Great Britain by Clays Ltd, Elcograf S.p.A.

MIX
Paper from
responsible sources
FSC® C104740

Headline's policy is to use papers that are natural, renewable and
recyclable products and made from wood grown in well-managed
forests and other controlled sources. The logging a
processes are expected to conform to the environn
regulations of the country of origin.

HEADLINE PUBLISHING GROUP
An Hachette UK Company
Carmelite House
50 Victoria Embankment
London EC4Y 0DZ

www.headline.co.uk
www.hachette.co.uk

We dedicate this book to our Noom coaches—you are Noom's soul!—and to our whole Noomily (that's Noom family), who relentlessly seek to expand and improve life in the Noom-iverse. But most of all, we dedicate this book to each and every Noomer who has come to us for help and found community, support, self-confidence, and better health. You are the beating heart of Noom.

Contents

THE
NOOM
MINDSET

INTRODUCTION

Hey, Noomer!

Welcome to the very first-ever Noom book. Whether you are already a tried-and-true Noomer or just Noom-curious, we are so glad you're here.

Noom is most known for our digital health platform that has helped millions of people lose weight, gain energy, feel better, and get healthier. We constantly strive to share—dare we say—lifesaving techniques, technology, resources, and information with people who could benefit from our health-changing, behavior-shifting tools. That's because, in the Noom-iverse, we're obsessed with growing, changing, and evolving to discover what works best and what helps the most people achieve their health goals. It's all integral to our mission to help people live better lives, and, in terms of our grand vision, we believe we've achieved only a fraction of what's possible. We're constantly envisioning what Noom can be and considering how many avenues we have yet to explore, how many places we want to go, and how many ideas we have about how to help people take their health into their own hands. Helping people to achieve weight-loss goals is just the beginning.

While we are always improving and developing our digital resources, we recently had a brilliant idea (if we do say so ourselves): What if, along with all our technological tools, we also went old-school and wrote a book? This book could complement the interactive and coach-supported Noom digital course by delving even deeper into the psychological concepts that are so effective, and by creating a new entry point for how to make some of our best techniques stick. It could

1

also serve as a stand-alone guide to the psychology of weight loss and behavior change for those who aren't familiar with us yet. As soon as we thought of it, we admit, we all got pretty excited.

Now, we love technology, and we know a lot of you do, too. If that's your thing, then we warmly welcome you to join us on the Noom app (head to the back of the book for information on how to get a free trial). But there are things a book can do that an app can't do, like taking more time and space to expand on the science and psychology behind the concepts that make Noom work so well for so many. The app has a lot of information about cool science, it's true, but this book includes even more research (we conducted some of it ourselves!), more examples, more strategies, and more opportunities for self-experimentation. It's a peek behind the curtain. We've also got lots of thoughts, psych tricks (our best psychology-based tips), and best practices from our incredible coaches. Everything we do in this book is based on what we've learned through our constant experimentation. We've got quizzes for you to take, questions for you to reflect upon, and sage advice—all of which will help you understand and put into practice the psychological concepts that are the foundation upon which Noom is built.

Whether your goal has anything to do with weight loss is totally up to you. You can use the wisdom in these pages to change any habits or behaviors in your life that you want to change, in ways that can make your life better.

We will show you how to feel more empowered, how to set goals for yourself, and how to stay motivated, and we'll give you tools to ditch old habits and create better ones. We'll also help you monitor your progress and celebrate *all* the victories that behavior change can bring—not just weight loss but also more self-confidence and personal autonomy, better self-awareness and intuition, more energy, less pain, a more positive mood, better fitness, and a calmer, more peaceful mind. We call these NSVs, or non-scale victories, but they apply even if your goals have nothing to do with weight loss. Whatever you want to do, this book is a place to start, or a place to dive deep, and we think both of those options are pretty awesome.

Noom is about options. You can take what you want and leave the rest, since the combination of factors that leads to success for one person will be different for another person. This book is just one more tool in the Noom toolbox, among many others that can help you achieve better health and wellness. We hope you'll browse through all our offerings, but that's 100 percent up to you. For now, you're here, and we love that.

How Noom Was Born

If you'd rather just skip straight to the science, head to chapter 1! If you want to hear the story of Noom, read on.

How did this whole Noom thing get started in the first place? We're relatively new to the weight-loss scene, in the scheme of things (considering that the first actual book about how to lose weight was published in Italy in 1558 and other weight-loss programs have been around since the 1960s or even before), but we think that gives us an edge because we base all our material on the latest science and developments in behavioral psychology. Our jokes may be old-school at times (sorry about that in advance), but our information is best in class.

Yet Noom, as it is today, was a long time coming. Maybe you want to know more about us, since we're going to be hanging out for a while. Maybe you're wondering who even thought of this whole Noom idea in the first place. Well, then, you are in luck!

Long before this book was a twinkle in Noom's (metaphorical) eyes, there were two young men on a collision course to become business partners, best friends, and founders of Noom: Saeju Jeong and Artem Petakov.

Saeju was raised in a small town in the southern part of South Korea, and from a young age, he wanted to be an entrepreneur. He tells us that he didn't watch cartoons as a child. He watched documentaries about entrepreneurs. Saeju's father was an entrepreneur—he was the founder and CEO of a hospital, and also an extremely industrious ob-gyn who delivered four to six babies every day. He had a contagious energy and he naturally motivated everyone around him. Saeju calls him a zero-to-one-hundred kind of person. The hospital he created grew into a chain of hospitals; and even as a young child, Saeju paid attention to how his father had created a hugely successful business out of nothing.

Saeju and his father were very close. Every night after dinner, they would sit together and drink tea and talk. Saeju's father watched the nationwide daily news in his big chair, and Saeju sat in what his father called "the apprentice chair," right next to his father. When Saeju asked his father questions about what was happening on the news, his father would say, "Let's listen first." After they listened, he put the television on mute and explained what the news story was about, and asked Saeju's opinion. That made Saeju feel important and lucky to have that kind of relationship with his father.

The first sign that Saeju's life was going to be different from how he had imagined was when he wasn't accepted into medical college like his father and so many other members of his family had been. Instead, he enrolled in electrical engineering college, but he quickly lost interest in his classes and eventually stopped studying. The only thing that he was really enthusiastic about was heavy metal music, so at just nineteen years old, he started a heavy-metal record label in South Korea, BuyHard Productions. It was a surprising success, but then fate dealt him another blow: Saeju's father was diagnosed with lung cancer, and Saeju's whole world changed.

Saeju spent a lot of time with his father in the hospital, and much of their conversation turned to lessons Saeju's father wanted to impart to his son. Sometimes, Saeju's father lamented that as a doctor, he had always felt frustrated that so many of his patients came to him when it was too late to help them. He wished the medical profession were focused on helping people to maintain their health, rather than on trying, often unsuccessfully, to save those who were already sick and had sought help too late.

Other times, the conversation focused on Saeju's career. "I hear your business is a great success," his father said one day.

Saeju proudly admitted that it was true.

"Saeju, what is the purpose of your business?"

Saeju paused, then answered: "I want to prove myself. I want to be an entrepreneur."

"That's a good answer. But why do you want to prove yourself?" his father asked.

"Well . . . I think it's a good thing to have money," Saeju said.

"Why is it a good thing to have money?" his father said.

"Because . . ."

Saeju had to think. He doesn't remember what he said exactly, but he produced some reply; and to that reply, his father asked, "Yes, but why?" And to every reply after, his father kept asking, "Why?" until Saeju finally couldn't answer him anymore. (This was the origin of the Why Test, which you'll get to try for yourself on page 56.)

Saeju had gone from feeling proud to feeling completely stripped down and vulnerable in front of his father. He knew his father wasn't scolding him—that wasn't his way. What he was doing, ingenuously, really, was demonstrating to Saeju that behind every great business is a great passion—a true reason. A purpose. He wanted Saeju to find his. Saeju's *liking* heavy metal music, it seemed, didn't quite pass his father's litmus test for changing the world. But what would?

Finally, Saeju's father said, "Always think about your company's mission and how you will impact the community." He wanted Saeju to have a real *why*. He wanted his son to figure out his own core values in this life, before he left his son and his own life behind. This conversation would change Saeju's life.

Not long after, at just fifty-one years old, Saeju's father passed away. Saeju was twenty-one, and he felt like the sun that had always lit up his life with meaning had stopped shining.

Confused and grief-stricken, Saeju decided to enter the South Korean Army for his three-year service—something required of all young men in South Korea—as an IT specialist. This experience helped him deal with his grief, clear his head, and get his priorities straight. After he returned, he realized college wasn't going to help him accomplish what he needed to do in the world, so he dropped out and did something daring that his father had always encouraged him to do: He moved to the United States.

He chose New York City for its diversity and international atmosphere, and he vowed that he would change the world. He decided he would do this not through electrical engineering or even the music business but by trying to improve the state of health care that had so troubled his father. And if he couldn't do it as a doctor, well then, he would do it as an entrepreneur.

Saeju still loved heavy metal music (and does even today— really, he seriously *loves it*), but he realized that what he did in this world had to be important. It had to help people. It had to matter, and he had to know why it mattered. He had an ambition to start some kind of business that would put the power of health back into the hands of the individual, so they could avoid becoming like so many of his father's patients, seeking "sick care" when it was too late. He had the business savvy, but Saeju had an inkling that he needed someone with serious technology skills, so he began looking for potential business partners.

If we turn the clock back a few years, we find a young boy from Ukraine who had begun programming computers at the tender age of nine in his spare time, when he wasn't shepherding goats. He might not call himself a genius, but anybody else would (we think even the goats would agree). He came to America when he was thirteen years old, but unlike Saeju, who as a child wanted to be an entrepreneur, Artem tells us his initial dream was to become a farmer. However, his fascination with both technology and psychology won out over animal husbandry, and Artem soon found himself at Princeton University studying computer science, psychology, finance, and theater (because even tech nerds have their dramatic side).

During Artem's freshman year at Princeton he built a chess program, called Golch, with machine learning, which became part of his senior thesis; but one of his favorite classes was the psychology of decision-making, a class taught by Daniel Kahneman, a renowned psychologist and economist who won the 2002 Nobel Prize in Economic Sciences. During college, Artem interned at Microsoft's SQL and Sun Solaris server groups and learned a lot about running software teams. After college, he began working as a software engineer and tech lead at Google, where he founded and then led the Geosearch Project, which became an integral part of Google Maps.

Artem loved working for Google, but for him the job was missing one thing that had always been so interesting: the study and exploration of psychology. He didn't think there would ever be a world where he could pursue both his love of technology and his interest in psychology—until he met Saeju at a dinner party for Princeton graduates.

Artem was a friend of Saeju's cousin, who introduced them, and they connected right away. Artem told Saeju about all the things he wanted to create, including a fitness product that would reinvent the gym experience. Saeju told Artem about his frustrations with the health-care system and his desire to empower people to take control of their own health. Soon they were brainstorming, as if they had known each other and worked together all their lives.

Saeju saw in Artem exactly the partner he had been seeking, even if Artem hadn't yet considered becoming an entrepreneur. They both had a vision: From the beginning, their unwavering primary purpose and compass was to have the largest possible positive impact on human health.

They began working together informally in 2005, while Artem was still at Google and had just won the RoboCup World Championship (because that's the kind of brain he has). It took

Saeju two years to convince Artem to leave Google and commit to their business full time. In 2007, they started a company called WorkSmart Labs, Inc. Their first company office was in a dorm room. Their next office was a bit bigger—a two-bedroom apartment, from which they launched their first ever prototype: the CyberTrainer. It consisted of tracking technology installed on a stationary bike. Their first employee was Artem's robot-building buddy Mark Simon, another tech-minded genius type, who became their senior software engineer (he would later be Noom's chief architect). They raised money to build more prototypes for other kinds of gym equipment, but they soon saw that the future was in mobile technology.

In October of 2008, they launched CardioTrainer, a fitness tracking app, and by 2010, CardioTrainer had one million users. CardioTrainer was initially for hard-core runners, but through user testimonials and feedback, the team noticed that most of the users were actually logging more moderate exercises like walking into the app, for weight loss rather than fitness goals. So, in 2010, they launched a calorie-tracking app called Calorific. Soon, that app had a half-million users.

A year later, Saeju and Artem decided to pivot again. They wanted to combine the best features of both their popular apps into one single app that could help people lose weight and keep it off through both fitness and weight tracking. They tell us it was a bit like boiling the ocean, but with a lot of research and analysis, they discovered that behavior change requires more than tracking. Consumers wanted something—or someone—to help them with some of their health problems. Saeju and Artem needed to do more.

In 2011, they changed their company name to Noom. Why Noom? "We played around with a lot of name ideas," Artem tells us, "and one name our designers liked was Moon because it was interesting from a design perspective. At first, it seemed like an unnatural choice for us. What does health have to do with the moon? It's not a word you see associated with companies, and it felt like a strange fit—a little like how trying a new health behavior can feel strange or unnatural at first because you aren't familiar with it or used to it. But instead of going with our gut on this one, we experimented with it, testing it on people to see how they responded to it, and were surprised by the positive response."

Artem says that as the concept became more familiar to the team, they got more comfortable with it and liked it more and more. "We liked it because the moon is a presence that's always there, even when you can't see it," Artem says. "It appears to wax and wane, grow and shrink, just like goals do, just like visions for companies do. Then someone suggested flipping the word to spell 'moon' backward. It tested really well, and so 'Noom' became our name."

They launched the Noom Weight Loss Coach on Android soon after, and a year later, the app debuted on iOS. A year after that, Noom began the Noom Group Coach program, while also expanding globally.

Never complacent, Saeju and Artem often discussed the fact that people knew what to do to be healthy, but they still had trouble actually doing it. Then they met Tom Hildebrandt, who worked at Mount Sinai Hospital's Eating and Weight Disorders Center, and they realized that their missing element was psychology. Noom needed to provide psychological solutions in addition to purely physiological solutions. It was a revelation.

In 2014, Dr. Andreas Michaelides joined the team as Noom's chief of psychology. In 2015, Saeju and Artem began to hire professional coaches, and in 2017, they introduced the Noom Healthy Weight program. This, as they discovered from their research, was what people were seeking: an effective weight-loss tool with real human support systems built in. By then, they had over one hundred Noom coaches and an ever-increasing number of people engaging with the program.

Since then, the Noom team has continued to expand and keeps internally experimenting, researching, developing, and innovating. In 2019, Noom hired their one-thousandth employee and hosted their first Noom Leadership Summit in New York City. By 2020, Noom had more than three thousand coaches, multiple programs, and a vision for the future that included—and still includes—expanding in ways that can help people manage or even improve chronic conditions like anxiety, diabetes, and hypertension.

At Noom, we continue to broaden our behavior-change platform to help people change their lives in all kinds of different ways—in whatever ways they wish. As Artem puts it: "If you know how your brain and body work, you can outsmart yourself and reach the goals that have been difficult to reach before. Put the guilt down. When you understand the psychological principles behind your behavior, you can make changes more easily. Noom is here to help you be the best version of yourself and unlock your potential. We aim to save years of life for all of humanity. It's a big goal and we aren't there yet, but we're always trying new things and looking through the lens of our mission. We want to inspire you to do exactly the same thing for yourself."

Our Wish for You

Our company has changed a lot, but our mission never has. It has always been to help as many people as possible live healthier lives through behavior change. We pride ourselves on the long-term results our program has helped people achieve. That's why we don't consider Noom to be a diet; it's a method for changing behavior and developing a healthy lifestyle. Our curriculum has been meticulously created and is continually updated by psychologists and researchers, all experts in the fields of health and psychology. We want to help you get to the root of your weight-loss or other health struggles and to prevail. It's not about numbers. It's about life. Ever since we brought psychology into the fold, we have been about so much more than numbers on the scale.

With Noom, you'll learn about social eating, stress management, cognition and food, managing emotions in relation to food, how exercise and sleep affect you, and most important, why we eat and act the way we do as humans. You'll explore how to take back the reins rather than feeling like you're being controlled by your emotions (although sometimes your emotions are just the guide you need; we'll talk about that, too).

Engaging with Noom in any form (whether this book, our online curriculum, or both) will help you start forming new neural connections, and over time this will help you change your habits. Habits are powerful and ingrained, but the more you retrain your brain to practice and even default to the healthy habits you *want and choose* to practice, the more likely you will find weight-loss success, better health, and an easier mind. We'll show you how, and we'll help you understand why. It doesn't do much good to give someone an instruction manual if they don't understand why they're using it or if they're not motivated to follow through. Instead, mastering change involves sampling lots of different tools and trying them out with guidance and curiosity. Noom offers you those tools. We have discovered the right combination of psychology, technology, and human coaching that empowers people to take control of their health.

Noom's goals are expansive, we admit. We start with weight loss, but the more you know us, the more you will see that weight-related goals are just roads to understanding yourself better. Our real mission is to share with you how to use psychology to change your behaviors in ways that can make your health and your whole life into what you dream they can be. Noom has become a tool to help people master stress, anxiety, confidence, and self-care, in addition to health.

In short (or is it too late for that?), we are here for you, with powerful tools for change. We are here for you, as you learn how *you* can change *yourself.* We are not about rules. We are not about "shoulds." We are certainly not about guilt, shame, punishment, or any of those things science has proven do not work to help people change. We are only about helping and supporting your goals to live a happier, healthier, stronger, more confident, *Noomier* life. That's what we wish for you.

Are you ready to go there with us, to explore the Noom-iverse, to embrace the changes you've longed for, and to empower yourself to make it all happen? We know you're going to accomplish great things for yourself, and we will always have your back.

You truly are the greatest force and biggest asset in your own journey. As you transform your own health, you will become part of the solution: a world where people know how to create health for themselves. No matter where you are on your journey, thank you for making us a part of it.

And happy reading!

1

You Rule:
Your Role in the Change
You Want to Make

Nothing changes if nothing changes.

—Anonymous

We suspect (since you are here) that there is something about your life that you would like to be different. Maybe you would like to get back to a healthy weight, where you felt so good in your body. Maybe you would like to get fit, or break some bad habits, or feel better, or just feel more like yourself. Maybe you know what you need to do, but you're having trouble doing it; maybe you're not sure where even to begin. Maybe you've already made some positive changes, but you want to make sure they stick.

Whatever story brought you here, you are in the right place, because Noom is all about helping people make changes. Our methods may not be like the ones you've tried before. We don't throw a bunch of rules at you, control what you eat or how you work out, or even say that you need to change at all. Instead, we approach behavior change from a psychological perspective: What do you want to change about your life, and why do you want to change it? And why haven't you changed it already?

We're all about the *why* of behavior. Knowing your *why* is motivating. According to self-determination theory, or SDT, people are most successful at meeting goals when those goals relate to their innate psychological needs,[1] especially autonomous motivation.[2] Autonomous motivation is about doing something because you've decided to do it for yourself, and because it is consistent with your personality and values. Making that connection between *why* and your inner reasons for making a change—reasons that come from you, not from what someone else tells you that you should do—will, according to SDT, increase your motivation and make you more successful at achieving what you set out to achieve, whatever you decide that will be. This is what we here at Noom believe to be true based on the research we've done,[3] and what we have seen in our most successful program participants. Understanding your *why* is an integral part of our program. In fact, "Why?" is our favorite question. Why do you make certain decisions, have certain thoughts, or form certain habits? To begin answering this question, we help you develop your self-awareness and learn how to experiment on yourself. We love experiments, as you'll soon see! Our entire program is rooted in experimentation, and everything we implement is rigorously tested. Experimentation is key, not just to how we run our company and develop our curriculum but to how you can quickly and efficiently figure out what works for you. "We've purposefully optimized Noom to maximize learning speed via experimentation," says cofounder and president Artem Petakov. "Experimentation is how I figure out what works in my personal life. It's how we figured out what works for Noom. And it's how you can figure out what works for you."

But we don't experiment just for the sake of experimenting. We base our experiments on research. We pull from cognitive behavioral therapy (CBT), dialectical behavioral therapy (DBT), and a lot of other psychology concepts we'll introduce you to along the way. We teach you how to identify and change destructive thought patterns that keep you from reaching your greatest goals, achieving your biggest dreams, and having the life you want for yourself, but the *way* we show you how to do this is always based on the evidence. We're here to help you reach *your* goals *your way*, rather than trying to make you do things our way. There is no one right way to do anything because everyone is different, so we help you pay more attention to your own body and tune in to your psyche—because that is where all the answers lie. You just have to access them. Noom doesn't give you a program. Noom gives you the tools to access the success "program" that's already running in your own brain.

That's how you build a life you love. We can show you how to shift painlessly into a calorie deficit that will lead to weight loss, how to have more fun moving, or how to feel calmer or more energized. Whatever your goal, we will always encourage you to ask "Why?" and we will always let you take the lead. We're just here to hand you tools when you need them so you can set goals that are in line with who you are, and so you can stay motivated, inspired, and reassured that science is in your corner. You know yourself better than anyone else ever could, so while it's your life, your plans, your goals, we're in your corner. Because we trust you, and we want you to trust yourself. Because we believe in you, and we want you to believe in yourself. Because we know you can do whatever it is you decide you want to do for yourself.

Because *you rule*. You are the single greatest force in your health and in your life. You are the most influential, are the most powerful, and have the most control over what you will and will not do. All you have to do is understand, unlock, and harness that superpower you already have within you. Our goal—because we have goals, too—is simply to help you figure out how to do that.

If you've struggled in the past with how to eat healthier, exercise more effectively, lose weight you don't want to be carrying around, or have a more comfortable relationship with food or your body, fear not. Noom has a ton of new tools. We can help you reframe how you look at food, exercise, weight, and even yourself, so you can stop fighting with food, the scale, the mirror, or your inner critic and start living in a way that can help you feel more confident and comfortable in your own skin. We like to say we are lovers, not fighters, and we want to help you put the battles aside so you can start truly enjoying your beautiful self and your beautiful life.

Here are some of the ways we do that:

- **We use psychology** to help you change your habits and behavior in ways that can make you healthier and better able to reach your goals, rather than just giving you food lists and meal plans and rah-rah talk (okay, we take that back, we do sometimes use rah-rah talk).

- **We will never tell you what to eat,** or what not to eat. We're cool with carbs, fine with fat, and pro-protein. We're not even going to tell you to quit sugar (mmm, sugar) or require that you eat two pounds of kale every day. Veggies are awesome, but you don't have to do wheatgrass shots or even make smoothies in the morning if you aren't into smoothies. We want you to eat what you want to eat. We want you to enjoy it, not feel guilty about it, and to choose foods deliberately and with knowledge and forethought so that what you eat can help to make you feel great, physically and psychologically. Because no matter what your goals, feeling great will make them easier to achieve.

- **We work with any eating style.** If you're an ethical vegan or a lacto-ovo-vegetarian or you're totally into paleo or keto or low-carb or high-carb, that's cool, too. You can be on any of those things and still "do Noom," just as you can if you are a regular omnivorous-type human. Remember, we care more about why you eat than what you eat.

- **We don't require exercise.** We encourage healthy movement throughout the day because we know it's beneficial to your physical and mental health;[4] whether or not you do formal exercise, and how you move your body, is your business. You can, if you want, use Noom to help you make exercise a habit, or to inspire you to move more intuitively in your life, but we promise we will never make you go to the gym (although if you like going to the gym, go for it—gyms can be fun, and besides, we are not your boss).

- **We know that how and why you eat** isn't just about food. It's also about stress, sleep, relationships, and a lot of other things that could be going on in your life. We don't ignore that stuff. We know it's important.

- **We don't believe in failure.** Noom is a no-punishment zone. We focus on all the great things that can happen to you when you make changes that can improve your health and how you feel. We even go so far as to say that there are no mistakes and no failures. Just because you don't always do what you intended to do doesn't mean you have failed. Challenges and obstacles are inevitable, and they're opportunities to learn. All change involves a wave pattern of motivation surges and dips—days when all goes smoothly and days when all your plans fall apart. That's how change (and life) works. Change is an active and dynamic process, not a straight line, and a perfectionist mentality can be self-defeating because, well . . . *nobody* is perfect, and we believe in progress, not perfection. Slip-ups are a sign of normal.

- **We believe in cooperation, not competition.** We don't use "leaderboards" in the app and we don't encourage a competitive mindset in this book because we believe that positive reinforcement and personalized support from coaches, groups, and individuals is more productive and better helps you to stay positive and focused on your goals. When someone wins, someone else loses, and that's not what Noom is about. Every step toward your goal is a win in our book!

- **You can use the Noom methods for any behavior change.** Maybe you aren't concerned with weight loss at all. That's cool, too. You can use the tools in this book for anything you want to change. Whatever your goal, we are here to help. It could be to gain more self-confidence, get more sleep, make yoga or meditation a new habit, or work on getting your blood sugar or blood pressure or cholesterol back into the normal range. The bottom line is that Noom can help you make a change, no matter what kind of change that might be.

This time can be different because Noom is different.

But enough about us. Let's get back to you, and one of the most important *first* steps you can take when you want to change your life: believing in yourself.

Why We Need Psychology More than Rules

Noom has always taken a psychological approach to behavior change rather than a rules-and-restrictions approach because what happens when you want to change something has less to do with what you *do* and more with how you *think* about what you do. That's why, in our experience, making rules to change behavior doesn't work very well. Rules address the *what* but not the *why*, and humans aren't very good at following rules that go against human nature.

For example, human nature tends to cause us to act based on in-the-moment feelings, rather than on what might happen in the future. There is a really good reason for that. In-the-moment decisions ("Run now!") and immediate rewards ("Eat that food while you know you can get it!") in times of danger and food scarcity probably significantly determined the survival of humans, back when there were a lot fewer of us and life was a lot dicier. Thinking about and acting based on a distant future (like next week) just wasn't as important back then, in terms of making it to tomorrow.

Also, human nature, according to researchers in psychology who study the evolutionary roots of human decision-making,[5] tends toward these ways of thinking:

- Paying a lot of attention to irrelevant information ("Squirrel!")
- Being easily influenced by what's happening around us even when it's not in our own best interest ("I guess everyone else is doing it, so . . .")
- Skillfully rationalizing our bad decisions ("It's just this once . . .")

People like to do what feels best in the moment, what's easiest, what's most pleasurable, and what everybody else is doing.

That's all totally normal and, to some extent, is hardwired into our brains, so if we make a rule and say, "Don't look at the squirrel" or "Don't eat sweet things" or even "Don't do what everybody else is doing," what do you think most people will immediately want to do?

However, we also have fairly evolved brains here in this twenty-first century, which means we don't always have to act on what we want *now* when we use our considerable intellects to determine that doing something differently could mean getting something even better *later*. When those delayed desires are more desirable than those immediate desires, that is when we can exercise our also very human ability to change our behavior.

But it's difficult to override the instinct to take what you can get while you can get it, especially when acting on instinct has also become a habit. Let's say you're in the habit of eating a couple of chocolate chip cookies or a candy bar for your snack in the mid-afternoon on most days. You probably do that because, in the moment, those foods sound awesome. Or they used to. Now it's just a habit and you don't think much about it. And maybe that's no big deal.

However, maybe you think it *is* a big deal. You think it's a "bad habit." You think sugar is bad, or cookies are bad, or whatever. Or you're trying to get into a calorie deficit to drop some weight, and that afternoon snack has a whole lot of calories for very little nutritional payoff, so you think that changing that snack could help you reach your goal. So, you make a rule for yourself: "No more cookies or candy for a snack."

The next day, when it comes time for a snack, suddenly you want those cookies. But you made a rule! So, you can't have them. But as soon as you tell yourself you can't have them, you want them more than you have ever wanted them before. So, you eat the cookies. Maybe even more cookies than you usually eat.

This is where psychology can come to your rescue. One thing you could do is to focus on *mindfulness*, a core concept of dialectical behavioral therapy, or DBT. When it comes time

for a snack, you can tune in to your body and ask yourself: "Are cookies *really* what I want right now? What is my body telling me? What is making me want cookies? Is it habit? Is it stress? Does something else actually sound better today?" How you really feel in the moment, physically and emotionally, might be more important than a blanket rule. If you determine you really want the cookies, then you might decide to enjoy every bite of cookie, no guilt! Or you might realize you don't really want the cookies; what you really want is to decompress, so you go outside and sit in the sun for fifteen minutes. Or maybe, when you really think about it, what your body is actually craving is a nice, fresh, crisp, juicy apple with a dab of peanut butter, and you realize you'd rather have that than a cookie. This is psychology at work.

Or, let's say you do want the cookies, but decide to stop before you nosh and consider the short-term and long-term ramifications of having cookies for a snack. First, you think about how those cookies usually make you feel later in the afternoon (hello, three o'clock slump), or how they might be keeping you from your much-desired longer-term goal of dropping those ten pounds you gained in the last year, pounds that make you feel uncomfortable when you zip up your jeans. Then, keeping all this in mind, you might decide that, even though you may want those cookies in the moment, what you *really want* is to choose a snack that will help you reach your goal. That goal might be feeling chipper at 3:00 p.m. when the people around you are all nodding off, or feeling great in your clothes, with no uncomfortable stomach feelings when you zip up.

How we think can cause us to make decisions *against* our own long-term best interest, but it can also be used to make decisions *in* our long-term best interest. This is a basic principle of cognitive behavioral therapy, or CBT: to examine and question ways of thinking and behaving that are unhelpful so you can change those thought patterns and behavioral habits in ways that benefit you. Immediate gratification is a powerful force. So is habit. But neither is as powerful as you and your very capable brain. If you can learn something, you can unlearn it. If you can choose to do something, you can choose to do something different instead.

When you weigh the costs and benefits, you may decide that the benefit of feeling better later will be greater than the benefit of enjoying cookies for a few seconds, when—if you are honest with yourself—you sometimes don't even taste them because eating those cookies is just a habit.

Maybe you'll even do a little experiment. Is it really the cookies causing that three o'clock slump? You could switch out your snack to an apple with some peanut butter for one week, and take notes about how you feel each day at 3:00 p.m. If you feel better, that may be evidence that your body responds better to the new snack, and that realization could motivate you to swap out those default cookies for that more energizing apple. And if you don't feel any different? Maybe it's all that coffee you've been drinking that's causing you the trouble, and you could experiment by swapping some of your coffee for green tea or water.

This is just an example of some of the many wonderful ways Noom approaches behavior change.

Self-Efficacy— aka Believing in Yourself

Self-efficacy is a scientific term that simply means believing in yourself. It's like that famous old quote, "Whether you think you can or think you can't, you're right." The first step to changing something in your life is to believe you can do it. Obviously, that's not the *only* step. You can't just kick back with a pint of ice cream and think yourself into triathlon-level fitness or magically write the Great American Novel with no effort. Effort is definitely part of the equation, but self-efficacy is foundational. If you never really believe it's going to work, then why would you put in the effort to try? But if (when) you believe, then you can move ahead with confidence, energy, and the willingness to put in the work it's going to take to reach your goals.

Self-efficacy isn't a quality that is set in stone. It's not genetic, like your eye color or whether you think cilantro tastes like soap. It comes from what has happened to you so far in life. If you have had a lot of experience succeeding at things (lucky you), then you may have a lot of self-efficacy. If you have experienced a lot of challenges or haven't always met your goals, you may have lower self-efficacy,[6] and this can make it really difficult to visualize success. It's hard to have high self-efficacy when most of your attempts at, for example, weight loss have not worked out. You have already learned from past experiences that you "can't" lose weight, so this becomes your belief.

But you can cultivate self-efficacy, and that's one of the things Noom helps you do because (at the risk of immediately launching into a cheer-squad moment): *You can do this*, whatever it is you have decided you want to do, even if you haven't really believed you could do it before. Even if you tried to do it before and didn't succeed. Every time something doesn't work, you learn what doesn't work. The lesson isn't that it's not possible. You are smart (you read books!), you are flexible (even if you can't touch your toes), and you know that doing something one way doesn't mean you can't do it another way going forward. That's another big Noom principle: This time is different, because Noom is different. And you're different, too, because with every new lesson, every new experience, you become someone smarter and more experienced.

NOOM IN ACTION:
ASSESS YOUR SELF-EFFICACY

Psychologists have various ways they help people to measure their self-efficacy, so let's start out by measuring yours.[7] Answer each of the following questions, giving yourself one point for every "strongly agree," two points for every "agree," etc., all the way down to five points for every "strongly disagree." Don't worry if the questions seem similar. Just answer each one as well as you can. And remember, even if your self-efficacy seems low right now, this is something you can definitely improve.

1 – strongly agree

2 – agree

3 – not sure one way or the other

4 – disagree

5 – strongly disagree

1. If I set a goal for myself, I know I can achieve it.
2. If I know something is difficult, I mostly likely can still do it.
3. I usually do what I set out to do.
4. If I really want something, I believe I can get it, one way or another.
5. Life is full of challenges, but I always find a way to get through them.
6. I'm confident in my abilities to do most things pretty well.
7. When the going gets tough, I get tougher.

Now, tally up your answers. Total points: _____

If you scored between seven and fifteen, you have excellent self-efficacy. You are confident that you can achieve goals and are good at being your own best cheerleader. We'll chime in: *Give us a Y, give us an O, give us a U!* Now, the next step will be to start figuring out what goals you want to tackle next and making a game plan to achieve them. You already *know* you can do it, so let's go for it!

If you scored between sixteen and twenty-six, you have pretty good self-efficacy, but you could gain even more self-confidence about your ability to achieve your goals. You already achieve goals every day. Do you brush your teeth? Do you eat breakfast? Do you sometimes give junk food a pass? Are you polite to others, even when they aren't so polite to you? Every one of those things is a success, a goal achieved, a win. If you can brush your teeth every day, you can do anything every day. Throughout this book, we'll help you prove it to yourself, one day at a time.

If you scored between twenty-seven and thirty-five, you may not be super-confident about achieving your goals, perhaps because you haven't always met the goals you were going for in the past, like trying to lose weight or starting to exercise or cutting back on sugar. No worries! We've got great psych tools to help you change that, and we're going to give you an exercise right now that will immediately build your confidence in your abilities.

Right here, as you read this, think of one small thing you can do *right now* that is good for you. Just one small thing. Can you go eat some fruit? Can you do ten jumping jacks? Can you sit with your eyes closed and breathe deeply for one minute? Whatever it is, stop reading and do it right now. We'll wait. Okay, go!

Are you done? How was that? Not so hard, right? And guess what? You just achieved a goal. And if you can achieve that goal, you can achieve one that's just a tiny bit more challenging. And then you can go from there. Awesome job, you!

The good news about self-efficacy is that there are some great tools anybody can use to start building it in themselves.[8]

One tool is to find proof that you *can* achieve things that are meaningful. Transfer your thoughts about those experiences onto the thing you are trying to do now. Think: "I did this, so I can do that." Another strategy is to break your goal down into smaller goals. Big goals are exciting at first but can soon become overwhelming.[9] Instead of saying "I'm going to run a marathon!" or "I'm going to lose seventy-five pounds," which can seem unlikely or impossible when you begin to hit roadblocks, ground your self-efficacy in smaller victories rather than the end goal.

You can determine where to start by asking yourself: "Do I believe I can run ten miles? Do I believe I can lose fifty pounds?" If the answer is no, lower the number. "Do I believe I can run five miles? Do I believe I can lose twenty-five pounds?" No, based on past experience? How about "Do I believe I can walk for one and a half miles and run for half a mile?"[10] or "Do I believe I can lose five pounds?" Once you get to a yes, you've found the perfect goal for now, even if you know in the back of your mind that you would eventually like to run much farther or lose more weight than that.

When you've accomplished that, no matter how long it takes, celebrate that Big Win! Then ask yourself again: "Do I believe I can lose five more pounds? Do I believe I can run half a mile?" Now you know you did it once, so you can do it again. So do it again! Once that starts to feel easier, ask yourself if you believe you can lose ten pounds, or run a mile and a half, or however it makes sense for you to progress toward your ultimate goal.

This is how you can look at the small picture to build self-efficacy. Every small goal you achieve will reinforce your brain's belief in your ability to do what you set out to do. Every small success pings your brain, and it begins to adjust its perspective— and that's how you make progress.

Cultivating a Growth Mindset

Do you have a growth mindset or a fixed mindset? These are psychology terms related to self-efficacy that have to do with whether or not you think you can change. Having a growth mindset, according to Stanford psychologist Carol Dweck and her team,[11] means believing that your effort will increase your abilities, whereas a fixed mindset means believing that your abilities are fixed, no matter what effort you might make. Someone with a growth mindset might say, "Math is hard. I need to practice more." Someone with a fixed mindset might say, "I guess I'm bad at math."

Do you have an "I can learn to run five miles if I put my mind to it" or "I will always be this out of shape so I guess I could try but the odds are not in my favor" kind of attitude? Dr. Dweck explains, in her book *Mindset*,[12] that people with a fixed mindset believe their intelligence, personality, and talents are set in stone. They don't think they can change, so they focus on doing what is familiar and easy for them, and they avoid doing what is challenging. They also tend to be less resilient when they think they have failed. They let it discourage them from trying.

On the other hand, people with a growth mindset believe they can change their intelligence and their personality with effort, so they are more resilient when they fail. They think they just have to keep trying, so in the end they are more likely to succeed.[13]

You may already have a sense of what kind of mindset you tend to favor based on the self-efficacy quiz you just took, but let's go a little deeper. Maybe you want to achieve something—run a 5K or eat more vegetables or start meditating for ten minutes a day. If you have a fixed mindset, you likely see all the obstacles standing between you and your goal and then struggle to see a path around them. If you have a growth mindset, you'll recognize that there are some obstacles, but you'll also believe that you can figure them out. You know that the power to achieve your goal comes from you, not from somebody else.

But other people are influential, make no mistake! It's important to practice telling yourself that nobody is forcing you to behave one way or another. Nobody is forbidding you from getting in some exercise or meditation, although they may be trying to distract you or make you what seems like a better offer, like girls' night out or a Monday Night Football watch party. And you can always do those social things if you want to do them. Always! But you are empowered to make choices about what is in your own best interest and what you really *want* to do, both in the moment and for your future. You are your own person.

That doesn't mean you can't ask for help. If it's hard to do alone, enlist a friend. Talk to a counselor. Having a growth mindset doesn't mean you can do everything by yourself. We are social animals, and we all tend to do better when we work together.[14]

An environment change can also be a great supporter of a growth mindset: Surrounding yourself with people who are supportive of your goals or have similar goals can be influential and powerful in shaping what you choose to do. Our resident chief of psychology, Dr. Andreas Michaelides, told us a story about how he used to smoke when he lived overseas, where everybody smoked. When he came to the United States for graduate school, he had a much easier time quitting because he was in an environment where smoking was not normalized. He says, "Changing the people you're with can rewrite the script on your environment that maintains the habits you're wanting to change or you're wanting to emulate. Being around other people who act a certain way that you would like to act will motivate you and help you act the way you want to act." Let's say you have a family with some less than desirable eating habits. You're surrounded by people who maintain and reinforce eating habits you wish you didn't have. But surrounding yourself with other people who have eating habits you *do* wish you had can help you adopt some of those behaviors. People are influenced by those around them, so this can be a good way to help support your desired behavioral changes.

Of course, you can't just ditch your family, or your friends for that matter, if you truly love them. That doesn't mean you can't also cultivate other peers whose goals are in line with yours.[15] Dr. Michaelides says: "When you see other people doing something, you get ideas about how to do it yourself, and if you get praised for doing the things that other people are doing because that's what's considered normal in that environment, that reinforces what you're doing.[16] Those other things you used to do, at the same time, may often be discouraged in some way and don't get reinforced, and that helps extinguish that behavior." Cultivating an environment that will help you reach your goals, even if that means something super simple, like creating a habit of meditating on your goals every morning or getting all the candy and chips out of the house, will bolster your growth mindset in powerful ways. And remember, there are always obstacles to success. Understanding your circumstances and the obstacles you face, then using a growth mindset to do your best to succeed in spite of those circumstances and obstacles, is a rational and healthy way to leverage a growth mindset for goal achievement.

The Ever-Changing Brain, aka Neuroplasticity

One of the most awesome things about human brains is that they are plastic. Not made-out-of-synthetic-material plastic, but plastic in that they can change according to your experiences. Scientists used to think we had a fixed number of brain cells throughout life, and once neuronal connections were established, they stayed that way; but now we know that's not true at all. Brains are dynamic and responsive to stimuli from the environment and from what's going on inside your body.[17]

Knowing your brain responds to experience, you can change your brain by changing your experience. Eating certain foods that benefit brain health—for example, omega-3 fatty acids from fatty fish or algae can strength the membrane of nerve cells and protect the brain from degeneration,[18] and polyphenols (antioxidant plant compounds) from brightly colored fruits and vegetables— can modify the brain's ability to adapt to stress and prevent degeneration.[19]

Exercising changes your brain by releasing brain-derived neurotrophic factor (BDNF, a molecule that helps your brain be more plastic and adaptive, and also improves learning and memory) into the brain.[20] It even triggers neurogenesis, or the creation of new brain cells, in the part of the temporal lobe in your brain that is largely responsible for learning and memory.[21]

How well you sleep influences how well your brain self-cleans at night, getting rid of dead cells and waste in the brain via the glymphatic system (like the lymphatic system in your body, but just for your brain),[22] which does its work during deep sleep. Being angry, negative, or sad changes your brain, and so does being optimistic, joyful, or friendly. Emotions influence how well your brain works, including how well you can perceive things, pay attention, learn, reason, and solve problems.[23] If your brain gets injured, neuroplasticity means that in some cases, your brain can even reroute neural functions from an injured area to a healthy area.[24] If your brain can do that, just imagine what else it could do for you! Changing your mindset is a snap in comparison.

Environment and the brain influence each other in a two-way conversation. It's a *feedback loop*—another fancy-ish psychology term for when the output of any system (like your brain) in the past or present becomes an input for that same system in the present or future.

So, maybe your brain is telling you to look on the sunny side of things. That teaches your brain to do that more often, so in the future you'll be more likely to think optimistically. Another example would be riding out a craving. When your brain is craving something, like chocolate or potato chips, and you give in to the craving even if it isn't in your plan, your brain might be more likely to give in next time, depending on the cause of the craving.[25] (Cravings are complex—there is much to consider regarding the causes, which we will cover in more detail in Chapter 5.)

But, if you wait to dig in, you will be more likely to wait longer next time. And if, eventually, you ride out the craving (which rises, crests, then falls away like a wave), then the next time you have a craving, your brain will know you've got this, Self-efficacy in action! You will have strengthened your mental muscles, and it will be easier and easier, every time you do it.

The Brain-Changing Power of Visualization

Another way to bolster your self-efficacy is with a technique we love here at Noom: visualization. One of the many amazing things brains can do is visualize things that aren't happening. According to Dr. Michaelides, "The ability to visualize things is part of how we are wired, and what's interesting is that when you hook up someone's brain to see what it's doing, the parts of the brain that light up when you visualize doing something are the same parts of the brain that light up when you are actually doing it." How cool is that? Dr. Michaelides tells us that you can get better at doing something *just by visualizing it*. Athletes do this sometimes, imagining they are practicing their sport before playing it, and the evidence suggests that this actually improves performance.[26] According to a review of the literature comparing how this works in athletes and how it works in surgeons, this kind of mental practice, also known as *guided imagery*, can even help surgeons perform better, taking their skills to the next level.[27] If it works for athletes and surgeons, why not for you?[28]

How about trying it right now?

NOOM IN ACTION:

VISUALIZATION

Sit comfortably, close your eyes, and visualize yourself, your goal achieved, in as much detail as you can. How do you feel inside? How do you act? How do you look? What is your life like? Really get into it and imagine exactly what it feels like to have achieved your goal. Think about how you knew you could do it all along. Feel proud of yourself. Hang out here as long as you like, then slowly let the image fade and open your eyes. Hey, you just visualized self-efficacy and success. Your brain is already making new connections.[29]

Patience, Noomer!

Behavior begins in the brain, and as you now know, you can change your behavior because you can change your brain. And just knowing that can improve your confidence in your own abilities to change. However, this isn't necessarily a "lose ten pounds in two days" scenario (in fact, we guarantee it's not, and we would never advise that anyway!). All good things take time, and slow changes are more likely to stick. You aren't going to achieve your entire goal by tomorrow. That's because behavior change, while 100 percent possible (unlike "ten pounds in two days"), isn't a quick fix. Real, meaningful, lifelong change that becomes part of who you are takes a bit of time, and that can require some patience.

But what you can do, just in the time it has taken you to read this chapter, is to lay the foundation for change by adjusting the way you think about yourself and your ability to achieve whatever it is you want for yourself and your life. You and your brain are amazing and capable, and if you really want to change something, you can do it.

There is plenty of research on how long behavior change takes. Experts estimate it can take anywhere from eighteen days to almost a year to change a behavior, such as starting a new habit or quitting one. The average, according to a 2009 study from the *European Journal of Social Psychology*,[30] is sixty-six days. You will almost certainly notice positive, exciting changes before then, but sixty-six days may be about what it takes to solidify those changes and make them a permanent part of your lifestyle. And in the scheme of things, sixty-six days really isn't that much time if you think about how long you've been wanting to make a change.

If you want to change something about your life—get healthier, have more energy, increase fitness, become a chess master—stick with us, because while we won't try to trick you into believing in instant miracles, we do have the tools to help you make change happen. Even if it takes a year, that's a year well spent, wouldn't you say? But it might take sixty-six days . . . or even less! Three months, give or take, isn't long at all in the scheme of your long, healthy, happy life.

The "You" Experiment

Improving your self-efficacy is just one of many strategies we'll tell you about in this book, but we always want you to remember that at the heart of what we do lies experimentation, and that can be the key to your own behavior change, too. At Noom, we conduct research all the time to figure out what works best for people and how to best evolve our platform—and not every experiment is a success. The same is true for anyone, including you. No one way of eating or exercising or sleeping or living is suitable for everyone. You won't use all our tools, and the ones you do use won't all be equally as beneficial or useful for you. How will you tell the keepers? Self-experimentation is the best method for finding out what will be both enjoyable and sustainable.

But we don't just experiment for the sake of experimenting. We experiment to figure out what to do, and we consult the research to figure out what to experiment on, and then we experiment to figure out what works. In the same way, you might read a research study, but that won't necessarily tell you what to do because it might not apply to you. To find out if it does, you can do an experiment. Artem explains, "Let's say you want to feel more energetic, and you read a study that says meditation helps with energy. Some people might think, 'Okay, then I'm going to start meditating because a study says meditation helps with energy.' But we don't think that's the best approach. The Noom approach is to do an experiment—to start meditating and keeping a record of your energy levels to see if meditation gives *you* more energy. You can base your hypothesis on the study, but then you still need to experiment to see if that hypothesis works for you. This is why at Noom, we say our experiments are research-*informed* rather than research-*directed*. It's a subtle difference, but it makes all the difference."

Let's say you want to be healthier, and you've read a lot of different articles or research papers about what improves health. The truth is, there are probably a million and seven ways a person could become healthier in a million and seven different ways. Which ways appeal to you? What would work for you? What results do you want? You may not know until you start trying things, and begin keeping track of what works and how, and what doesn't work and why.

Think about (or write down) all the things you might already be thinking you want to try or that you've heard could work. Jogging? A salad for lunch every day? Deep breathing? A sleep tracking gadget? A workplace weight-loss challenge? Running a 5K or embarking on a yoga handstand or plank challenge? You can record when you tried things, how well they worked, and whether you'll definitely keep doing them (lunch salads are awesome!) or not so much (we aren't all born to do handstands, and we include ourselves in that group).

Another reason we like experimentation so much is because it takes the pressure off. "Experimentation emboldens you to act because it's not really a commitment. It's just an experiment," Artem says. "It's just something you're playing around with, so you may not feel like you have to wait to get started, and once you get started, you can be more aggressive about the intervention you're experimenting with. You can make larger moves in order to get results from your experiment, and that can result in faster and more obvious results. Pick something that really moves the needle and put a lot of effort into it to see if it works. You're most likely to see results that way, and when you do, that's reinforcing. If you don't, that's evidence that what you're testing might not be for you. Once you decide to do something regularly, you can settle into it, but if you're just testing, you don't have to worry about sustainability yet. You can go harder with your test because it's just a test."

For example, let's say you want to experiment with intermittent fasting. Maybe the idea of eating only within an eight-hour window and fasting for sixteen hours (such as finishing eating in the evening by 8:00 p.m. and not eating again until noon the next day) sounds too hard and too extreme for you to do forever. That's okay. Try it as an experiment. If you don't like it, you don't have to keep doing it. But maybe you *will* like it, and then your experiment has paid off because you found a new health behavior that works for you and that you really enjoy.

Knowing how to experiment on yourself is also important, because people change and grow. Self-experimentation can help keep your goals updated according to your current needs, keep you from getting into a rut, and keep your progress visible and motivating. Throughout this book, we'll be giving you lots of opportunities for self-experimentation, along with information about what we've learned has worked with our Noomers and what science has discovered about the most powerful tools for health and behavior change. What you do with this information is all part of your journey, and we're honored to be a part of it.

What do you experiment on? That's totally up to you, and don't worry that you'll pick the wrong thing. "Anything can be improved," says Artem. "Any little area of your life, any part of our program, anything you want to change, can probably be done better. That's just life, and that's how we learn and grow. Experiment in any area of your life you want to improve. Maybe you try to exercise to get better abs, but maybe you don't get the results you want from exercise alone, so then you think, 'Maybe abs are made in the kitchen, and I have to change my diet, too.' That's good data, even if the experiment didn't necessarily work the way you wanted to. And you still increased your ab strength. You just realized you might also have to do something else, or two other things, and then you can triangulate to get to the best solution. We generally expect that one out of five or even one out of ten experiments will succeed, but they're all worth trying. I think of experimenting as playful, not heavy. Don't get discouraged! Take a playful approach, and you'll see how fun self-experimentation can be."

The journey to change may have its challenging moments, and we won't ever try to tell you it's not difficult, but we will tell you (because it's true) that you are stronger than any habit you have right now that you want to change, and you are stronger than your resistance to change. When you approach challenges with a sense of adventure and an intact sense of self-efficacy (getting stronger every day!), you can actually enjoy the process as much as the results. We know you're anxious to see changes, and we're anxious to see you seeing them, but if you keep yourself busy with the thrill of getting there, you'll be so engaged with the *how* that you might not even notice the length of the road to the finish line. And then, before you know it, you're at your healthy weight, or you're running that 5K, or you're a chess master, or you're standing on your hands *away from the wall* (show-off).

Go, you!

Keep visualizing you achieving your goal, and how it feels to be there already. Think about it, write about it, draw it, dream it.

The more you keep it in your mind, the more motivated you'll be to get there, and the more your brain will believe you can do it, as much as we believe in you.

Now, the next step toward making a change is to know exactly what your goals are. Where are you going, and why? And we mean *exactly*. Like, put your finger on the map, and let's start charting the course.

2

Setting Goals and YBP
(Your Big Picture)

What you get by achieving your goals
is not as important as what you become
by achieving your goals.

—Zig Ziglar

Self-efficacy can help with generating the energy and motivation to enact a big life change or a small habit change, but now let's get down to thinking more specifically about what exactly it is you want to change in your life right now. We're guessing you already have a goal or three in mind. Maybe your goals are pretty specific, like "lose ten pounds" or "start a running program." Or maybe they're more general, like "get healthy" or "reduce stress." What you might not have thought about before, though, is that there are different kinds of goals and different levels of goals, as well as benefits to creating different levels of goals.

Beyond just "goals," there are higher-level or Super Goals, and lower-level or sub goals. They go together: Beneath every Super Goal are sub goals, and above every sub goal there's a Super Goal, even if you haven't really thought about it or defined it yet. And beyond even your highest-level goals is something we call YBP, or Your Big Picture. It's beneficial and productive to think about all these levels, and there is science behind doing this in order to achieve your goals more effectively, so let's consider what all this could mean for you.

We did a lot of research to get to the point where we were able to determine that having YBP is a powerful motivator for goal achievement. "YBP is less about goal setting and more about the goals you set in context," says Dr. Michaelides. YBP increases motivation around goal setting because, from a psychological perspective, having a goal isn't enough to stay motivated long-term. YBP helps people discover the driving force behind their goal, and we discovered that Noomers were more likely to come back after slips and keep going in spite of plateaus, with an ulti-mately increased likelihood of reaching their goals.

Creating YBP is a powerful strategy, so let's look at how you can create one for yourself. This is a process you can do interac-tively in the Noom app (our coaches are a big help with reinforcing YBP and encouraging people to stay motivated on the journey), but we'll also walk you through the basics here. It's a multistep process, so to get from what you're thinking of doing now all the way to a YBP, we like to start with sub goals.

Your Sub Goals

We find that most people who first engage with Noom have what are actually sub goals, even if they don't feel like they are sub-ordinate to anything in particular. Maybe you want to lose ten (or twenty or fifty or whatever number) pounds, period. It's your goal. There's nothing "sub" about it. Or is there . . . ?

Sub goals are goals that are very right-now and often based on something tangible, like a number on the scale or a clothing size or being ready to participate in an event, like a wedding or a vacation or a 5K. These kinds of goals are legitimate and real! But they usually underlie (when people really examine them) larger goals. Wanting to lose ten pounds, for example, could really be a sub goal that underlies a larger goal of wanting to feel more comfortable in your body, have more confidence, or live longer—all of which, when you get really into the nitty-gritty of your own psychology, may not require losing ten pounds at all.

"Sub goals are really helpful as a component of YBP," explains Dr. Michaelides. "I think a lot of times, especially with weight loss but also with all goals, people want to go straight from A to Z. But there are always those steps in between—the B, C, D, E, etc. What sub goals do is allow you to take a big, daunting thing and break it into small pieces so you can feel success all along the way. And failure, too, which is all about learning how to get to your goal, as well as learning how to recover when you miss a goal. That's just as important."

Your sub goal doesn't have to be a requirement of a larger Super Goal, but it is something that, in your own estimation, will help you get there. Seeing your goal as a sub goal may cause you to reevaluate it. Maybe feeling more comfortable in your body (higher goal) doesn't require that you lose ten pounds (sub goal), and when you realize that, you may decide to shift your focus to fitness or stress management instead of weight loss. Or you might decide to keep that sub goal because you personally *want* to lose ten pounds and know that you will feel more comfortable in your body when you do. You still see it as a good way to get where you're trying to go. The point is that a closer examination can help you understand the reason behind your goals a little bit better, and that's motivating.

But you may not know exactly what your larger goal or Super Goal is at first. Investigating your sub goals is a great way to start this thought process. Our cofounder Artem Petakov describes how this worked for Noom, and how it works for other companies as well. "One of Noom's first products was CardioTrainer, and even though we didn't necessarily think of ourselves as an exercise company, even though we had a bigger vision, we focused on exercise as a first step while we worked out what the bigger picture was. At some point, we realized that this was an important step for us. We boiled things down to a critical area and improved there, as part of the process of reaching our larger vision."

You can spend a lot of time improving a particular area, and when that gets to where you want it, you can step back and broaden your vision. Then maybe you'll find another area to focus in on and improve, then you zoom back out again. "It's like how Amazon wanted to be a company that sold everything, but they really focused first on just selling books," Artem says. "Or how Steve Jobs spent so much effort on the packaging of Apple products. Those were sub goals that were important to get right. Putting all the energy into those sub goals didn't mean those companies didn't have a bigger vision in the background that was still in play." In the same way, you can have sub goals that become primary foci, but that doesn't mean you don't still have an active and important big picture going on behind the scenes that's fueling the pursuit of your sub goals. Both are important, but, especially at first, sub goals can feel more manageable as you figure out your Super Goals and your big picture.

If you want to change something about your life, you need to be clear with yourself about *what* and *why*, and a sub goal is your initial clue to the *what*. It provides a general direction to explore. If your sub goal is about weight loss, you can begin to think more closely about why you want that, even as you are already working on it. Your sub goal gives you a destination, even if it's not the final destination. As our favorite psychologist Dr. Michaelides says, "Nobody really jumps into a car and starts driving without at least some idea of a destination in mind. Usually, people know at least approximately where they want to go, even if they aren't exactly sure how they're going to get there just yet."

Another thing we discovered through our own experiments with our coaches: When goals are too complex or too difficult, they don't work as well. Simpler goals seem to work better, and easier goals keep motivation higher, because achieving small goals acts as positive reinforcement for continuing to set more goals and working toward them. Sub goals can also serve this purpose: Each small sub goal is another win and more progress toward a larger goal.

Sub goals are the baby steps that point the way. But to make really useful and meaningful sub goals, you need to be very clear about your Super Goal.

Your Super Goal

In psychology, a lot of goal-setting theory is based on research involving small, short-term goals or sub goals. Practically, this is because those are easier to study. There are fewer variables, and short-term goal experiments are simpler to set up and execute. Smaller or sub goals are great for organizing your actions in ways that can help you to reach your Super Goal. For example, if your Super Goal is to get to a healthy weight, a sub goal might be to eat more vegetables, go for a walk on most days, or work on getting more quality sleep. You might take on several at once, or tackle them one at a time as you work on changing your eating and other health-related habits.

Both Super Goals and sub goals are important, and they work together. Super goals can feel overwhelming without a plan, and sub goals can feel pointless without a Super Goal. The sub goals can get you there, making the Super Goal feel more achievable, but the Super Goal is your guiding star as you work toward what you want in smaller steps that will eventually get you to your desired life change.

You may not always know what your Super Goal is, but you can use sub goals to find your way there by asking yourself:

"Why?" (Just as Saeju's father did to Saeju—we tell that story in the Introduction.)

Let's say you have a sub goal of getting back to the weight you were when you graduated, or on your wedding day, or some other time in the past when you felt really good and healthy. That's a fine sub goal, but why is that your goal? Ask yourself: "Why do I want to get back to that weight?" Really think about this and figure out what your answer is. Maybe it's because you saw a photo of yourself from that time and you like how you looked. So, your answer might be: "So I look as good as I did back then." The next step would be to ask yourself why again: "Why do you want to look like you looked X number of years ago?" Again, really think about this. The answer might be: "Because I don't feel as young as I did then." Why don't you feel as young as you did then? "Because I'm not as young as I was then." Clearly, you can't be whatever that age is again now, but what could you be? Maybe it's not so much about looks as it is about how you feel. You might realize that your real goal is to *feel* as good as you felt then. Because when you feel good, you feel happier and even younger. And there, suddenly, is your Super Goal: "I want to feel healthy, good, strong, and energetic."

Once you have a Super Goal, you can reverse engineer that goal to figure out what sub goals could help get you there. This may no longer be about the scale but rather about how you live your life. Sub goals to feel healthy, good, strong, and energetic might include eating healthier food, getting more exercise, sleeping better, and managing your stress. Suddenly it's not about the scale—it's about *your life*. Now we're getting closer to Your Big Picture . . . but we're not there yet.

Goal-setting is a very important part of changing your life, your habits, and your behavior. It gives you tangible benchmarks you can track so you know when you are making progress, and both Super Goals and sub goals are useful for this purpose. A 2018 study out of Switzerland published in *Frontiers in Psychology* reinforces this idea that combining superordinate goals with smaller goals that are related to achieving the larger goal is more effective than having either specific goals without a big-picture focus or having a big-picture focus without goals.[1]

This paper surveyed a lot of different goal-setting research projects over the years to draw theoretical conclusions about what works. They use as an example the superordinate (Super) goal "create less garbage." (This obviously wasn't health related, but it was a good goal for the purposes of this study.) Creating less garbage isn't something you do in a week and then forget. It's a goal to make a lifestyle change. It requires a sustained, longer-term effort, with smaller, supporting habit changes accomplished through sub goals, such as buying food in bulk, prioritizing products with minimal packaging, and recycling more. Without the sub goals, you would never get to the Super Goal, but without the Super Goal, it can be easy to lose sight of that long-term goal when it becomes inconvenient, such as when you don't feel like schlepping your cast-offs to the recycling center or buying in bulk.

Having a Super Goal is, to put it another way, motivating. A study on the goal-setting theory of motivation[2] published in the *International Journal of Management, Business, and Administration* claims that "goal setting is the underlying explanation for all major theories of work motivation." We think that applies not just to work but also to your personal life. You can have a general idea of what you want, but when you set a goal, you're setting up the framework for an action plan. A Super Goal can guide your decisions and help you determine what sub goals can get you there, as well as helping you stick to your plan when it gets difficult.

So, hooray for both Super Goals and sub goals! Are you ready to nail some down?[3]

Formulating Your Goals

Begin by thinking about your goal in terms of a destination. Where do you want to go? Or, to put it a slightly different way, what about your life do you wish were different? For a moment, let's set aside the goals you already have in mind. Think about what you would like your life to look like. Really think about it. Don't limit yourself. What's your dream life? Be specific, but dream big.

Your first impulse might be the low-hanging fruit: lots of money, true love, adventure, a perfect body (whatever that is), perfect health, your dream house, athletic prowess, fame, fortune . . . fun to think about, right? But the next question to ask is: "What would it take to get there?"

You may not know the exact answer, but when you think really seriously about what you would actually have to change to get those things you're dreaming about, you might start thinking in a different direction, in ways that surprise you and help you get down to a more realistic version of your heart's desire—something that's really *you*.

It can also be helpful to think about what you would be willing to do to get what you want. You may think you want a billion dollars, but would you want to live the life and be the person who would have to do whatever it takes to get a billion dollars? You may think you want to run a marathon, but do you want to be the person who puts in the effort and training to be able to do that? You may think you want to weigh what you did in high school, but do you want to live the life of someone who has to do what it would take to get to a weight that you haven't seen in decades? Maybe the answer to these questions is "Yes, I do!" and maybe it's "Wait a minute, maybe not!" Either way, asking yourself the question will teach you something about what your goals *really* are.

Scientists have studied this matter and determined that when your vision of your future self is in line with, and shares similarities with, your present self—when your dream life is exciting and vivid but also realistic and feels achievable to you, and when you see it in a positive light, as something you're really motivated to do—then you're likely to be more willing to make choices now that will ensure that future self becomes a reality.[4]

Remember self-determination theory from Chapter 1? Self-determination theory, as you may recall, is based on the idea that autonomous motivation drives behavior change. In other words, you are more likely to be successful when your motivation to change comes from within, rather than externally. At Noom, we call this intrinsic motivation: when your motivation is about something relevant and meaningful to you personally.

Research shows that when it comes to successfully changing health-related behaviors, intrinsic motivation—like getting healthier to live longer or to be an example to your kids—is more powerful than motivation based on external factors, like people's approval or looking good in a bathing suit in front of others.[5]

Are your goals intrinsically motivated? This is something to examine because you can always tweak them to make them more meaningful to you. That doesn't mean your goals have to be easy or perfectly in line with your current life. Maybe they are part of the life changes you want to make. It also doesn't mean there can't be external motivators at play as well. Sometimes, having some external motivation can turbo-charge your intrinsic motivation. We don't want you to put any limits on your imagination or the dreams you have for your life! But consider where your motivation comes from, because that can influence how likely you are to succeed.

But maybe you're still hazy about the specifics. Another way to look at this question is not to ask yourself what you want to *have* but, instead, what you want to *be*. You might say you want to have perfect health, a billion dollars, a flashy car, or a luxurious life, but asking yourself *who* you want to be can bring you to more meaningful things—more intrinsically motivated things. Do you want to be more energetic so you can get more done? Do you want to be less stressed about money? Do you want to be a fitter person so moving doesn't take so much effort and is pleasurable? Do you want to be calmer, or kinder, or a better partner, parent, or friend? Do you want to be someone who changes the world in a positive way? You could become any of those things, no matter how much money or what possessions or privileges you may have. What could get you to *those* end points?

Ask yourself: "What is the most amazing life I can imagine

that I would actually want, could actually achieve, would actually be willing to achieve, that actually feels like *me*, and that would actually bring me a sense of happiness and fulfilment?" Those are much deeper questions than "What do I want?" When you have that picture in mind, you can start thinking seriously about what goals you really want, and you'll have a lot more psychological infrastructure to support them.

After you've thought about all the questions we've posed so far, some Super Goals may be forming in your mind. A Super Goal might be something like, "I want to get healthy so I can live a long life and be around to see my kids and grandkids and great-grandkids grow up," or "I want to get fit so I can avoid losing my mobility the way my grandparents did." But it doesn't have to be that long-ranging. It could be something like, "I want to get back down to a healthy weight so I can have the energy and confidence to reach my full potential," or "I want to be a role model for my family so we can all get the most out of life," or "I want to be a calmer, more peaceful and centered person, and good health will help me achieve that."

Here are some examples of Super Goals with sub goals that support them. Maybe one of the goals on this list will coincide with yours, but if not, let these be inspirational.

Potential Super Goals you could set today:

♦ **Become a runner.** Possible sub goals: Start a walking program, work up to a running program, sign up to run your first 5K.

♦ **Get into great shape.** Possible sub goals: Start taking a fitness class, join a gym, go to the gym on a schedule, work with a personal trainer.

♦ **Become a regular yoga practitioner.** Possible sub goals: Try a yoga class at your gym, find yoga videos online, find a yoga buddy and sign up together at a yoga studio.

♦ **Feel confident and comfortable in your body.** Possible sub goals: Work on eating less calorically dense foods (see

Chapter 4), begin a walking program, start lifting some weights a few times a week, make a shorter-term goal to feel body-confident, as for an upcoming wedding, class reunion, or vacation.

◆ **Have healthy eating habits.** Possible sub goals: Start eating more vegetables, dial back sugar and fried food, pay more attention to your food choices, start noticing how you feel after eating different foods.

◆ **Avoid chronic disease.** Possible sub goals: Ask your doctor about getting some labs done to see how you are doing, work with your doctor to make changes to get your labs into normal ranges, get a clean bill of health from your doctor, learn what works for you and keep it up to maintain your progress.

◆ **Become an expert at managing your stress.** Possible sub goals: Develop a meditation practice or other concrete stress-management practice (by the way, we have an app for that; for more on Noom Mood, see page 275).

Whatever you choose as your Super Goal, know that it will likely change over time as you change and your life changes, and that's okay. Nobody says you have to keep the same goal forever. Whatever it is *right now* is a product of what your real priorities are right now. Now, let's refine your goal further by checking to see what psychology says about how to make the most motivating and achievable goals possible.

What Makes a Great Goal?

Most of the research on this agrees that a well-constructed goal with a good chance of success is both *motivational* and *achievable*.[6] According to an article about the neuroscience of goals and behavior change published in *Consulting Psychology Journal*,[7] a good goal gets you excited when you think about it. You want to do it. You also believe you *can* do it. It doesn't require you to become a completely different person, but it's challenging enough to inspire you to action. We do a lot of our own research here at Noom, and one of the studies we've been working on is showing that more positive emotions linked to weight-related Super Goals result in more weight-loss success.

One set of criteria for effective goals that we really like is to make those goals smart. Or, make that SMART.[8] SMART is an acronym for a set of goal-making criteria that have been studied and shown to be effective in many different goal-setting scenarios.[9] SMART stands for specific, measurable, attainable, relevant, and time-based, as follows:

- **Specific goals.** Research on goal-setting theory demonstrates that having specific, concrete goals is more effective than having vague goals. In their 2002 summary of thirty-five years of goal-setting research,[10] Edwin Locke and Gary Lathan used the example that people are more likely to accomplish specific goals like "I will lose ten pounds" than vague goals like "I will lose weight."

  This is reflected in Noom's own research,[11] where we've found that specific goals were linked to more positive emotions than abstract goals. It's not that abstract goals are necessarily bad. What we think, based on our own research with Noomers, is that specific goals—at least when it comes to health changes and weight-loss efforts—are more motivating because they are trackable, so you can see concrete proof of progress.

  Now, it's true that Super Goals may not be as specific as sub goals that will get you there, but you can make Super Goals more specific, too. Maybe you want to get healthy. That's a great Super Goal (and we'll talk about the Ultimate Why for your Super Goal later in this chapter), but "I want to get healthy" isn't very specific. In what way do you want to get healthy?

Maybe you want to get into the normal BMI (body mass index) range for your height. Maybe you want to be physically fit. Maybe you want to eat a healthy diet most of the time. Those are all more specific goals than "I want to get healthy."

Sub goals can also be made more specific. Let's say your Super Goal is to improve your diet. A sub goal of "I want to improve my breakfast" is vague, but maybe what you really want is to swap your typical breakfast of cold cereal and red licorice for something more nutritious, like fruit and oatmeal. "I want to eat more vegetables" is vague, but "I will eat at least two servings of vegetables every day" is more specific.

By the way, one reason people sometimes hesitate to make specific goals is that they can sound like rules. We here at Noom are not sticklers for rules. We like flexibility and choice. Rules do work for some people, but sometimes they just beg to be broken, so think about that when you are making your goal more specific. Your goal isn't a rule; it's a good thing you are adding to your life. It's not something you tell yourself you *have* to do. It's not a "should." It's a new habit you've *chosen* to establish for yourself.

- **Measurable goals.** These goals are quantified so you can clearly determine whether you have met the goal or not. You can't quantify "I will exercise more" or "I will start meditating," but you can quantify "I will do some kind of exercise for 150 minutes every week" or "I will start my morning with ten minutes of relaxed mindfulness."

  These goals are still flexible because you can meditate in any way you want or break up that exercise in whatever way you like. You can do any exercise you choose, but you can also tally up, or quantify, those ten minutes in the morning, or those 150 minutes at the end of each week. Again, these don't have to be rules. They are goals you are setting out to achieve for your own benefit, because you want to improve your life. When you quantify and then achieve your goal, that's rewarding.

- **Attainable goals.** These are things you can actually accomplish with some hard work, rather than things that are, in truth, impossible for you or your lifestyle, or that go against the laws of physics. An attainable goal would be losing five pounds a month. Losing fifty pounds by your wedding in five weeks is not realistic, nor would it be healthy or sustainable if it were possible.

  Exercising thirty minutes per day, five days a week, is attainable, depending on your schedule. Exercising for two hours a day, seven days a week, probably is not (and doesn't allow for necessary recover time). Hiking the Grand Canyon is attainable if you have a trip planned. Convincing Richard Branson to take you up on his next space flight so you can hike the mountains of the moon? We're thinking that's probably not attainable (although maybe RB is your BFF—we don't know!).

  That being said, there is also some research showing that goals need to be at least somewhat challenging or people lose interest, so let your goal be attainable but not so easy that you lose interest or don't feel proud of yourself when you achieve it. Easy goals don't offer that same rewarding sense of accomplishment.

  For example, if you already eat breakfast most of the time, a goal of "I will eat breakfast every day" won't give you that same "I did it!" thrill. As you think of your Super Goal as well as your sub goals, consider about how to make them just challenging enough to get you excited about the change you will experience when you achieve them, whether that's going to the gym four times this week or finally reaching your healthy weight goal a few months down the line (woo-hoo!).

- **Relevant goals.** These are in alignment with your life as a whole. If you are really motivated to set a goal of getting to a healthy weight by eating better and moving more, then throwing in a goal to also master the piano or to get your PhD might be a little bit confusing in terms of sorting out your priorities. If you *are* working on mastering the piano, or finding your soul mate, or getting your PhD, then you will likely be most successful if you keep your other goals relevant to whatever your priorities are right now and save the "run a marathon" or "go vegan" goals until, well . . . at least after your first recital or your graduation.

  Then again, we will say that it's *always* possible to be working on good health, even if it's in the background of other goals. Let's say you're in the middle of working on that degree. If your coping mechanism for academic stress is beer and doughnuts, you might be making your degree goal more difficult to achieve. You can set health-related goals that will honor and facilitate *any* Super Goal, rather than compete with it. Every step you take toward better health can make the achievement of all your other goals easier, and you can *always* use Noom to create boundaries when the big things in your life threaten your health.

- **Time-based goals.** These are linked to a time frame, and that can make goals seem both more clear and more attainable. A Super Goal might be to lose twenty-five pounds in a year. A sub goal might be to get 150 minutes of exercise this week. While behavioral changes are really lifestyle changes rather than temporary, "ten-day diet" kind of changes, a time frame can help you plan how to best meet your goal. You might set up your goal, like "I will run a 5K on June 19" or "I will lose twelve pounds by my birthday" or "I will get my fasting blood sugar into the normal range by the end of the year." These might all support your larger Super Goal of "I want to feel healthy, strong, and fit after retirement so I can enjoy my golden years" or "I want to avoid ever getting diabetes."

HEALTH AS A SUPER GOAL

Health is instrumental to reaching so many goals people have. With health, you will have the energy, confidence, and mental clarity to go for all your other goals, so how might health factor into YBP? Maybe it's the primary focus, because when you picture achieving your Super Goal, you have boundless energy, or you are super fit, or you have successfully sidestepped a family history of some health condition. Or maybe health is a means to an end—something you need in order to score that promotion, or summon up the confidence to ask out that barista, or take your cover band on the road. (Great, now we have Nirvana songs stuck in our head.) Either way, better health makes everything better, so maybe factor that in as you formulate your Super Goal.

Let's practice what it might look like to make a SMART goal. Let's say your Super Goal is to have healthy eating habits and your sub goal is to eat more vegetables.

"I want to improve my diet by eating more whole foods and fewer processed foods" is more specific than "having healthy eating habits." Specific sub goals might be to bring a big salad for lunch on workdays. That's more specific than "eat more vegetables," and it gives you more guidance. Maybe your goal will be to have a salad for lunch every day that contains 4 cups of leafy greens, 2 cups of other chopped veggies, 4 to 6 ounces of any protein, and a tablespoon of olive oil mixed with a tablespoon of lemon juice. Now, that's *specific*.

Is it *measurable*? Yes, because you can know whether you had a salad by the end of the day, and you can keep track of how many days of the week you ate the salad.

Is it *attainable*? Maybe not having it *every day*, as many of us will get tired of doing the same thing day after day. Boring! A more attainable goal might be to have a big salad for lunch every other day, or four times a week. And while you're at it, mix up those veggies and add-ons. Salmon? Chicken? Marinated tofu? Carrots? Beets? Sliced almonds? Salads can be very interesting if you vary the ingredients.

The goal is *relevant* if your priority is to improve your diet quality or to feel better by getting more nutrients and fiber into your diet. However, the cool thing about health changes is that they are always relevant to any goal. If you are really focused on something else, the salad can still be a supportive way to eat.

To make it more *time-based*, you might consider this a test and reevaluate after six weeks. So now, your goal is to eat a big salad, with 4 cups of leafy greens, 2 cups of other chopped veggies, 4 to 6 ounces of any protein, and a tablespoon of olive oil mixed with lemon juice, for lunch four times a week for the next six weeks, to see if eating more vegetables makes you feel better or helps you eat less calorically dense foods (see Chapter 4). It's a test of a lifestyle intervention you may want to continue with, or alter, at the end of six weeks. It's just one new habit, so you can focus on it and get it into place before you take on something else. And it's delicious!

SMART, right?

WRITE IT DOWN AND TELL SOMEONE ELSE

If you write down your goal and tell someone else about it, you might be more successful than if you keep it to yourself and never write it down. As you set your Super Goal and sub goals, consider writing them down. The more you write about your goals and detail your planned strategies for achieving those goals, the more likely you may be to achieve your goals. A 2020 study showed that writing about goals, whether the goals are personal or professional, specific or abstract, increases performance and goal achievement. The more the study participants wrote and the more specific they were about their *strategies* for achieving their goals, the better they did.[12]

We're also big advocates of having an accountability partner or group. In the app, we found that a more generic social forum didn't have the same impact as what we do now, which is to put people into groups of others with similar goals and at similar places in their journey. That dramatically increased people's involvement and extended commitment to their goals. Research also backs up the effectiveness of having a knowledgeable and positive supportive coach to help people adhere to health-related goals. A 2020 study published in the *Journal of Medical Internet Research*[13] tested the supportive accountability theory with people working to lose weight through technology interventions. Those who had support and accountability, rather than trying to lose weight without any intervention from others, were more likely to stick to their new healthy habits and had more positive psychological coping when weight loss became challenging. This is just one more reason why we're so committed to including individual coaching support and group support on our app. If another person, or group of people, is there for you and is monitoring your progress, and they get what you're going through and have your best interests in mind, you may stay more engaged with your goals and be less likely to give up when sticking to your resolve gets difficult.[14]

Your Ultimate Why

You have a Super Goal. But why? You can have all the goals you want, but if you don't have a conscious and concrete answer to the question "Why?" to back up your goal, you may lose interest over time or find it's easier to make excuses for "Why not?" in the moment.

Your Ultimate Why is the driving force that will push you to work hard toward your goals every day. To get there, let's try an exercise that one of our founders, Saeju, learned from his father (we tell that story in the Introduction). We call it the Why Test.

Once you have established a Super Goal you feel comfortable with, ask yourself:

1. What is your Super Goal? Put it into words. Remember to make it SMART!
2. Now, why do you want to achieve this goal? Really think about this, then write down (or think about) your answer.
3. Let's dig deeper. You answered why you wanted to achieve that goal. But why was that your *why*? Get to the next level—the *why* behind your *why*.
4. Good, but can you go deeper? What is the *why* behind that last *why*?
5. You're doing great. But again, can you go deeper? Is there another *why*?

Keep asking "Why?" after each answer, until you can't answer anymore because you are into the deep-seated core of your reason for wanting to reach that goal. This is your Ultimate Why.

Write it down! You're going to want to remember it. You could even have your smartphone remind you of it every morning.

Let's look at how this might work in real life. Here's an example of how someone might work through these questions to get to their Ultimate Why:

1. What is your Super Goal? "I want to get to a healthy weight."
2. Why do you want to get to a healthy weight? "So I can feel good in my body."
3. Why do you want to feel good in your body? "So I can feel more confident."
4. Why do you want to feel more confident? "So I can stop holding myself back from the things I know I could do with my life."
5. Why do you want to stop holding yourself back from things? "So I can reach my fullest potential as a human being."
6. Why do you want to reach your fullest potential as a human being? "So I can live a long and healthy life full of adventures and experiences, and not regret that I missed any opportunities to really live!"

Aha! Now that sounds like an Ultimate Why! Wanting to get the most out of life and not be held back by issues of confidence or health is a great motivator for change. And isn't it interesting that, in the end, this person's reasons for wanting to lose weight ended up having absolutely nothing to do with weight? The Super Goal is a catalyst to achieve an Ultimate Why that is something much more meaningful than a number on the scale.

Here is another shorter example, because sometimes you can get there quickly:

1. What is your Super Goal? "I want to have a better-quality diet."

2. Why do you want to have a better-quality diet? "So I can lose weight and have more energy."

3. Why do you want to lose weight and have more energy? "So I can avoid getting a chronic disease."

4. Why do you want to avoid getting a chronic disease? "Because my mother had diabetes and it really reduced her quality of life, and I watched how it affected her and I don't want that to happen to me!"

That's another powerful Ultimate Why. If you have a family history of a chronic disease, whether it's diabetes, heart disease, dementia, or something else, remembering that living a healthy lifestyle could help you avoid that fate can be a powerful motivator.

Your process of answering all these "Whys?" may look quite different, but try it and see how far you can go. You might surprise yourself.

SET GOALS, NOT LIMITS

Some people find that when they're setting goals or thinking about their Ultimate Why or trying to imagine how their lives will be different, "Yes, but" limitations keep popping into their heads. You want to get to a healthy weight? "Yes, but I'll never be able to quit eating so much cheese." You want to get in shape? "Yes, but I really hate cardio." You want to feel calmer? "Yes, but my job will always be stressful."

Contrary to how it might feel, these thoughts are not reality checks. They are thought distortions. We have a whole chapter about thought distortions coming up (Chapter 8), but for now, know that there will always be obstacles to every really great goal. Obstacles are part of every process of change.

They're not proof of failure (or proof of anything, other than life).

Just because something didn't work before doesn't mean it can't work now. You will never be able to do the same thing exactly the same way twice because you, your environment, and your experience are always changing. Not achieving a goal teaches you things. What did you learn? Why do you think it didn't work last time? What could you do differently this time? That experience and hard-won knowledge can make it *more* likely that you will achieve your goal this time.

There is no failure, only information. As long as you know that there will always be obstacles, but that there are always ways around them, then they don't have to derail you as you work toward your goals. Your Super Goal and your Ultimate Why are more powerful than any obstacle, including your own worries about what "might" happen and all the "can'ts," "won'ts," "buts," and "what-ifs." When the obstacles come, we'll be there with more psych tricks to help you.

How Your Life Will Be Different

The last step on the journey to YBP is to ask yourself: "How will your life be different when you have achieved your goal?" (Note that we say "when," not "if," because we *know* you can achieve your Super Goal!) Of course, you can't tell the future, but you can imagine the future. To do this, we like to employ a powerful technique called *creative visualization*.

Creative visualization is a method of using your imagination for a purpose. According to a 2010 study in the *Journal of Psychology*,[15] students who formed a vivid personal vision of their lives set more ambitious goals and were more committed to those goals. We also found, in our internal experiments, that creative visualization was a particularly effective technique for helping people really get a sense of how their lives could be different when they meet their goals. Here's one way to try it:

1. Relax, get comfortable, and take a few slow, relaxing breaths.
2. Close your eyes and start thinking about your Super Goal and your Ultimate Why.
3. Once you've got them in mind, imagine reaching your Super Goal. You are at your goal weight, or you are fit and strong, or you are doing whatever it is you want to be doing with your life.
4. Think about how it feels to have achieved this goal. Do you act differently? Do you look different? How do other people respond to you? Try to imagine everything about your life with your goal achieved. See or describe your life in as much detail as you can. What happens when you are at home? At work? With family? With friends? What do you choose to do with your time? How does it feel to be you, in this scenario?
5. Hang out here in this awesome place for as long as you are enjoying yourself. Let yourself bask in that good feeling to have reached that goal. Marvel at the difference in your life. When you've had enough (or you really need to get to work or make dinner), take another few deep breaths and then open your eyes.

Maybe you'll see yourself feeling happy and free, moving with grace and ease. Maybe you'll see yourself eating healthy food and not worrying about it or even thinking about food that much. Maybe you've got a better job. Whatever it is, it feels *good*. Your Super Goal feels *so worth it*, because you can *see it*. Now let's put it all together: *what* your goal is, *why* you want to achieve that goal, and that clear picture in your mind of *how* your life will be different when you achieve it. Put together, this overview of the *what*, *why*, and *how* is *your big picture*, aka YBP, a powerful asset in your pursuit of change.

Your Super Goal + your Ultimate Why + how your life will be different = YBP

YBP is something bigger than a goal. If your goal is something like "get fit" or "lose ten pounds," you might express your YBP like: "I will get fit because I don't like the feeling of being out of shape, and I want to be healthy, active, and mobile for decades to come" or "I will lose ten pounds because I know I haven't been eating very well lately and I want to take better care of myself so I can feel more confident and comfortable in my body." YBP is the sum total of your biggest, most meaningful goal, coupled with your Ultimate Why for achieving that goal, plus some serious thought on how your life will be different once you achieve that goal. We like to make it into an equation that looks like this:

> your Super Goal
> + your Ultimate Why
> + how your life will be different
> _____
> YBP

Getting to a really compelling YBP takes a bit of forethought and planning. It involves choosing a Super Goal, digging all the way down to your Ultimate Why, and then really envisioning your life with that goal achieved. And we are here to help! By the end of this chapter, *our* Super Goal for *you* is that YBP will be clear to you, and it will feel exciting, motivating, and achievable.

Try yours on for size. Putting all the pieces together, you can express your YBP something like this:

> I will achieve [YOUR SUPER GOAL]
> because [YOUR ULTIMATE WHY]
> so that [A FEW OF THE BEST WAYS
> YOUR LIFE WILL BE DIFFERENT].

What's your YBP? Here are some we think are inspiring:

- "I will achieve my healthy weight goal because I want to have the confidence and freedom to live my best life, so that for years to come, I will be out there having adventures and experiences and staying healthy until the very end, when I will have no regrets."
- "I will eat a high-quality diet so I can fully support my body and give myself the best possible chance of avoiding the chronic diseases that have afflicted people in my family. Those health issues do not have to be my fate!"
- "I will become a vibrantly healthy person so that I can live a creative and fulfilling life full of love and success."
- "I will become a fit and strong person because I want to have the energy, strength, and mobility to play with my kids and watch them grow up, and to play with my grandkids and watch them grow up, too."

One of the biggest benefits to consciously knowing YBP is that it can help you stay the course when the going gets tough—and it will get tough. The best, most meaningful, biggest goals are usually challenging. They involve some significant work, and it's human nature not to necessarily want to put in that work because it's hard.

There's a concept called *temporal discounting* that psychologists use to describe the very human tendency to care less about future outcomes than present ones. The authors of a study titled "Is a Bird in the Hand Worth Two in the Future?" put it this way: "Humans and animals prefer rewards with short-term availability over rewards that become available in the long run."[16] This is one of the major reasons why behavior change can feel so challenging and why achieving goals feels so difficult. In any given moment, what you want for your future can feel much less pressing than what you want *right now*. That can make it a real challenge to stay goal-focused.

But there's another part of your brain—a more advanced part that's capable of more complex, higher thought and knows how to be forward-thinking. This is the part of your brain with the capacity for executive function. Executive function can override your in-the-moment impulses (like chocolate cravings or that feeling that you would rather watch TV than go to the gym) because it's more conscious and sophisticated, and it includes things like paying attention, switching from one task or focus to another, inhibiting irrelevant or distracting information, remembering things, updating your perspective based on what you learn, and planning for the future.

But executive function takes effort. It's not automatic, like breathing, and it's not instinctual, like hunger or fear. It's also limited.[17] The energy to keep focusing on using your executive functions needs to be replenished with rest and relaxation. You can't have it cued up 24/7/365. So, while your executive function can override temporal discounting, or your brain's tendency to default to desires in the present moment, this gets harder if you are stressed or tired. The less energy you have, the more your basic instincts and entrenched habits kick in and become harder to resist. (Just one of many reasons to get a good night's sleep! But we'll talk more about that in Chapter 6.)

When you're stressed or tired, you may start to experience things like *decision fatigue*, a term describing how decision-making becomes much harder when you have been making decisions all day.

At times like this, you may not have the power to gear up your executive function, look into the future, and think: "Wait a minute, I've had plenty of food today and I don't need ice cream. Ice cream is not in my best interest. It might compromise my sleep, it could set me up to want more sugar, and it might make me feel like I don't want to exercise in the morning. This could be bad for my health and interfere with my long-term goals for my life." After a long, hard day of work or conflict or stress, you may think, "Goals schmoals, I want ice cream." Enter YBP. This is when having your big picture clear in your mind can make a huge difference in how successfully you are able to maintain a longer-term perspective in the face of short-term desires. YBP takes the decision out of the equation. Dr. Michaelides tells us, "If you know your YBP, it can eliminate in-the-moment decisions. Questions won't just be about 'Should I or shouldn't I?' They will be about 'Does this fit into my YBP?'" This can be really useful when you have to make a choice and you don't have a lot of mental energy left at the end of the day. YBP can help you with decision fatigue by having a set strategy already in place when you have to make a decision, so you won't have to think about it. You might still think about ice cream, but there it is, YBP, like a shining star in your mind.

In psychology, construal level theory (CLT) is a theory that when people think about the big picture, the *why* behind their behavior, they are more successful at avoiding habits they are trying to change than when they look at the details of their present situation. This might sound like the opposite of temporal discounting, but the difference is in the way these two choices are weighted. Research on CLT and self-control showed that when people considered global, superordinate, big-picture aspects, they were more successful at avoiding unwanted behavior than if they considered subordinate, secondary, local features.[18]

Translation: When people think about their big picture, they are better at avoiding temptations right in front of them. Thinking about and visualizing a heathy, energetic, vibrant you doing all the things you want to do in your life while feeling confident and strong can be more compelling than food or a comfy couch in front of you in the moment. YBP is the difference between "I might as well eat this" and "I remember why I don't want to eat this."

And while you still might have the ice cream (we all need a treat now and then), at least you will do it in the context of your goals, rather than at the whim of your instincts. You might think, "I'll just have a small bowl, after I have a nice bowl of veggie-rich soup for dinner." Or, you might think, "I'll save the ice cream for another time. Thinking about how great I'll feel when I achieve my goals feels rewarding enough right now."

YBP can also help you when you encounter obstacles. Dr. Michaelides says, "If you hit a road bump or get a flat tire, you may give up and go back home because who cares? But if you have a final destination—YBP—and you care about it, you won't just wander off at the first exit or give up when things get hard. You'll sail past that first exit, you'll navigate around the bump, you'll fix the flat tire, and then you'll keep on heading down the road. There are always detours, but when you have YBP, you will stay focused on where you're going."

An everyday example might be going out to a restaurant. You may decide what to order ahead of time, based on what you feel fits with YBP. Then, as Dr. Michaelides adds, "if you have decision fatigue or you've had a glass of wine and your inhibitions are lower, or someone else orders something and you suddenly think you want that thing instead of your initial thought-out choice, YBP will have your back." You'll have an answer to the question "Why not get the triple chocolate cheesecake?" Your answer might be "Because that doesn't fit into my big picture" or "I really want two or three bites, and that is in line with my big picture. Who wants to split dessert?"

When you have YBP in mind, running like a mantra in the background of your life, you can call it up whenever you need it— in the morning, before meals, before workouts, before relaxing, before going to sleep. If you keep telling yourself (and your phone or other alerts keep telling you) that you *will* achieve your Super Goal because you know your Ultimate Why and you have imagined in great detail all the ways your life will be different when you achieve it, YBP will seem not so far away after all.

Most of all, we want you to remember the Y in YBP. This is *your* big picture. These are *your* goals, not anything anyone else told you that you should do. This is *your* Ultimate Why, not something anyone else told you should be your reasons. This is *your* vision of how your life will be more in line with your dream life, not someone else's vision, someone who thinks they know what you should want. *You* want something, and *you* have chosen to get out there and achieve it because *you believe in yourself.*

You can decide to change your goals, your why, your vision, any time you choose. YBP can evolve with you because you are driving this car, steering this ship, and running your life like a boss. You are the only one who can really decide how you will live your life. Every decision—what you eat and don't eat, whether you will move or rest, and how you will handle obstacles that come your way—is yours and yours alone. With the right information and the right psych tools (which we will keep providing), you can do this thing. We're right behind you, cheering you on, because we believe in you, too.

3

Habit Formation
and Habit Change

Habit is a compromise effected
between an individual and his environment.

—Samuel Beckett

Habits are behaviors people repeat over and over again without thinking much about them, like brushing their teeth before bed or always eating dinner in front of the TV. They can also be things you stopped doing (remember that gym membership you're still paying for?) because you started doing something else more rewarding (like napping). They seem to happen without any forethought, but in truth, they formed because of a largely unconscious multistep mental process that happened for a reason.

The reason is your environment. "Habits aren't good or bad," says Dr. Michaelides. "Habits are adaptive. You developed your habits because they did something good for you, or helped you overcome something." A habit is something you initially did just one time, but it helped you adapt to your environment in some way. If you repeated that behavior and it continued to benefit you, your brain decided that, as long as you're going to keep doing that thing over and over (bite your nails when you're nervous, eat candy when you read or study, take a shower before bed), it might as well put that behavior on automatic pilot. That's why trying to change habits is so difficult—your brain likes automatic processes because they take less energy than conscious, deliberate processes.

Let's say you're feeling stressed, so you decide to eat some ice cream. It tastes really good, and you forget about your stress for a while. Your brain notices this effective stress relief in the moment, so the next time you feel stressed, it reminds you: *Hey, maybe ice cream will help!* If you eat ice cream again, and it has a beneficial effect on your stress, and then you do it again and again, then your brain may create a habit: Whenever you feel stressed, you eat ice cream. You (and your brain) don't even have to think about it anymore. You write a mental program: 1. You feel stress. 2. You reach for the ice cream. And your brain has less work to do.

To use another example, maybe you sprained your ankle and had to stop running every morning. Your doctor told you not to go running until your ankle was healed, so you started sleeping in during that running time. Running was a habit, but now you've replaced it with sleeping. You may intend to start running again when your ankle is healed, but your brain isn't thinking about the future and how beneficial exercise is. It's thinking how easy it is to automate the process of getting up an hour later. You get out of the exercise habit and into the sleeping habit. That's why, when your ankle feels good again, it can still feel so difficult to start exercising again.

In general, many habits develop because of what causes someone to feel pleasure or avoid pain in the moment. These could be things like having a glass of wine every night while cooking dinner to unwind from a difficult day, smoking in social situations where you feel a little nervous, or getting that same candy bar from the vending machine every day at 3:00 p.m. These things may help you relax, calm down, perk up, or feel better as you do them, and that positive psychological reinforcement is strong—even stronger than your knowledge that the habit could have negative health consequences in the future.

It is exactly these habits easing difficult feelings in the moment but having negative outcomes later that people often wish to change. These are also the habits that are the most difficult to change because we don't like feeling uncomfortable. Humans are very simple: We avoid pain and we seek pleasure. It's no surprise, really, that we develop habits that help us do just that. But we also have brains with the capability to perceive future consequences, and therein lies that internal conflict about habits.

Dr. Michaelides explains, "When you are trying to change a habit, you're trying to do things that require monumental changes to your brain. But your brain doesn't want to change. It wants to stay just how it is, and it's designed to stay this way, for efficiency purposes. The brain seeks the path of least resistance, or least energy expenditure, so when you are trying to change a habit, you are essentially going against biology, and that can feel unnatural."

If you are struggling to break a habit, it's important that you know it's not because you're a failure; it's because you're working against an ingrained habit. "Your brain doesn't care that you've decided you don't like a habit anymore," Dr. Michaelides says. "Your brain isn't optimized for change. When you change a habit, you are essentially saying, 'I don't want my brain to operate in the way it's meant to operate. I choose inefficiency.' That's difficult. It's going against your biology in many ways. But that doesn't mean you can't do it, and it certainly doesn't mean you shouldn't do it."

So how do you work against your very smart, very powerful brain? Ironically, you do it by using your very smart, very powerful brain: You fire up your executive function (those conscious higher-brain functions we talked about in Chapter 3). Your higher brain in charge of executive function *can* change habits that are not serving you or that aren't in line with your goals.

Let's engage that executive function by taking a closer look at the process of habit formation. Habits are embedded in what psychologists call scripts, and scripts are formed through a process that we call the behavior chain. Once you understand how scripts and the behavior chain works, you can edit your scripts and reverse-engineer your behavior chains to undo a habit you want to change. You can also use these constructs to create new habits you want to adopt.

Becoming Aware of Your Scripts

If you're into, say, community theater, you've experienced what a literal script does: It tells you what to say and do during the performance, and you rely on it until you know it so well that you can repeat the lines and movements from memory without having to think about them. In psychology, a script also tells you what to say and do, but you are the playwright. You wrote the script that tells you what to do in particular situations—and that means you can change the script.

Just as we all have habits for a reason, we all have scripts for a reason. Brains love scripts just as they love habits, because brains are always trying to save energy, and conscious thoughts and behaviors require more energy than automatic thoughts and behaviors. People have scripts for many parts of their lives—morning routine scripts, lunch scripts, work scripts, leisure time scripts, family dynamic scripts, evening routine scripts, and more. Many of the scripts people have are functional and useful in their lives, but if you have a habit you want to change, you can rewrite the script.

One way to identify your scripts is to figure out where you've established (consciously or not) an "if . . . then" routine. Scripts generally follow an "if . . . then" format, such as: "If it's bedtime, then I wash my face, brush my teeth, and get into bed" or "If it's my lunch hour, I order a sandwich, chips, and a cookie, and I eat at my desk." When you find a script you'd like to change, you can drop different behaviors into the format.

Let's say you want to start having a healthier lunch. Look at your lunch script and see if you can make an edit, so that the sandwich, chips, and cookie become a big salad, crackers, and a banana. This way, you can change the habit but keep the script. Your brain gets the benefit of maintaining a mostly automated script, and you are essentially sliding in a new habit under the radar.

But changing a habit isn't always that easy. Sometimes it requires more of an overhaul, and that's when you need to take a closer look at how the script got created in the first place. Scripts generally emerge out of behavior chains, and a behavior chain is a series of events that lead to the creation of a script that contains habits. Deconstruct the behavior chain and you can figure out where your script got started. Behavior chains can help you take a script off automatic pilot to make it conscious again, which can then make it easier to edit.

Deconstructing Behavior Chains

The behavior chain is the process of script or habit formation, and every behavior chain begins with a trigger. This trigger leads to thoughts and feelings, which lead to actions, which lead to outcomes (we call these "consequences" in the app, FYI), which, over time, if the outcome is consistently positive, lead to the formation of scripts.

Here's how the behavior chain looks:

Trigger = thoughts/feelings = action = outcomes =
script or habit

Triggers

Every behavior chain begins with a trigger. Remember, habits are adaptive, and triggers are what habits are adapting to. They can cause you to do beneficial things, or neutral things, or detrimental things. There are many types of triggers that can kick off behavior chains:

◆ **Environmental triggers,** like the box of doughnuts someone put on the kitchen counter or the vending machine at work that you can see from your workstation.

◆ **Social triggers,** like your friends from work urging you to join them for happy hour or at the gym.

◆ **Time triggers,** like automatically reaching for a snack at 3:00 p.m. or cookies after dinner.

◆ **Biological triggers,** like those sugar cravings you get when you skip breakfast or only have a side salad for lunch.

◆ **Mental triggers,** like that urge to eat after doing something really difficult.

◆ **Emotional triggers,** like the proverbial ice cream after a tough breakup, or feeling defeated because you missed a deadline and ordering pizza instead of cooking that healthy meal you planned and shopped for.

Another common trigger is what *other* people do. People tend to eat at about the same speed and about the same amount as the people they are eating with,[1] dress in ways that others in their group dress,[2] even mimic each other's body language.[3] When people are together, their behaviors can start to sync up without anyone realizing it, and that can mean you start doing things you might not have chosen to do on your own. This behavior is called *norm matching*, and it's one of those things humans do that help us bond and get along in groups.

We are more likely to engage in unhealthy behaviors if other people around us are doing them. Fortunately, the flip side is also true: We're more likely to engage in healthy behaviors if other people around us are doing them. Doing what other people do makes us feel comfortable, but when we repeat these behaviors over and over, they can become habits that have nothing to do with our own preferences. They are habits shaped by what other people are doing, rather than what we want to be doing.

To some extent, we can't help doing what other people are doing. It's a natural behavior meant to keep us safely in groups, which used to be necessary for survival. Norm matching is normal and usually benign. Until it isn't. Think about some situations where you have observed, or participated in, this kind of seemingly harmless but ultimately potentially health-damaging norm matching:

- Your boss orders pizza for everyone, so you eat it, even though you brought a healthy lunch.
- Your workout buddies cancel on you, so you don't go to the gym either.
- Your roommate wants to stay up watching that late movie, so you watch it, too, even though you have to get up early.
- You go to a restaurant to meet friends and everyone is having jumbo margaritas. You were planning on having a club soda with lime, but . . .
- All your friends get riled up about something happening in the news and start forming a group opinion about its significance. You find yourself going along, even though you don't really agree with the view and it stresses you out.

All these examples can become scripts if you do them regularly, causing you to engage in habits you might not want for yourself. See if you can notice the next time you go along with something you wouldn't have done on your own. Do *you* really want to be doing that thing?

Thoughts and Feelings

When you encounter a trigger, the next thing that happens is that you will have thoughts and feelings. This is the next link in the behavior chain. These thoughts and feelings are reactions to the influence of the trigger. They might be simple observations or they might be emotionally charged, but they lead to doing something.

Let's say you tried really hard to meet a deadline, but you didn't finish on time. You're exhausted, feeling a little insecure, and you have no bandwidth left. You planned to cook a healthy dinner, but when you get home, it feels too exhausting. Not meeting the deadline was your trigger, but it made you *feel* defeated and it made you *think*: "I don't want to cook a healthy dinner. I want comfort food, and *fast*."

Action

This is what you actually do in response to the thoughts and feelings caused by the trigger. In the above example, the action is your ordering takeout instead of cooking. Sometimes, an action almost seems to happen before the thought. The server at the party walks by with a tray of fancy appetizers, you skipped lunch and you're famished, so you grab a chicken skewer or a cheese ball and down it before your brain has a chance to register that you're going to eat dinner in thirty minutes. You take a handful of chips or a hunk of bread from the basket on the table before you even look at the menu. You find yourself plugging quarters into the vending machine before you remember that you brought hummus and crackers to work for just such a situation. Those thoughts may race by at supersonic speeds in response to those triggers you weren't prepared for, and boom—you acted.

Outcomes

The next link in the behavior chain is outcomes. Outcomes are the result of the actions that were the result of the thoughts and feelings that were the result of the trigger. These outcomes can be positive or negative, and they are instrumental in whether the action you took will become a habit. They might be:

- ◆ **Physiological:** Mmmm, peanut butter cup ice cream. It tastes so good and now I actually feel calmer!
- ◆ **Physical:** That third slice of pizza gave me a stomachache.
- ◆ **Psychological:** I'm totally justified in taking a day off from the gym because I worked really hard today.
- ◆ **Emotional:** I felt so sad, but that peanut butter cup ice cream is making me feel a lot better.

If the outcomes of your action were reinforcing—they had a positive outcome for you, like making you feel good or causing you to get praised—then you are likely to perform the same actions the next time you encounter that trigger. If the outcomes of your actions were punishing—they had a negative outcome for you, like making you feel bad or causing you to get criticized— you're less likely to perform the same action next time you encounter the trigger.

As a behavior chain is forged, the "thought/feeling" part can change to weaken or reinforce the chain, depending on what the outcomes were. Next time, you might think, "The last time I was stressed, ice cream did make me feel so much better. I want to feel better *again!*" A more punishing consequence would have a different result: "The heartburn from that pizza kept me up all night. I think I'll just make the healthy meal I planned this time."

Your thoughts and feelings might not even be quite that conscious. If the ice cream was rewarding last time, you may feel an urge or a craving to have it again without really rationalizing why. That's because your brain has already started to automate the behavior. If the pizza wasn't very good (although, isn't all pizza at least pretty good?), the next time you think of pizza, your response might be more "meh" than "bring it on" (or at least "let me find a different place to order from").

Now, if you're like us, and we bet you are, you are already aware that outcomes are often a mixture of positive and negative, all in one. If the relief of ordering the pizza and the cheesy, pepperoni goodness outweighed the heartburn you had later, you still might order the pizza again next time. If the ice cream was amazing in the moment but you really hated how bloated you were the next morning, the bloating may win out over the treat. Whether a habit forms or not becomes a sort of contest to see who will win—the negative or the positive outcome.

However, for many of us, the treats win out over the downsides, more often than not. It has nothing to do with willpower or some internal moral flaw. It's just because brains are really good at convincing us to do things that make us feel good or relieve stress in the moment.[4] You may selectively forget the more negative outcomes, just to get more of the good stuff. The sugar rush or the relief of not having to cook dinner can override the regret about not sticking with your plan, or even the physical discomforts of indigestion.

A Habit Is Born

When your brain decides an action was worth taking, and you start to repeat that action, a script gets written. *If* it's Friday night, *then* you're ordering pizza, whether you actually want pizza or not. *If* work is over, *then* you join your colleagues for a margarita, even if you don't always feel like having one. *If* dinner is over, *then* you have dessert, even if you're full. Your script, and the habits it contains (ordering the pizza, drinking the margarita, eating the dessert), becomes more and more ingrained the longer you "rehearse" it.

It's important to understand, at this point, that none of the things you are doing are, in and of themselves, bad things. There is nothing inherently wrong with pizza, or ice cream, or margaritas, or takeout; there is nothing inherently wrong with not going to the gym, or staying up late, or drinking a lot of coffee. In fact, many scripts are beneficial. *If* it's Saturday, *then* you go for a hike with the family. *If* it's a weekday morning, *then* you take fifteen minutes to breathe or meditate before breakfast. *If* it's 11:00 p.m., *then* you go to bed.

However, there is something wrong with feeling like your habits are happening *to you* or are beyond your control. Automation is great for saving energy, but not for manipulating you to do things you don't really want to do. You have the power to change anything in your life that you want to change. You just have to make the unconscious *conscious* again. This is the secret to breaking a habit. And what's the secret to creating a new habit? Making the conscious *unconscious*, or automated.

Breaking the Chain

You can alter a behavior chain by working backward from the script or the habit, all the way to the trigger. Changing any element along the way, but especially changing the trigger or the thoughts/feelings related to the trigger, can cause the whole behavior chain to fall apart, so you become conscious of the script and the habit, thereby putting you back in charge. For example, one way we do this in the app is to use push notifications that serve as triggers for new habits people are trying to establish. You can create your own "push notifications" just by setting up your environment in an appropriate way. Let's practice how this would work. Starting at the end of the chain, choose a habit you want to break, and then identify the script around it (the "if . . . then" part). Name it, and then move backward along the chain:

trigger = thoughts = action = outcomes = **Habit**

Let's say your habit is always eating ice cream after dinner. Again, there is nothing wrong with eating ice cream after dinner, but because it's a habit, now you do it even when you are full. You do it even when you don't really want it. You do it because you always do it, or everybody does it, or just because it's comforting to do something the same way every day. This is the habit you want to break. (Substitute any habit *you* want to break.) You identify the script: "*If* dinner is over, *then* I have ice cream." Now, let's figure out how that got started.

Outcomes

Working backward, what are the outcomes that encouraged you to make eating ice cream into a habit? There are probably good ones and bad ones. Maybe you used to get a nice feeling of calm, or a happy feeling of treating yourself, and maybe you sometimes still do. That's nice! But maybe—more often than not—now that you really think about it, you notice that the ice cream often makes you feel overly stuffed and uncomfortable, or it leaves you feeling restless and not sleeping well because you ate too close to bedtime. Maybe it doesn't even feel like a treat anymore because it's become commonplace. Maybe you barely even taste it after the first few bites. Or maybe it's still really great, but you have a goal of getting back to a healthy weight and ice cream every single night is, you suspect, interfering with your goal.

Analyze: Are your outcomes now more negative than positive? Maybe they are and maybe they aren't, but it's good to determine whether or not they have changed over time (most things change over time), and to bring some of the more negative outcomes to the forefront of your mind.

Actions

Working backward along the chain, you get to actions. What are the actions you take that result in those outcomes? We don't just mean "eating ice cream." In this case, the action is actually getting up, going to the freezer, getting out the ice cream, getting a spoon (or a fork, if you're quirky like that), and if you're the fancy type, an actual bowl. It takes effort to eat ice cream after dinner—more effort than just sitting and not getting up, at least—and you have purposefully been making this effort just to maintain that habit. It's interesting to think about this. If you simply *didn't* do that action, you wouldn't have the habit. Of course, it's not that easy because a trigger caused thoughts and feelings that made the effort of getting that ice cream worthwhile, so let's look at those.

Thoughts and Feelings

What are those tricky, slippery thoughts that made eating ice cream *so* worthwhile? Do you remember what the thoughts were that led to forming this habit in the first place? If you don't remember, look at the pattern and start thinking about what it might have been a reaction to. When you really think about doing this action now, what kind of thoughts come to you? A list of these thoughts could look something like this:

- I deserve ice cream.
- I crave something sweet.
- I feel sad! Ice cream makes me feel happy.
- I feel nervous! Ice cream makes me feel calm.
- My dinner doesn't feel complete without something sweet at the end.
- I like ice cream. (A very good reason to enjoy it!)
- I'm still hungry.
- The person I'm with wants ice cream, so it seems chummier to eat together.
- I want to be the kind of person who can eat ice cream whenever and it's NBD.

The act of bringing your thoughts and feelings into your conscious mind is an important one. It allows you to analyze those thoughts and feelings for their validity, truth, and relevance for today. These are thoughts you want to challenge or at least understand, if you're going to break that habit. But before you even start to do that, remember: Be nice to yourself—this is not about blame or shame. It's about understanding the nuances of your thoughts to get to heart of what's really going on with your efforts to make a change that matters to you. Here are some ways you can contend with your behavior-chain thoughts and feelings:

- You do deserve good things! Are you sure the good thing you really want is ice cream?

- Think about all the reasons why you might crave sugar. Are you eating enough for dinner, or throughout the day? Is the craving really about food? (For more thoughts on this, check out the section on conquering cravings on page 132.)

- It's okay to be sad! Are there other things that could make you feel happier, like getting some emotional support from a real person rather than from a bowl of dairy product?

- It's also okay to feel nervous! We've all been there. Ice cream might make you feel calm, but would other things make you feel calm, too, that are more in line with your goals for yourself? What about a nice cup of tea, or wrapping up in a warm blanket, or cuddling with a pet, or watching funny videos, or listening to relaxing music? You could try some of these other actions to see if they help you feel as calm as ice cream does. It's great to like ice cream! It's delicious. Think about whether or not it would be more rewarding to have it less often.

- Would it be fun to shake up your routine a bit?

- What might be a good swap for ice cream, with a higher nutritional density or a lower calorie density or less sugar (if that's what you're going for)? What about Greek yogurt (mmm, probiotics) with a tablespoon of mini chocolate chips and chopped strawberries? A popsicle? Some peppermint or cinnamon tea?

- Why are you still hungry after dinner? Are you eating enough? What would happen if you increased your portion size of your dinners, then really tuned in to that feeling of fullness? Would you still want the ice cream?

- What if you are eating ice cream because your partner is, and they are eating ice cream because you are, and neither of you really wants to keep doing it? You could ask them.

- You *can* be that person who can eat ice cream whenever, and it's NBD. Imagine you are that person. If it's NBD, would you only eat it when you really wanted it?

We don't know the answers to these questions, and we can't promise any of these ideas will work for you. They are your answers and your self-experimentation, and these prompts are only suggestions. The point of this exercise, though, is to question thoughts that result in actions that you don't want to be doing. Questioning your thought process with interest and curiosity is a good way to check on whether those thoughts are still applicable to you or if they are no longer relevant.

Trigger

Finally, we are all the way back to the trigger. This is where it really all began. Maybe you can't remember the initial trigger, or maybe that trigger is still in place and triggering you daily. Think about what this might be:

- Boredom
- Fatigue
- Anxiety
- Sadness/negative feelings
- You started doing it in response to a crisis event, like an injury or a break-up
- Work stress
- Family/relationship stress
- Time: You always have ice cream at that time of day
- People: Someone you eat with always wants ice cream after dinner
- Hunger
- Norm matching

Whatever the trigger, look at it with a critical eye and unpack it a bit. If you can redirect the thoughts that happen after the trigger, then you can redirect the action—for a different outcome. For example, if fatigue is a trigger, can you work on how to get better sleep instead of turning to ice cream? Can you get help with anxiety or sadness? If the crisis event is over, is the script still helping? Are there ways to reduce your stress? Could you replace ice cream with something else at that trigger time of day or in response to those triggering people? If you're typically overly hungry late in the day, could you eat more food earlier in the day? If you're norm matching, could you bring awareness to that and consciously choose something different?

It may not be that easy to change a trigger but becoming aware of it is sometimes all it takes to collapse the whole behavior chain so you can put it back together any way you want to.

And voilà: Habit busted.

Exposure Therapy, or Feeling Your Feelings

Sometimes, the hardest part of busting a habit is recognizing that there are strong emotions going on and you developed the habit to cope with, or even mask, those emotions. If you break the habit, then yikes—*feelings!* Before you replace one habit with another one (eating a huge bowl of grapes in front of the TV instead of a huge bowl of buttered popcorn in front of the TV), think about whether there are underlying strong feelings that are driving the desire to have a huge bowl of *anything*. Facing those feelings can help you to deal with them, or get used to them, so you no longer need three hours of TV to end your day, let alone more food when you aren't hungry.

Dr. Michaelides says, "Habit change is the ability to push through discomfort." He also tells us that eating to block the discomfort of an emotion—aka emotional eating—is quite common. "We learn our eating habits throughout our lives, and if you learned that eating is a comforting response to emotional pain, then that habit can become entrenched. Breaking it can feel extremely uncomfortable. These habits can be even harder to break if you've had these associations throughout your life, from early childhood. They are a good example of a habit that is adaptive, but as you become an adult, you can learn that there are more sophisticated ways to cope with negative emotions. You no longer need food to adapt, but you may *feel like* you do and that feeling can be quite strong."

How do I control my eating habits when I feel stressed, sad, etc.?

A lot of Noomers have had success replacing the action of succumbing to a craving or impulse with a constructive, actionable task like going for a walk, journaling, doing some yoga, working on a hobby, or any other healthy, positive activity. Have it planned ahead of time so you don't have to come up with it when a craving hits.

Let's say you always eat after arguing with someone, and you've been doing that since you were a little kid, when you heard family members arguing. Those family arguments were an initial trigger, but you've kept that behavior chain going for decades. Now, when you hear people arguing (one of those people might be you), your emotions can feel more uncomfortable than the situation necessarily warrants because you're associating that arguing with the more traumatic arguing you experienced as a child. This can trigger a strong desire to eat something, which you know from experience could dull the uncomfortable emotions. All you want is for those feelings to stop, and if something as easily obtained as, say, a bag of kettle chips or a cup of vanilla pudding can calm those feelings and let you get on with your life, then of course you will be tempted to have it.

The alternative—actually feeling the feelings—may sound scary. You may even need a bit of help and support from a friend or even a therapist to help you through it. However, this is a powerful way to dissolve a habit. Feeling your feelings without resorting to angry crunching or the soothing sensation of something smooth and creamy can diffuse those cravings that really had nothing to do with food at all.

If you want to try this, we suggest a technique called *exposure*.

Exposure therapy is something psychologists use to help people deal with phobias, anxiety, and other uncomfortable feelings. They expose the patient to the unpleasant thing—the heights, the enclosed spaces, the spider—in small amounts, in a safe environment, gradually increasing the time they are exposed to the thing and the intensity of the exposure, until those feelings get less intense. For instance, maybe at first you look at a picture of a spider for one minute. Then you look at the picture longer. Then you look at a real spider for one minute. Then you get closer and closer to the spider. You stay at each step until the fear begins to increase in intensity before moving on to the next step.

This also works for dealing with strong emotions that cause you to engage in habits you want to stop. Exposing yourself to uncomfortable feelings a little at a time helps you get used to the discomfort, until it's not so uncomfortable anymore. It is a way to build up emotional tolerance or resilience.

Let's take the example of emotional eating, for which exposure can be very effective. Dr. Michaelides explains, "Every time you have anxiety and then you eat, you feed the anxiety, and that is reinforcing. The avoidance is fueling the anxiety. But if you learn to push through that anxiety and wait to eat until you have actual hunger, then you begin to build a different relationship with what hunger is and what it feels like in your body."

At Noom, we call this *urge surfing*. Urge surfing is a process of riding the wave (like a surfer) of discomfort that comes when you don't do something you're used to doing. Maybe your script is: *If* I go to a movie, *then* I eat a tub of popcorn. You don't want to do this anymore, so you go to the movie and you don't order the popcorn. You sit down in your seat without popcorn. And suddenly you get very uncomfortable. You're used to the popcorn. You like the popcorn. You want to crunch something. The previews are boring. You get the *urge* to get up and buy the popcorn anyway, because your current discomfort feels more pressing than your goal of breaking your popcorn habit.

But remember everything you've learned: how humans tend to default to the now over the later; how we prioritize pleasure and pain avoidance over more logical, goal-oriented behavior; how ordering popcorn is a script that's no longer in line with what you're trying to achieve. And then you can *ride that wave, baby*. Feel the discomfort. Notice it. Feel it growing and growing. And . . . wait for it . . . feel it subsiding. When the wave subsides, you know you've achieved something important. You've sent your brain the message that your habit is not in charge. *You* are. And suddenly, that popcorn doesn't feel so important, and you enjoy the movie without it. You've just experimented on yourself using exposure, and you've urge-surfed your way right out of your script.

Whatever your trigger, whatever your strong feeling, you can use this technique. Feel the distress until it subsides. Every time you do this, the feelings will start to have less power, and the compulsion to suppress them will become weaker and weaker. Exposures are most effective when the distress significantly subsides *before* ending the exposure, so see if you can wait until the intensity of the feeling subsides. It's valuable to feel that subsiding. It's the beginning of the end of that pesky habit.

Using the Behavior Chain to Build New Habits

You don't have to just stop an old habit. You can also start a new one. Quitting an old habit is a great opportunity to put a new habit in place where the old one used to be. It's hard to just stop doing something rewarding. It's a little easier if you replace it with something else that's rewarding. People are action-oriented, so we like to do things more than we like to stop doing things.

Your new habit may not feel quite as rewarding, at least at first, as the old habit was. Peppermint tea isn't going to push all the same buttons as chocolate-mint cookies, but it may help create a bridge between a habit you're trying to break and a new one you're establishing.

As you begin working on breaking habits, also think about new habits you would like to have. Now that you know how habits are built, you can purposefully build a new behavior chain. You can design **triggers** that will lead to **thoughts** that will lead to planned **actions** that will lead to irresistibly wonderful **outcomes**, and then you've reverse-engineered your very own new habit.

Let's say you're trying to quit drinking so much soda, and in its place, you want to start drinking more water. That's your new habit. As you deconstruct your old habit by looking at the outcomes from drinking soda, back through the actions, the thoughts and feelings, and the trigger, you can go the other way to establish a water habit.

First, what was your soda trigger? If it's a craving for that sweet taste, think of something moving in the right direction toward water that you could put in soda's place. You're looking for something that could give you a similar outcome as soda. Maybe that would be pomegranate tea or a piece of fruit. This choice could satisfy your desire for sweetness while also reducing the intensity of the sweetness you got from soda, so you get used to less. You can use some exposure experimentation here, as you drink the tea and feel the urge for soda. As your urge for sweetness decreases, you can start introducing less sweet tastes.

Meanwhile, you can start thinking about how to engineer a new "trigger." It's not really a trigger if you create it; it's more of a cue. But that's okay. What cue could you set up to make you think the thought that would lead to the action of drinking water? Maybe mealtime is a cue. Or you could set an alarm on your phone. Maybe waking up in the morning is your cue, or your break at work. Every time your cue happens, think about drinking water and how good it will make you feel. Then, take action and drink a big, refreshing glass of water. Finally, bask in the outcome: Water gives you more energy, you'll be less likely to mistake thirst for hunger, it gives you a chance to take a break from work, and studies show that people who drink more water tend to have healthier eating habits and get better nutrition.[5] Hooray for luscious water!

To make this even easier, set yourself up for success by removing soda's environmental triggers and adding water triggers. Get all sugar-sweetened beverages out of the house, put a nice pitcher of cold water in the fridge (maybe throw in some lemon or cucumber slices so it has some extra flavor), or get an awesome water bottle you'll enjoy carrying around. Time can also be a trigger, so you could set a reminder on your phone or watch for all the times during the day when you start thinking about sugary beverages, and you make a point to get yourself a glass of water instead.

Now, you are set up for success: Your watch alarm dings. Ah, water time! You take a break from what you're doing, go to the fridge, and pour yourself a refreshing glass or fill up your water bottle, sip contentedly, think actively about how good you feel and how much energy you have . . . and then you do it again, and again, and again. Pretty soon, you'll be in the habit and drinking more water will be just another part of your daily routine. You may still drink soda sometimes, but your water habit has filled the hole where the soda used to be—and it also fits with your health goals.

NOOM COACH Q&A

Can I drink alcohol on Noom?

Like all macronutrients, alcohol has calories. Seven calories per gram, in fact, compared to four calories per gram in carbs and proteins and nine calories per gram in fat. In other words, it's pretty calorie-dense. Moreover, unlike healthy fats, proteins, and carbs, alcohol isn't a necessary part of a balanced diet. Essentially, drinking booze adds empty calories to your diet, increasing your calorie intake without making you feel full. Does that mean you can never have a glass of wine? Of course not! It's just important that before imbibing, you work those calories into your daily calorie budget. They aren't free! As long as you've planned in advance, a drink or two shouldn't derail your progress.

Habit Bundling

Another of our favorite methods for developing new habits is called *habit bundling*. This is a great method for helping to establish a new habit. Habit bundling is when you pair a habit you already have down pat with a new habit you want to have. For example, if you always eat breakfast, then pairing your new "drink more water" goal with breakfast makes it easier to remember and do. You're already eating; you might as well drink some water while you're at it.

In short:

Current habit
+ New habit
_____

Habit bundling

Habit bundling can reduce the time it takes to develop a new habit because it's like the old habit gives the new habit a boost. It's a support system for your new habit—a habit buddy, if you will.

Maybe the new habit you want to create is to eat more vegetables. You already have a habit of having hummus and crackers for your afternoon snack. It's your favorite snack. Pairing the old with the new, you could add some chopped raw veggies to your snack, to dip in the hummus. You don't have to ditch the crackers; you're just adding the veggies. Habit piggybacked!

This can work for any habit. Maybe your new habit is flossing more (you know you want to). Since you already brush your teeth, adding flossing to your existing tooth-brushing routine is easier than just randomly remembering to floss during the day.

If your new habit is deep breathing for stress reduction, and you already read a book before you go to sleep, bundle your deep-breathing exercise with your reading, right before or after.

There are a billion ways to bundle your habits, so use your imagination, but whatever you do, match your new habit with a friend. You don't want it to get lonely.

And remember, the more you do something, the more your brain detects that it should be automated. Let that programming work for, not against, you and get those new healthy habits automated ASAP!

Final Thoughts

Even though the brain's pull to maintain old habits is strong, you can gain traction by taking apart the behavior chain, link by link, using your extraordinary logic skills. Your brain may still complain a bit, with erudite arguments like, "But I *want it!*" Even if you have replaced your habit with a different habit (like the Greek yogurt, the herbal tea, Sudoku, an evening stroll, learning a new vocabulary word every night—we're just spitballing here), you're still going to want that ice cream or pizza or soda sometimes, maybe a lot. Fortunately, you are the boss so you can have those things when you decide consciously that you really want them. And, whenever you choose, you can also say to your brain: "Sorry, brain, but we're not doing that right now. I know what's best for you." (And, of course, it's your brain saying that to your brain. So meta.)

And what if you sometimes still eat ice cream at the end of a hard day, or order takeout instead of cooking, even when you don't intend to? Well then, guess what? You're a normal human being. People don't always do what they intend, and the only permanent changes you will ever be able to sustain in your life require you to know that and not punish yourself when it happens. What matters is what you do next. You always have the next decision to make a different choice, and that's how you practice taking back the reins of your actions and your life from the habits that seemed to control you.

Breaking habits and making new ones can feel overwhelming, but figuring out why you do what you do, feeling your feelings, and breaking down those tired old habits and replacing them with shiny new ones really can change your brain and your behavior. Knowledge is power when it comes to habits, so the more you start paying attention to how you feel about what you do, the more aware you will become about your behavior and the easier it will be to do what you actually want to do, big picture.

A lot of examples in this book have been about food, glorious food. Now, it's time to take a closer look at food—that thing so many love and fear, label, and ruminate about. Instead of all that, let's get real. Let's get face-to-face with food.

4

Face-to-Face with Food

Tell me what you eat, and I shall tell you who you are.

—Jean Anthelme Brillat-Savarin

Food is complex. We need its energy to live and its nutrients to be healthy. Food is fuel, but it's also much more. People are culturally, socially, and emotionally involved with food, and there is nothing wrong with that. Of course, we would form an emotional connection with something we engage with multiple times every day, that is so closely associated with social bonding, and that is so physiologically important for life.

But there are also plenty of problematic issues with food culture. Big companies profit from making junk food irresistible. They bombard us with advertising that can send us straight to the drive-through line, despite our best intentions. People may eat a lot more, or a lot less, than their bodies need, for many complicated reasons, and feel bad about it. Then there's diet culture, with its impossible standards. It's no wonder we need help trying to navigate a world that makes it so hard to stay healthy.

So, what should you eat? That's a question for you to answer, not us, but the more you know about food, the more you can answer that question for yourself with the knowledge you need to use food for what you want it to do for you: keep you healthy, give you energy, help you heal, bring you pleasure, serve as a means to bring family and friends together, or all of those things and more.

Some people try to answer the question about what to eat by exploring what humans ate for most of human history. That makes sense, logically, because it appears to be a question about what the "natural" human diet is. But that's not an easy thing to discover. The human diet evolved differently depending on where people lived and what was available, and what part of human evolution you look at. Some people during some periods, in some locations, ate mostly fish or meat, while others lived mostly on starchy root vegetables. Overall, humans have eaten a lot of plants, fruits, seeds, nuts, fish, meat, grasses, leaves, fungi, and, yes, insects over the millennia, and we evolved to be able to survive on a wide variety of foods. This is why humans are considered omnivorous: We can eat, and survive on, many different kinds of diets. Eventually we figured out how to cook food, and then to farm it. But the one thing all food had in common, at every time period and in every part of the world, throughout the vast majority of human history until very recently, was that it came from nature, not a factory.

Food processing is a very recent phenomenon. It makes eating more efficient and convenient, and in some cases safer (such as with pasteurization), but it has also made food less natural and, in many cases, less nutritious. Ever since big food corporations started manufacturing processed food, or what author Michael Pollan calls "edible food-like substances,"[1] people began to develop more chronic diseases.[2] Highly processed foods tend to be unnaturally high in sugar, fat, and salt compared to whole foods (foods in their natural state, like fresh vegetables and fruits, whole grains, fresh meat, etc.—i.e., minimally processed). They tend to have more calories, less fiber, and fewer nutrients than whole foods. While there is nothing wrong with eating something fun once in a while (candy is dandy), taking in too many calories without the nutrition that comes with whole foods could result in unwanted health problems down the line.[3]

Then again, eating isn't all about health. Sometimes we eat for pleasure, entertainment, or celebration, not for nutrition. Sometimes we have to eat quickly or on the go. What's even more complex is the human relationship to food. Ideally, we would all intuitively know what we need, eat the amount of food our bodies require to have sufficient energy and nutrients, enjoy our food, and share meals with loved ones, have treats and food-based celebrations sometimes, not obsess about it, and generally get along fine with food. But that can feel a long way away for someone who struggles with their relationship to food.

One of Noom's top priorities is to help you work through your understanding of and relationship with food so you can eat in a way that includes nourishing foods and fun foods in a balance that feels good and is in line with your goals. To accomplish this, we educate you about the nutritional aspects of food and different dietary strategies, but we also help you to personalize your diet by teaching you about why you get cravings, how to distinguish different kinds of hunger, what emotional eating is all about, and how to begin bringing more mindfulness to how food affects *you*. In this chapter, we cover nutritional information, and in the next chapter we cover personalization. So, let's start with the basics: What do you really need to know about food, so you can get what you want and need, physiologically, from the foods you choose?

NOOM COACH Q&A

What are some suggestions for meals that I can quickly eat on the go?

With our busy schedules, having more than fifteen minutes to prepare a meal is a luxury, but time shouldn't get in the way of enjoying a nutritious meal. Almost any meal can be eaten on the go. The key is to have food prepared and ready to throw together. Here are some helpful hints:

- Double, triple, or quadruple a recipe to have multiple meals for the week, or meals to freeze for a later date.
- Cook multiple servings of your food (lean meats, rice, potatoes, vegetables, etc.) at once and toss together different combinations every day.
- Clean and chop fruits and vegetables in bulk so they're always ready to snack on or add to any meal.
- Prepare your breakfast and lunch the day before and leave it in the fridge overnight.

Calories: Just the Facts, Please!

First and foremost, we eat food for the energy it provides our bodies. Different foods have different amounts of potential energy in them. Sometimes you need a lot of energy, and sometimes you need just a little energy. That can help you determine what to eat.

Kilocalories, or calories, as they are more commonly called, are a measure of the energy in food. Uh-oh, did we say the dreaded C-word? Calories! But yes, reality check—food has calories. Different foods have different amounts of energy—that is, different numbers of calories. People attribute a lot of emotion to the word *calorie*, but a calorie is just a unit of energy. Specifically, it's the amount of heat energy required to raise the temperature of 1 gram of water by 1 degree Celsius.

But you are not a test tube, and how energy works in your body will be unique to you. Energy is processed differently in different people, according to their age, weight, muscle mass, activity level, and so on. How your elderly aunt uses three hundred calories will be much different from how it's used by a toddler, or, let's say, Dwayne Johnson.

You also process calories differently according to what kind of food they come in. Some foods have more units of energy than other foods. For three hundred calories, you could have a small scoop of ice cream, *or* you could have a plate of grilled fish, a small sweet potato, and a pile of steamed asparagus. How much sugar, fat, and fiber a food has influences how, and how quickly, those calories get processed.

But calories are controversial. People argue about whether you should be counting them.

Should you count calories? The answer to that is: It's complicated.

Some health experts say yes, and some say no. Counting calories really does help some people stick with their goals. They find it motivating and rewarding. For others, it's too time-consuming or discouraging, or can even trigger them to overeat or undereat. It all depends on who you are.

In the Noom app, we do ask people about their goals and time frame for achieving them, and then we set a calorie range for them. We get some pushback on this, but we do it because research shows that people who self-monitor their diets by tracking food and calories are significantly more likely to succeed in their weight-loss goals and in sustaining healthier, long-term habits.[4] That being said, counting calories is *not* an app requirement. It's a tool people can use, or not. The reality is that if someone wants to lose weight, they must eat fewer calories than they burn. A calorie deficit is necessary for weight loss.[5] But whether you count the calories in order to get there or not is less important than actually achieving that calorie deficit, if weight loss is your goal.

Just as with weighing yourself, if counting calories helps you, then we're all for it. If it makes your relationship with food more difficult, then don't! Your health goals will be harder to reach if you do anything that makes you uncomfortable. We are here for you, whatever you need, and you can absolutely achieve your greatest dreams of health without counting anything at all.

NOOM COACH Q&A

How is my calorie budget determined?

The app automatically calculates your budget based on the Harris-Benedict Equation, which takes into account activity level and rate of weight loss desired. It does a pretty good job, but calorie calculating can never be 100 percent accurate. If you're feeling like you need more fuel than your current budget gives you, you can adjust that budget anytime in your Noom app.

Calorie Density: An Easy Way to Choose Foods Without Counting

What we have found more useful than the number of calories in food, in real-life sustainable scenarios involving food decisions, is caloric (or calorie) density. *Calorie density* is how densely packed those calories are in a food, by weight or volume. It's calculated by dividing the calories of a food by the weight of a food. A grape and a raisin have the same number of calories, but the raisin is smaller and weighs less because it has had all the water taken out of it.

That makes it more calorically dense. Because they still have all their water, grapes are larger and heavier than grapes. And yet, a raisin comes from a grape. They are the same food, differing only in water content. One isn't "good" and one isn't "bad." They simply have different calorie densities. The water dilutes the calorie density, and that makes grapes more filling than raisins. For the same number of calories, you can eat a lot more grapes in terms of weight or volume than you can eat raisins. So, if you are really hungry, you might choose the grapes. If you just want a little bite of something sweet, you might choose the raisins.

Here's another example from a different perspective. A quarter-pound hamburger (without the bun) and a quarter-pound of salad greens (without the dressing) weigh the same, but the quarter-pound of hamburger has about 290 calories and the quarter-pound of salad greens has about 9 calories. If you ate 290 calories worth of salad greens, the salad greens would be more filling because that would be a *huge* amount of salad greens (like, about eight pounds of salad greens!). The 290-calorie hamburger would be less filling because it's just one-quarter of a pound, rather than eight pounds. The hamburger, therefore, is much more calorie dense than the salad greens.

You don't have to know exact caloric density to use your knowledge of the energy density of different foods to your benefit. When you need more energy (calories), like if you have been going hard with exercise or if you are trying to get back up to a healthy weight, you can choose to eat more energy-dense foods. If you don't need as much energy—maybe you are having a sedentary day (week, month, year), or you have a goal of getting back down to a healthy weight—you can purposefully fill up on less energy-dense foods. Grapes and raisins, hamburgers and salad greens—all have their place. Sometimes you want a hamburger, sometimes you want a salad, but understanding the caloric density can help you satisfy your hunger and balance your food choices to reach your healthy weight goals.

It's important to note that calorically dense foods are not bad foods. You can still eat them whenever you want to (you can eat *any* food whenever you want to), but knowing a food is calorically dense can help you make meal decisions. "Thinking of foods in terms of caloric density helps people get away from thinking about food in binary terms, with 'good' and 'bad' labels. Foods aren't good or bad. It's all about context. Caloric density can help people to move toward seeing food as existing on a spectrum that facilitates an easier decision-making process and doesn't require or forbid any food," Dr. Michaelides says.

NOOM COACH Q&A

What are some ideas for snacks I can eat?

Whether it's during a hectic workweek or a jam-packed weekend, finding nutritious, convenient snacks can be tough. Many snacks are either full of salt and saturated fat or might appear healthy but are actually loaded with added sugar. It's best to pack your own snacks. Here are some great options you can pick up at the grocery store or make ahead of time:

- **Fruit:** This is a no-brainer. Fruit comes in its own packaging, making it easy to grab and go. Fruit provides healthy carbs that are perfect for an afternoon pick-me-up. Go for citrus fruits like oranges or grapefruit if you're craving something sweet. Bananas or pears can be more filling if you need a more substantial fix.
- **Greek yogurt:** Full of protein and low in calories, Greek yogurt is a great snack. Go for the nonfat options, and instead of grabbing those "fruit on the bottom" types (which are full of sugar), add your own sweetener, like honey, natural jam, or a spoonful of chopped dried or fresh fruit.

- **Nuts:** These are a classic snack option. Nuts provide healthy fats and protein, and are great for keeping your brain fueled. Choose roasted nuts for maximum crunch, but watch out for salt. Trail mix with nuts is also a great option. Just remember that nuts are calorie dense, so keep an eye on portion size.
- **Hard-boiled eggs:** Though you'll probably have to prep these ahead of time, hard-boiled eggs are super portable and filling. Shell them once they've cooled and throw them in a storage container for later. Add some flavor with a sprinkling of salt, or even a bit of mustard.
- **Protein bars:** True, many bars are full of sugar and unpronounceable ingredients, but there are also many that are made from ten ingredients or fewer. On days when time is running short, they're an easy alternative to chips or a candy bar. Remember to check labels for added sugar.

Nutritional Density: The Source of Food's Power

Nutritional density is related to caloric density, in a way. Some foods are nutrient-dense, meaning they have a lot of nutrients (like vitamins and minerals) for their calories. Other foods are not nutrient-dense, meaning they don't have a lot of nutrients for their calories. Kale, for example, is more nutrient-dense than iceberg lettuce. You will get a few more calories from a cup of raw kale (just under nine calories) than from a cup of iceberg lettuce (just under eight calories), but you're going to get a lot more fiber, vitamin C, vitamin A, vitamin K, B vitamins, calcium, iron, and potassium from the kale than you would from the lettuce.[6]

But wait . . . does that mean that kale is good and iceberg lettuce is bad? What if you love iceberg lettuce and, for you, kale is a hard pass? Not to worry! We here at Noom staunchly believe and tirelessly remind our Noomers that *there is no such thing as a good food or a bad food*. Food is just food. One food (say, an apple) having fewer calories or more nutrients than another food (say, a hunk of apple pie . . . mmm, pie) does not in any way indicate "goodness" or "badness."

The caloric density and nutritional density of foods are simple concepts that you can use, or not use. We only want you to know about them so you can decide for yourself what to eat. Your goals and desires might be health-related today and pleasure-related tomorrow. Sometimes an apple, or a kale salad, might be exactly what you want; other times, what you really need might be some apple pie, or a salad made of crispy, juicy iceberg lettuce with ranch dressing and bacon.

HYDRATION HACKS

One of the things that alters caloric density—like the difference between kale and iceberg lettuce, or a grape and a raisin—is the water content of a food. Water, of course, has zero calories in any amount, so the more water a food has, the more those calories are diluted. This is why 100 grams of watermelon, which is 90 percent water and about thirty calories, is less calorically dense than 100 grams of banana, which is 75 percent water and about eighty-nine calories.

The fact that water is filling is another tool you can use to your benefit. A study that suggests people often eat in response to thirst[7] demonstrated that people responded "inappropriately" to thirst and hunger cues (such as by eating when thirsty, or not drinking when thirsty) 62 percent of the time, and responded "appropriately" by drinking water when thirsty only 2 percent of the time (as opposed to drinking sweetened drinks or eating food). Drinking more water might therefore help settle and clarify your hunger and thirst signals, which can help with mindful eating (see pages 153–54).

Here are a few of our favorite hydration hacks:

- Start your day with a big glass of water to restore water you lost during sleep.
- Fill up faster and feel more satisfied by drinking a glass of water before or along with your meals.
- Try kicking off your morning coffee break with a glass of water. After, do you really want the coffee? (If so, go ahead; we would never get between a coffee lover and their morning cup!)
- A warm cup of herbal tea or water with lemon in the morning or on a chilly afternoon is comforting and hydrating. (Herbal tea counts as water—warm, cozy, flavorful water.)
- Try sparkling water for a treat during the day. Bubbles are fun!
- For more flavor, add citrus or cucumber slices or a few berries to your water.
- Get a nice water bottle you enjoy looking at and drinking out of, to carry with you. Some high-tech water bottles can keep track of how much water you are drinking and remind you to drink more.

These are all pleasurable, zero-calorie hacks that will keep you hydrated, and staying hydrated feels good and helps your body work better and stay healthy.[8]

Cheers! (Clinking water glasses.)

Macronutrients Under the Microscope

There is a lot more to food than just calorie density, of course. Foods consist of three primary nutrients, called *macronutrients*. These are fat, carbohydrates, and protein. Food also contains *micronutrients*, which are vitamins and minerals. We all need a balance to stay healthy and keep our bodies humming along as they should without nutritional deficiencies. Any eating program that has you drastically increasing or decreasing particular macronutrients may not be balanced. Before you make any rash decisions about macronutrients, let's look at what each one of them does for you, and debunk some common macronutrient misconceptions.

Don't Fight the Fat

Fat is not the enemy. We repeat: *Not the enemy!*

Fat is often unfairly maligned, but fat isn't bad. It's simply more calorically dense than carbohydrates or protein. A gram of protein and a gram of carbohydrates each have four calories, but a gram of fat has nine calories. Nevertheless, you need fat to function, and your brain is mostly fat (we are all "fat heads," if you want to get literal). Fat also helps your body absorb some very important vitamins, called fat-soluble vitamins (like vitamins A, D, E, and K). Fat supplies energy, helps nerve cells work better, lubricates the body, and is generally essential to life.

Fat can be saturated or unsaturated. Unsaturated fat comes mostly from plants, like olives, avocados, and nuts, and from fatty fish like salmon, in the form of omega-3 fatty acids. There are subtypes of unsaturated fat: polyunsaturated and monounsaturated fat. Saturated fat comes mostly from animals and processed foods. Red meat, dairy products (butter, ice cream, etc.), and eggs are mostly saturated fat. Coconut oil, despite being plant-based, is also mostly saturated.

Which fat is best? That is a point of contention for many.[9] Some say unsaturated fats are best, and many studies have shown that replacing saturated fats with unsaturated fats significantly decreases the risk of heart disease.[10]

Others say exactly the opposite, claiming that there is no link between saturated fats and heart disease,[11] and that polyunsaturated fats like corn, sunflower, and soy oil that contain a lot of omega-6 fatty acids are inflammatory.[12] The research is so conflicting, and fat itself is so biochemically complex, that trying to resolve the saturated versus unsaturated fat debate is virtually impossible at this point—and as we keep saying, no food is "bad" or "good," anyway. It is likely more important to limit processed fats (especially trans fats) than whole-food fats. We do know for sure that trans fats, which are (for the most part) the human-made "franken-fats," contribute to heart disease risk.[13] Trans fats are so risky that the government is taking steps to make them illegal food additives. (Your tax dollars at work!) We also know that eating a lot of fried food correlates with a higher risk of heart disease.[14] It seems that interfering with natural fats is what causes the problem—again, that pesky food processing!

On the other hand, "healthy fat" usually refers to the types of fat we know actually contribute to good health (rather than just *not* contributing to disease).[15] These fats lower LDL ("bad") cholesterol[16] and raise HDL ("good") cholesterol,[17] and consist of mostly whole-food fats from plants and fish: avocados; olives and olive oil; nuts like walnuts, almonds, cashews, and pistachios; seeds like flax seeds, sunflower seeds, chia seeds, hemp seeds, and pumpkin seeds; and fatty fish, like salmon, mackerel, tuna, and sardines.[18] There are those who say that saturated fat from foods like fresh beef and pork are also healthy fats, and there is some newer research showing that saturated fats may not contribute to heart disease the way we once thought.[19]

Until we know more for sure, it's probably just fine to get a combination of saturated and unsaturated fats in moderate amounts, in as close to their natural form as possible. Fat is more

calorically dense, gram for gram, t... ...
hydrates, so if you are trying to cut bac... ...
you could do it by moderating your fat inta... ...
tiple research studies have shown that high-... ...
and high-carb, low-fat diets are about equally effe... ...
loss,[20] so you may find that a lower-carbohydrate, hig... ...
works well for you.

The bottom line is that fat doesn't make you fat any ... ...
than protein or carbs do. It's more about whether you are eatin...
more calories than your body needs.

NOOM COACH Q&A

I'm breastfeeding. Should my calorie budget be higher?

It's recommended that you increase your budget by four hundred to five hundred calories per day for each child you're breastfeeding, and always refer to your doctor or lactation consultant's guidance. In the Noom app, you can manually adjust your calorie budget to be in line with your physician's recommendation for calorie intake.

Making Peace with Carbohydrates

Back in the 1980s, everybody got mad at fat and went bonkers for nonfat cookies. Now, people tend to be merely slightly suspicious of fat. But carbs? Carbs are practically canceled these days! But carbs, like fat, are innocent—*innocent, we tell you!* (Food judge rapping gavel.) Carbs are your body's favorite fuel, and your brain loves carbs because they are so easily converted into glucose, which feeds the active and hungry brain.

Every vegetable, every fruit, every grain, every nut, and every bean contains carbs, and you can't get fiber without carbs. Fiber is essential for keeping the digestive system moving along also good food for the friendly bacteria in your intestine (aka your microbiome). Most of the non-calorically dense but nutritionally dense foods in Noom's color-coding system are carb-y, and carbs often come "packaged by nature" with vitamins, minerals, and lots of phytonutrients (a fancy term for all the antioxidant and anti-inflammatory compounds in plants that help fight off diseases and make us healthier).[21]

That being said, carbs, just like fat, come in many forms: pears and pizza, carrots and cookies, white beans and white bread. Some carb-rich foods are great allies in the quest for health, helping to dull cravings, promote weight loss, improve heart health, and steady blood sugar. These star players are all the whole-food carbs: veggies, fresh and frozen fruits, legumes like black beans and lentils, and whole grains like oatmeal, quinoa, wild rice, and barley.

Processed foods are also carb-rich, and these are the foods that people are really thinking about when they rail against carbs: white bread, white pasta, cookies, crackers, bagels, pizza, pastries, breakfast cereals, doughnuts, chips, fruit juice, soda, and anything with sugar. These are processed foods and the sources of carbs in them are typically highly refined (not in the fancy way, drinking tea with their pinkies up, but in the processed way, like stripping all the fiber out of fruit or the bran and vitamins out of flour).

But you love pizza, bagels, cereal, doughnuts? You enjoy your morning orange juice or your afternoon fancy coffee drink with whipped cream and all the syrup? *These foods are not bad*. What they are, usually, is calorically dense and nutritionally sparse. They are fun treats to enjoy, but they aren't staple foods for nourishment. They're like tuxedos and ballgowns—great for special occasions, but not for every day.

There are nutritionally dense swaps for many of these foods, like whole-grain pizza crust, whole-grain pasta, whole-grain bread, whole-grain cereal, and so on, which can move them back closer to their whole-food origins and get them out of the red zone. White pasta is moderately calorically dense but not nutritionally dense, for example, but whole-wheat pasta is nutritionally dense, even if it has slightly more calories (worth it!).

When we talked about fat, we mentioned that science has shown that low-carb, high-fat diets are about equally effective for weight loss as high-carb, low-fat diets. (Some studies show that low-carb diets are more effective for weight loss, and other studies show that low-fat diets are more effective for weight loss, while still other studies show no statistically significant difference.[22]) If you love your carbs, you don't have to fear you'll never be able to lose weight. Exactly the opposite! You may find it is easier to maintain a calorie deficit, and therefore lose weight, if you arrange your diet around whole-food carbs, which are nutritionally dense but not calorically dense. There is plenty of research to support this.

SINISTER SUGAR?

Talk about sugar, or offer a sugary treat to someone, and you are likely to get some combination of delighted anticipation and worried guilt. "Oooh, a delicious doughnut? Oh, no, I can't possibly!" Sugar may have the reputation as the bad-boy carbohydrate, but sugar isn't inherently bad. It's simply calorically dense and nutritionally sparse.

Most sugar has the fiber and nutrients removed and is a refined food. But some sugars also come naturally packaged with their fiber, vitamins, and minerals; they're inside fruits, veggies, and grains. This is natural sugar. Sweet fruits like bananas and grapes have more natural sugar than less-sweet fruits like berries and citrus. Corn, wheat, barley, and oats all contain natural sugar, too. Foods with natural sugars are much less calorically dense than foods with added sugars. An ear of corn on the cob is not calorically dense, but a hunk of sweet cornbread is.

When people talk about the negatives of sugar, they usually mean processed sugar, which comes from sugarcane, sugar beets, dates, or corn, commonly in the form of crystals or syrup. If you are watching your sugar intake, keep an eye on those food labels. Sugar goes by many names: dextrose, fructose, sucrose, lactose, molasses, nectar, honey, or anything coupled with the word *syrup*, so scan those food labels. Sugar is in a lot of processed foods, including those you might not expect, like condiments, pasta sauce, soup, nut butter, and salad dressings, as well as foods that are obviously sweet, like breakfast cereals, flavored milk and yogurt, granola and protein bars, and flavored coffees.

If you are working on eating more mindfully, you might also want to notice how you feel if you eat a lot of sugar. In some people, sugar can cause bloating, stomachache, headache, jitters, fatigue, or excessive thirst, or can make you hungrier. It could also lead to problems with blood sugar and insulin over time, which are risk factors for diabetes. The more you notice sugar's effects on you, the more information you have to help you make decisions about your sugar intake.

Preaching About Protein

People rarely demonize protein. It's essential for life and it helps rev up metabolism, fire up the immune system, and heal and grow the body's very substance: muscles, skin, organs. While there are those who claim we don't actually need fat or don't actually need carbs (we don't agree with either of those claims, by the way), nobody says we don't need protein. We may not need as much of it as we get, but most of us, with the possible exception of body builders, probably don't have to worry about not getting enough.

According to the experts, most adults need about 0.36 grams of protein per pound of body weight, so someone who weighs two hundred pounds should eat about 73 grams of protein every day. That's not hard to accomplish because most foods contain protein. The richest sources are meat, seafood, eggs, and dairy products, and the leaner they are (lean cuts of meat, low-fat or nonfat dairy products, egg whites), the more protein they have.

Vegetarians needn't be concerned—there are many protein-rich plant-based foods, too. Tofu and other soybean-based products are great sources, since soybeans have so much protein, but other legumes (black beans, white beans, lentils, split peas, kidney beans—basically all the beans and peas) are protein-rich. Nuts and seeds have protein, and peanuts and peanut butter are good sources, too. Even leafy greens like spinach and other green vegetables like asparagus, broccoli, and sprouts have some protein, so if you eat lots of veggies, those smaller amounts add up.

Protein is filling, so we recommend including a source of protein (animal or vegetable) in most of your meals and snacks if you have a healthy weight goal. Protein also has a higher thermal effect, which means it takes more energy to digest it than it takes to digest carbohydrates or fat. A study reported in the *American Journal of Clinical Nutrition* showed that the increased satiety from protein results in reducing the amount of food people eat when their food isn't restricted and also helps maintain lean muscle in people who are in the process of losing weight.[23]

◆

There, in a nutshell, are your macronutrients: fat, carbs, and protein. They all contain energy (calories). They all contain micronutrients (various combinations of vitamins and minerals). They can all be part of a healthy diet, and while there are many ways of eating with greatly differing ratios, it's important for health—and the key to a balanced diet—to get them all.

SALT SENSE

You may often hear that salt is "bad" and that a low-sodium diet is better for heart health and blood pressure. Like sugar, salt isn't a "bad food." We all need it. It helps our bodies maintain an electrolyte balance in the blood, and unprocessed salt (like sea salt, pink salt, etc.) is a good source of trace minerals. The health hazards of salt are still hotly debated, but the current consensus seems to be that moderate intake is fine for healthy people, and strictly limiting salt is most important for people who already have certain health conditions, such as hypertension.[24] However, since salt is in just about every packaged food, is liberally used in restaurant food (fast food and fancy food), and serves as a flavor enhancer, it's easy to eat a lot of it, and too much salt isn't good for anyone. Overdoing the salt could cause water retention, which can make you gain five pounds overnight. It could also increase blood pressure in some people. It's not something to eliminate, but it is probably something to moderate.

Food Philosophy Round-Up

So, which foods should you choose? We know we keep saying that's up to you, but some people want more guidance, and we get that. Dr. Michaelides says: "I recommend developing a food philosophy, whatever that is for you. A food philosophy is different from a diet. It's something sustainable you believe in and follow for life. A diet is temporary. If you're thinking about going keto, or vegan, or Mediterranean, consider whether it's something you could do over the long term. Will you feel full? Will you be satisfied? Will you enjoy it? Can you see yourself eating this way in ten years? Is it in line with your values? Is it something you are interested in or believe in? If so, then go for it. No matter what it is, it will still work with Noom."

Your food philosophy can be something simple, like "balanced" or "omnivorous," or it can be centered on keeping your heart healthy or dealing with a health issue you already have, like celiac disease or diabetes. It may be that you want to learn to eat whatever you want with mindfulness, so you obsess less about rules and listen to your body's cues (see Chapter 9). Maybe you are already a staunch practitioner of a particular food philosophy, or maybe you aren't sure what your food philosophy is, but you are interested in learning more. Let's look at some popular ones with a lot of followers. Maybe one will stand out to you as "The One!" (We love matchmaking.)

Vegetarian/Vegan/Plant-Based/WFPB/ WFPBNO/WFPBNONSNS

You thought you knew what we were talking about with this section title, with vegan and vegetarian, and then saw all those acronyms and you were like, "Wha . . . ?" (Or maybe you were more like, "Wow, I'm so impressed that Noom understands my WFBPNONSNS lifestyle!") These diets are all variations on a theme, with some distinct differences:

◆ **Vegetarians** eat mostly plants, but often also eat dairy products and/or eggs. Technically, vegetarians who eat dairy products are called lacto-vegetarians, and those who eat eggs are ovo-vegetarians, and those who eat both are lacto-ovo-vegetarians, but seriously, it's not the 1970s anymore. Nobody says that. It's just "vegetarian."

◆ **Vegans** eat no animal products of any kind, including dairy products, eggs, or honey. Vegans also consider veganism to be more than a diet. It's an ethical position. Even if the animal is supposedly not injured, vegans consider using animals for human pleasure and consumption to be unethical. They also avoid wearing and using animal products (like wool sweaters and leather shoes) as much as possible.

◆ **Plant-based** means your diet is based on plants, but it may not contain 100 percent plants. It is also a term to distinguish people who eat only plants, but do so for health reasons, not for animal-rights reasons. There is some crossover, when people talk about this subject, between the terms *vegan* and *plant-based*. For instance, many people call plant-based diets vegan diets, even if they are not ethical vegans.

◆ **WFPB** stands for "whole-food, plant-based," and it refers to people who eat only whole foods, not processed foods. These people are often, but not always, 100 percent plant-based.

◆ **WFPBNO** stands for "whole-food, plant-based, no oil." If a food is naturally fatty, like avocados, that's okay, but people following this diet don't ever add oil to their food. Not even olive oil is allowed, no matter how healthy people say it is.

◆ **WFPBNONSNS** is for the truly devoted whole-foodies out there—it stands for "whole-food, plant-based, no oil, no salt, no sugar." They eat only food the way nature made it. No additives of any kind. Hard-core!

There are a lot of pros for all these variations on the plant-based diet. First is that they typically include mostly non-calorically dense but nutritionally dense foods, so plant-based eaters tend to get more vitamins and minerals than meat eaters, especially more vitamins C and E, folic acid, potassium, magnesium, and phytochemicals. They also tend to eat much more fiber than omnivores, and usually get plenty of protein from plant-based proteins like tofu, tempeh, beans, mushrooms, whole grains, nuts, and seeds.

Plant-based diets have also been associated with lower rates of heart disease[25] and cancer.[26] The only nutrients they tend to be low on are vitamin B_{12} (found only in animal foods) and sometimes vitamin D, which is hard to get unless you drink vitamin D–fortified milk. People who don't eat meat often take B_{12} and D supplements.

If you're interested in plant-based eating, meat substitutes (burgers, brats, "chickn," ground "meat") and plant-based dairy products (like almond and oat milk, cheese, yogurt, and ice cream) are easy ways to transition from animal to plant foods. To minimize caloric density and maximize nutrition, make veggies the centerpiece and supplement with whole grains, legumes, and fruit.

Gluten-Free

You've probably heard of gluten-free diets, but for the many who aren't aware, gluten is a protein in wheat, rye, barley, spelt, and other relatives of wheat. In some people, gluten induces an autoimmune reaction that causes the body to attack its own small intestine, producing a cascade of health problems. These people have a condition called celiac disease, and gluten-free eating has to be a way of life for them to avoid damage to the digestive tract.

Others find that avoiding gluten relieves irritable bowel syndrome (IBS) symptoms or other digestive problems, and increases their energy, even if they don't have celiac disease. They may have a recently recognized condition called non-celiac gluten sensitivity.[27] Other people have no apparent problem eating gluten, but may think they should jump on the trend. There are no apparent benefits to going gluten-free for people without gluten sensitivity. It isn't a weight-loss diet. Many gluten-free food replacements are not any more nutritious or lower in calories (read: gluten-free cookies). Eating gluten-free can be perfectly pleasurable, with all the gluten-free substitutes out there, but it's probably not necessary if you don't have a sensitivity.

Paleo

The so-called Paleolithic or ancestral diet, called "Paleo" for short, is an often misunderstood eating philosophy centered on eating foods that mimic, as closely as possible in this modern world, those our ancestors ate in the Paleolithic era, before the days of agriculture and domestication of animals. We can't exactly match what our ancestors ate because it's a different world, but nobody *has* to eat processed food or agricultural food, and that is the Paleo way.

The focus is on fresh, preferably organic meat and fish, vegetables, nuts, seeds, eggs, small amounts of fruit (usually what is seasonal), and added fats that are minimally processed, like butter, coconut oil, olive oil, and avocado oil. Off the menu are all processed foods, added sugar, all grains (thought to have only meaningfully entered the human diet during the agricultural revolution), beans and legumes, and processed vegetable oils like canola, corn, and sunflower oil. Many Paleo enthusiasts also cut out dairy products.

The good thing about the Paleo diet is that its whole-food emphasis tends to include a lot of healthy foods that could help with weight loss, blood sugar control, and blood pressure control. However, the devil is in the details. Some people who eat this way focus mainly on meat, rather than on all the plant foods our Paleolithic ancestors probably ate most of the time. This could result in a diet low in nutrients and fiber and very high in saturated fat (for better or for worse). Contributing to the low-fiber risk is the absence of all whole grains, beans, and legumes, which are fiber- and nutrient-rich.

If you like the idea of trying a "natural human diet," we recommend getting in enough plant foods for fiber and phytonutrients, balancing the meat intake, and choosing natural, organic food as much as possible. Some people thrive on this diet, while other people feel it is too restrictive (eliminating all grains and dairy cuts out quite a lot of common foods).

Mediterranean

Probably the most well-studied diet, and the one most often proclaimed the healthiest diet in the world, the Mediterranean diet comes in as the #1 best diet, year after year, on the widely circulated *U.S. News & World Report* annual ranking of popular diets.[28] It's true that some of the countries where people live the longest and have the lowest rates of chronic disease follow this kind of diet (like Sardinia, an island off the coast of Italy, and Ikaria, an island off the coast of Greece). There are a lot of variations on this eating style, but in general, it's characterized by a lot of vegetables, fruits, whole grains, nuts, seeds, and legumes, as well as a lot of seafood and small amounts of poultry and red meat. The main dairy products are yogurt and cheese, in small amounts, and minimal sweets. Instead of butter, olive oil is the star, and moderate amounts of wine are also a common feature (but not required). Processed food is out. Also probably key to this way of life is a lot of social support, time outdoors, natural movement, and prioritizing family life, all of which are not insignificant factors in a healthy life (see Chapter 6).

This is an easy, balanced, and delicious way of eating. If you want to try it, it helps if you enjoy cooking. Stick to home-cooked meals most of the time, with lots of vegetables and fish, and yummy foods like hummus and whole-grain pita bread; unsweetened yogurt with fruit; Greek salad and vegetable soup with pesto and whole-grain bread; pasta with tomato sauce and fresh herbs; pizza with fresh mozzarella, olives, and artichoke hearts; and nuts and fruit for snacking. Mmm, now we're getting hungry . . .

Low-Carb

Low-carb diets have been around for at least five decades. They first got really popular with the Atkins diet craze, but have been a feature of many other popular diets (including the Paleo diet, typically). They may be good for people who overeat carbs and want to cut back. A standard low-carb diet gets about 20 percent of its calories from carbs.

This way of eating emphasizes meat; fish; eggs; full-fat dairy products; non-starchy vegetables like leafy greens, mushrooms, and broccoli; nuts and nut butters; and added oils and fats. It may also include beans and legumes, and lower-sugar fruits like berries. Low-carbers tend to avoid all grains and grain-based products, starchy vegetables like potatoes and corn, and high-sugar foods, including fruits like bananas and grapes.

As we've mentioned, low-carb diets can be successful for weight loss—about as much as low-fat diets are[29]—although some studies proclaim low-carb diets to be more successful for weight loss.[30] The low-carb life may also help to control blood sugar and lower triglycerides, which are risk factors for heart disease.

"Keto"

Ketogenic diets are very low-carb, very high-fat diets. Some may get up to 75 percent or even more of their calories from fat, and fewer than 5 percent of their calories from carbs. That may not sound healthy, but ketogenic diets have been proven effective for weight loss, at least in the short term. One meta-analysis of randomized controlled trials (an analysis of multiple research studies) showed that the ketogenic diet beat out a low-fat diet for achieving long-term weight loss (meaning a year after the studies analyzed, participants had retained their weight loss better on a keto diet than on a low-fat diet).[31] Another study reported in the *International Journal of Environmental Research and Public Health* concluded that a ketogenic diet can reduce hunger in people with obesity and may help speed fat loss,[32] although this article did describe the ketogenic diet as a temporary diet, not a permanent way to eat.

If you have any health issues, such as a history of heart disease or diabetes, discuss whether this kind of diet is appropriate for you with your doctor. If you want to try the ketogenic diet, just be sure to include plenty of non-starchy vegetables and fruits to get enough fiber and nutrients into your diet.

Intermittent Fasting

This last eating philosophy isn't about what you eat, but when you eat. Intermittent fasting involves setting a window of time during which you can eat and a window of time during which you fast, or don't eat. People often start with twelve hours on and twelve hours off. For example, if you finish dinner at 7:00 p.m., then you wouldn't eat breakfast until 7:00 a.m. Since you'll probably be asleep for much of this time, a twelve-hour fast isn't too difficult for most people.

Those who want to progress may widen their fasting window to fourteen, sixteen, eighteen, or twenty hours, leaving themselves just ten, eight, six, or four hours (respectively) to get all their caloric and nutritional needs met for the day. Some people go even longer, taking one or two days off eating every week. A more extreme form is to eat every other day.

The theory is that time free from digestion gives your body a chance to heal and repair. Most studies on intermittent fasting do show some weight-loss effects and improvement in metabolism;[33] that is, intermittent fasting may help to reduce body fat and inflammation and improve insulin sensitivity.

Some people eat like this naturally. They wait to eat until about noon, or they stop eating in the late afternoon. If you know you get hangry (hungry + angry) if you haven't eaten in a few hours, this way of eating may not be for you. It seems to fit some people's lifestyle, and possibly metabolism, better than others.

If you want to try intermittent fasting, start with a twelve-hour overnight fast, and if you like how it feels, you can work up to greater amounts of time gradually. But listen to your body! How you feel will tell you whether fasting is for you. If fasting feels great and you love it, then your body probably responds well to it. If you hate it, then don't worry about it. There are plenty of ways to eat (as you've just seen) that are at least as effective as intermittent fasting for improving health and getting to a healthy weight.

◆

We hope by now you've got some good ideas about food and are inspired by the power of food to influence your health and weight, but what we haven't yet covered is the psychology of eating. Knowing what eating style you want to follow is one thing, but contending with the complicated relationship between humans and food is another. Why do you eat? How do you eat? What about cravings, and emotional eating, and mindful eating? In the next chapter, we're going to put a pause on food-as-nourishment and look more closely at what's going on in your brain when you eat food.

5

The Psychology of Eating

Good food is like music you can taste, color you can smell.
There is excellence all around you. You need only
to be aware to stop and savor it.

—Chef Auguste Gusteau (from the movie *Ratatouille*)

If you take one thing from these food chapters, we hope it's this: Food is meant to be enjoyed. Food is an integral part of life, and no matter what your health goals are, you can relish, savor, and anticipate food; you can look back on your meals and feel good about how enjoyable they were. But that's easy to say and not so easy to do. To master this deceptively simple relationship with food requires a little bit of psychology know-how. Fortunately, that's our specialty!

Food gets complicated when we begin to project feelings, judgments, and values onto it. People often think about their relationship with food in terms of *I can't, I shouldn't, I mustn't, I won't, I should, I must, I have to*. They ask themselves, "Why did I eat this?" "Why didn't I eat that?" "Why can't I eat what I intend to eat?" "Why do I eat what I didn't want to eat?" All this "should-ing" and second-guessing and labeling leads to fear, guilt, regret, and a sense of a lack of control around food.

Unfortunately, diet culture promotes many of these attitudes, then makes people feel dependent on diets, either constantly deprived ("I have great willpower!") or guilty for eating "too much" ("I have no willpower!"). All this black-and-white thinking is human nature, to some extent. Dr. Michaelides says, "People like to put things in buckets, categorizing things to make sense of the world." But it's one thing to categorize and another thing to judge.

You've already seen how we here at Noom sometimes put things in buckets, like categorizing foods as non-calorically dense or calorically dense. This makes a balanced diet easier to navigate. But what we don't do is say that non-calorically dense foods are good and calorically dense foods are bad. You can have clear-cut health goals (SMART goals). You can have a big picture (YBP). You can work on getting healthy or getting to a weight that feels good to you, but what you don't need to do in order to achieve these things is to put value judgments on food.

This is, admittedly, a hard pattern to break. It might require reframing your thoughts, feelings, and attitudes concerning food in ways that will support, rather than thwart, your goals. To get started refreshing your relationship to food and your thoughts and feelings about eating, let's begin with a little psych trick we like to call *metacognition*.

Intro to Metacognition

Here's a brain-bender: You are not your thoughts, and you are not your feelings. You are the one who *has* thoughts and feelings.

Metacognition is a fancy term for an awareness of the separation between you and your thoughts, and the acknowledgment that you are the one observing your thoughts.[1] It's the process of planning, monitoring, and assessing your own understanding or performance, and includes a critical awareness of your own thinking and learning, as well as an awareness of yourself *as* the thinker and learner. Technically, metacognition means "cognition about cognition," or thinking about thinking. (Are we blowing your mind yet?) Metacognition sounds like a cool concept they might make a sci-fi movie about (a thought within a thought within a thought . . .), but it's actually a tool you can use to handle thoughts about food (or thoughts about anything) that feel problematic.

Before you can have a good relationship with food, you may need to deal with some of your less helpful thoughts about food, and the way to do that is to begin noticing those thoughts and reframing the thoughts as things you are having, rather than things that you are. It's also useful to question whether the thoughts are true.[2] For instance, after a day of eating a lot of vegetables and fruits, and going to the gym, you may have the thought that you were "good" all day. Then, when it came to dinner, you were really hungry and ate second helpings and had a big dessert. You may have the thought that you ruined everything and are a failure and were "bad."

But with metacognition, you can stop and examine those thoughts apart from yourself. Is it true that eating vegetables makes you good and eating dessert makes you bad? Of course, it's not true, even if you have that thought or that feeling. Remember, you're *having* the thought that you were good or bad, but that has nothing to do with your actual goodness or badness.

If you employ metacognition whenever you feel your thoughts going negative, you can stop the spiral of despair that is so common when people are trying to eat healthier and think they have failed. Metacognition can help you step back from your thoughts so you can (1) deconstruct them to discover whether they are true or not, and (2) reframe them in a way that is more positive and in line with your goals.

Here are some ways you can pluck some of those thought distortions out of your head and reframe them:

- **"I was good all day."** What does that even mean? Good all day? Really? See this thought as a thing apart from you, floating around in the ether. "I was good all day." Look at it for too long and it can start to feel absurd. Now, reframe that thought into one that is more useful for you, such as: "I stuck to my goals today. I'm so proud of how well I was able to do that! I really can practice healthy habits."

- **"I was bad tonight."** Do you really believe you were "bad"? If so, is that a rational thought? Would people who love you agree with that? Instead, you can reframe this thought as: "I had a long day and by dinnertime, I had decision fatigue. My willpower felt like it was all used up tonight, and then I ate more than I had planned to when I started the day." The end. No judgment, just fact. If you're going to add a helpful thought, rather than a discouraging one, you could also think: "Well, it happens to everyone now and then. It doesn't mean it's going to happen to me all the time. Now I know that it's more difficult to act according to my long-term goals when I'm tired. What plan could I put in place to help me next time?"

- **"I blew it. I'm a failure!"** Let that one float around for a minute and you can see how untrue it is. You're a failure because you ate more food than you had planned to eat hours before that specific meal? Of course, that doesn't make you a failure. You have plenty more chances to work on your goals. Instead, you might reframe this thought as: "I know there are reasons why I did what I did. Maybe I didn't eat enough earlier in the day and let myself get too hungry. I didn't follow my plan tonight and sometimes plans don't work out." You could also look on the bright side and remember that you enjoyed that ice cream. You could even have the thought: "It's okay to really enjoy an ice cream treat."

- **"I'll never be able to get healthy."** Are you a fortune-teller? You can see the future? This negative thought should look extra untrue when you view it from the distance you can get with metacognition. How can you possibly know what you won't be able to do in your life? Instead, you could reframe that thought as: "Getting healthy is a journey, and I'm on that journey because I want to feel good. I don't feel so good right now though, so that's information that can guide me."

You can do this with any thought distortion. Just step back. Have a look. Your brain is wise, but sometimes it can produce thoughts that are overly dramatic, pessimistic, or frustrated. At other times, it can be a cock-eyed optimist, bubbly and cheerful, or full of hope and ambition. It's up to you which thoughts you will take as guidance and which ones you can roll your eyes at and say, "Oh, come on now, thoughts. Let's get real." (We'll talk more about metacognition in Chapter 9, which is about mindfulness.)

THAT'S YOUR WORK

A trick we like a lot to counter and reframe frustrated thoughts and feelings is a simple phrase with a lot of power behind it: "That's my work."[3] Whenever you find yourself thinking that your goals are too difficult, you can't accomplish them, you feel stuck, or you just want to give up, all you have to say to yourself is: "That's my work."

We all have work to do in this life, and it isn't always fun, but we have chosen to do it because it will result in something re-warding, whether that's a paycheck, or a feeling of pride and accomplishment, or feeling better and becoming healthier. You don't want to go to the gym? "That's my work." You are feeling a strong sugar craving you want to resist but it feels impossible, even though you already had a big dinner and you are not actually hungry? "That's my work." You are tempted to give in to a food pusher to go along with the group, even though you would like to think you have the strength to say no? "That's my work."

Somehow, this reframing of your goals as a job that you are doing can make them feel more important, more necessary, and harder to ignore. It also makes it easier to recognize the daily steps you take toward your goal as cumulative.

Types of Eating

Metacognition, as it turns out, happens to be a great tool to apply to eating in order to understand the many reasons why and how we do it. It can help you notice when you are eating because of hunger, when you are eating for pleasure, when you are eating out of boredom, or when you're eating driven by strong emotions. There is nothing wrong with eating for reasons other than hunger now and then, but if you begin to feel like you're out of control with food and not eating in a way that supports your health goals, metacognition can help.

To use this tool more effectively, we've identified four types of eating that most of us dip into and out of at different times, in different situations, and in different moods. As you read these, see if you recognize doing them (most of us have done them all), so that when you are doing them next time, you can think about them and notice how and why you are eating. The four types of eating we've identified are these: fuel eating, fun eating, fog eating, and storm eating. (Dr. Michaelides reminds us, and would like to remind you, that evocative as these names may be, these are not psychology terms. We named them this way to help you remember and recognize them, but we'll be sure to explain the psychology behind these, too.)

Fuel Eating

Fuel eating is eating for the purpose of fueling your body. Fuel eating means choosing foods that are nourishing to the body and that provide the right kind of fuel for good energy and good health, in the form of complex carbohydrates, healthy fats, lean protein, fiber, vitamins, and minerals. Fuel eating is eating to live (as opposed to living to eat), and it feels great because these are foods your body likes to use for fuel. When you make that conscious choice to have that big salad with lots of veggies topped with grilled salmon, you are fuel eating.

Fuel eating helps your body work better, and it's also good for your mental health. A 2017 study published in *Scientific Reports* looked at how happy and satisfied people felt after eating, using a smartphone-based assessment over the course of eight days.[4] Surprisingly, they found that vegetables contributed to the most eating happiness over the course of the eight days, and that people generally were just as happy after eating vegetables and fruits as they were after eating sweets. The study also found that people were just as happy after eating dinner as they were after snacking, which surprised the researchers, who expected that snacking would make people happier. So, no worries that fuel eating is a bummer. It's just the opposite!

Because it's healthy, however, be aware that it's easy to label fuel eating as "good" or "virtuous." It's good *for you*, but it's not the only food game in town.

Fun Eating

Fun eating is eating for pleasure. If fuel eating is eating to live, fun eating is living to eat (and, yes, you can do both—variety is the spice of life). Fun foods are things like comfort foods (mom's mac and cheese!), indulgent desserts (chocolate lava cake, anyone?), holiday and celebratory foods (birthday cake!), and any food you eat more for pleasure than for nutrients.

That doesn't mean fun foods aren't nutritious. According to 2019 research published in *Health Psychology Open*, the moderate consumption of pleasurable foods can be a healthy way to eat, as opposed to constantly fretting over food, trying to be a perfect eater, and thinking of pleasurable food in negative terms. Just as it can be easy to think of fuel eating as "good," it can be easy to think of fun eating as "bad," but that can result in unnecessary stress.[5] There is absolutely nothing wrong with having a little fun in life! Mindfully eating fun foods that are shared with family and friends, enjoying cooking, appreciating the food experience, and prioritizing high-quality food and dinner rituals are all great ways to achieve moderation without constantly having to worry about self-control, according to the study. We approve of this theory! Just remember that fun foods tend to be calorically dense, so keep that in mind as you make deliberate decisions about portion size.

Fog Eating

"Fog eating is really just mindless eating," says Dr. Michaelides. "You aren't paying attention to what you're doing." We've all been there, right? You're totally into your show and suddenly the whole bowl of buttered popcorn is gone and you're looking suspiciously at the dog and the dog is like, "Hey, that was all you, dude."

It's not that surprising that something we do multiple times a day is also something we stop noticing after a while. The first time you ever ate ice cream, you were probably bowled over by this miraculous concoction, but over time you got used to it. It's hard to pay close attention to something that happens so frequently, and so people tend to switch to autopilot and eat while doing other things, whether that's checking messages, or watching TV, or even engaging in lively dinner conversation.

You can't completely avoid fog eating. "Really, paying close attention to every single bite you eat every single time isn't very realistic," notes Dr. Michaelides. "But that doesn't mean a little mindfulness can't improve your eating experience." Paying attention when you eat might mean you make more considered choices, notice when you're full, and enjoy eating more.

It can also help you tune in to how much you're eating. Did you notice the server refilling your wine glass? Did you mean to polish off the whole basket of tortilla chips? Portioning out what you're eating, eating it intentionally, and paying enough attention to say, "No, thanks, I've had enough" when you really have had enough can help to avoid overeating in situations where you have decided you don't want to overeat.

Storm Eating

Storm eating usually occurs around strong emotions, or as a backlash to food restriction. You come home furious about a work situation and start tearing through the snack cabinet. Somebody left a box of doughnuts on the table, and although you "quit sugar," everybody in the house is gone, so you go to town on the doughnuts. No witnesses! You've had nothing but salad and fruit all day, and then someone orders a greasy, cheesy pepperoni pizza and you dive in head-first.

Storm eating isn't about actual hunger. It's more about rebelling against food restriction and/or self-medicating with food. When it happens, you feel about as in control of it as you would feel if caught in a hurricane. Most people have experienced storm eating at some point, and some people do it frequently. It's normal for it to happen every now and then, but if it becomes a habit, it can definitely work against reaching your health goals. (And if you often feel out of control with storm eating, you could check in with a specialist in binge eating or a dietician for some professional assistance to get this kind of eating under control.) If storm eating is feeling problematic for you, think about whether you are eating enough, whether you might be overly restrictive in your eating, or whether you are eating for emotional reasons, and what you might do instead (because in the long run, food isn't, unfortunately, able to solve anybody's emotional issues).

Emotional Eating

Since we've brought it up, and it's often associated with storm eating (and can also be associated with other types of eating), let's talk about emotional eating. Emotional eating is eating in response to strong feelings, and the reason people do it is that, in the short term, it feels like it helps. Food can be comforting, interesting, pleasurable, and distracting; sometimes that might feel like just what you need. And maybe it is!

But when emotional eating is happening more than you want it to, there are some ways you can redirect your emotional energy. Wait, don't worry—we're not going to tell you to "take a bubble bath" or "call a friend" or any of those things you've heard a million times before. We're not even going to tell you to "feel your feelings," because the whole point of emotional eating is *not having to feel them!* You can always do that later, but in the moment, when all you want is cake, feeling your feelings probably isn't going to cut it.

What you really need are coping strategies,[6] and guess what? We are *flush* with coping strategies![7] In fact, we have an acronym for them: EMOTE. Technically, *emoting* means "feeling your feelings," but that's not what this is about. Our version stands for

Explore, Meditate, Observe, Talk/Text, and Exercise. EMOTE-ing is more like a replacement for actual emoting, when that feels too difficult in the moment. When you want to eat and you know it's coming from an emotional place, here are some things you can do:

E Is for Explore

Exploring is fun! It's engaging, it's interesting, and it can even hit that dopamine button and fill you up with good vibes. If you are feeling the urge to eat because of a strong emotion and not because of hunger, turn to something else you're interested in that makes you feel good. This could be reading a compelling article or going down an internet rabbit hole (conspiracy theories!) or watching something on TV you've been wanting to see. You could put in those earbuds and check out that hot new band everybody's talking about. Remember that hobby you love that you haven't had time for? Play the guitar, draw a picture of your cat, immerse yourself in that woodworking project, start your memoir (you are *too* interesting enough!), go on a hike and try a new trail, start designing your dream house, plan your next vacay—or anything else that's new and exciting, that sparks your imagination and passion. Let that exploration and newness take over your brain, so there isn't room for anything else.

M Is for Meditate

Drop and gimme Zen! Meditation isn't as hard as people say, and it feels really, really good. It can calm your anxious mind, relieve stress, cheer you up, and make you feel serene. There are many ways you can meditate, from just sitting and noticing how your breath feels going in and out, to repeating a calming phrase, to visualizing a relaxing environment. Ahhhhh . . . Pick any strategy you like.

MEDITATION MENU

Anything that helps you relax could be considered meditation, but sometimes a little structure helps. Here are a few easy meditation techniques to try when you're feeling a strong emotion and the urge to blunt it with food:

- **Fallout breathing:** Inhale deeply through your nose, taking in as much air as you can, then let it all fall out of your lungs through your mouth, with a big sigh. Repeat five times or more, until the strong feeling passes.
- **Box breathing:** Inhale for a count of 4, hold your breath for a count of 4, exhale for a count of 4, and hold your breath after the exhale for a count of 4. Repeat as needed.
- **Counting:** Choose a number. Slowly count up to the number, then count backward down to 1. Repeat as needed.
- **Visualizing:** Imagine a peaceful environment and imagine yourself in it, interacting with it. Try to picture it in as much detail as you can. Where are you? Walking through a peaceful forest or a flowery meadow? At the beach, in your favorite city, or in a place from your past where you loved to be? Imagine your ideal meditation garden, yoga studio, or designer kitchen. Whatever sounds like a fun and relaxing place to be, make it happen in your head. Fun!

O Is for Observe

Sit still for a few minutes and observe everything around you, running through four of your senses (you can skip "taste"). Mentally notice everything you see (get detailed), smell (aromas can be subtle, but try to detect some), hear (from traffic noise to the hum of the dishwasher), and feel (your clothes, the air on your skin). This can be distracting in an interesting way and really ground you in the present moment.

T Is for Talk/Text

You don't have to reveal your most vulnerable or complicated feelings to reap the benefits of reaching out to a friend. Strike up a casual chat or send a text just to say hello. Asking someone else about what's going on with them is a great distraction. There's nothing like listening to someone else to get you out of your own head. And if you end up talking through your feelings anyway, then cool! But it's not required at all. Sometimes, interrupting the intensity of an upsetting feeling is as simple as remembering that other people are out there going through stuff, too.

E Is for Exercise[8]

No, you don't have to go to the gym, or do thirty minutes of cardio, or whatever else we're pretty sure you don't feel like doing in this moment. But what could you do, physically, for one to five minutes? Set a timer. Even one minute is enough to shift your mind to something else and get the blood flowing. See how many squats, push-ups, lunges, jumping jacks, or anything else you can do in one minute. Or, set a timer for five minutes and go on a quick walk outside. Even if you only make it to the end of the walkway or driveway, you've done something physical.

And what if, after trying one (or more than one, or all) of these coping mechanisms, you realize you're actually hungry? Then for goodness' sake, eat something! Eating is *always* an option. EMOTE is only for those times when *you* (and nobody else) have decided that eating isn't your best or healthiest option right now. For more help with fog eating and storm eating, as well as emotional eating, check out the keystone habits starting on page 140, especially "Lose the Labels" and "Mindful Eating."

As you continue to examine and play with your relationship with food, you may find that you are contending with another pesky food phenomenon: cravings. Everyone gets them, but if you feel that they are controlling your eating behavior in ways you don't like, you may want to get to know them a little better. Because you know what they say: Keep your friends close, but your enemies closer! (Although, as you'll soon see, cravings are not actually your enemy. They can help you with body awareness.)

Conquering Cravings

When scientists have asked people what derailed their attempts at eating a healthier diet, one of the most common answers has been "food cravings." Cravings feel physical, but they often (not always) have a psychological trigger behind them. What really causes cravings, why do we give in to them, and most important of all, what can we do about them so we don't feel helpless in the face of them?

There are a lot of opinions, many scientifically based, about what causes food cravings. We suspect they are all right some of the time, to some degree, and depending on the situation. Here are some of the most common theories—do any of these feel like they might be true for you?

- **Nutritional deficiencies cause cravings.** There is a widely circulated theory that when you are low on a nutrient, you will crave a food with that nutrient. This would be a physiological reason for a craving, rather than a psychological one. The theory is that if you are low on iron, for example, you might crave steak. If you are low on magnesium, you might crave dark chocolate. If you are low on vitamin C, you might crave oranges.

This may be true in extreme cases, but it's generally been disproven. While your craving for potato chips could theoretically be due to sodium deficiency, most people get more than enough sodium and still crave salty snacks. In fact, the opposite is more likely to be true: Research has shown that people who eat a lot of salt are more likely to crave salt, while people who cut their salt intake get used to less and are less likely to crave it.[9] People who eat more sugar also tend to crave more sugar, perhaps because it releases opioids and dopamine in the brain,[10] and this pleasant response can become habit-forming. In general, the current consensus seems to be that while nutritional deficiencies could theoretically cause food cravings, and might be the cause of cravings occasionally, other reasons for cravings are more likely.

- **Food rules cause cravings.** If you aren't eating enough, or you are depriving yourself of certain foods, it is quite common to have cravings, especially for food you've decided you can't have. It's our naturally rebellious natures. "I can't have chocolate? Oh, yeah? I'll show you! Just watch how much chocolate I can eat!" While you may not actually say or even think this, that feeling could be behind your cravings. But this is probably only the case with very strict food rules and undereating. Sensible calorie reduction for healthy weight loss probably doesn't have this effect, at least in the long term. A 2020 study published in *Nutrition and the Brain* found that while cutting calories causes cravings at first, this is a short-term phenomenon and, like a habit, it can be unlearned.[11] Long-term calorie reduction actually results in *reduced* food cravings, perhaps because you get used to eating less, and once you adjust, that becomes your new normal.

- **Overeating causes cravings.** What may be more likely to cause cravings is regularly eating *too much* food. A 2020 study published in the journal *Appetite* showed that people who tended to eat a lot of food during the day also tended to eat more calorically dense food.[12] They also tended to eat for a longer period during the day (such as eating late at night), had a higher BMI, and were the most likely to experience food cravings. This may seem counterintuitive, until you look at this from a habit perspective. Getting into the habit of eating more, not less, does seem to cause cravings over the long term.

- **Cravings are attempts at altering mood.** We all know the stereotype of drowning one's sorrows in a pint of ice cream, and there is some evidence that people do eat in response to stress (storm eating, emotional eating). One study from 2001 published in the journal *Appetite* showed that eating carbohydrates relieved feelings of distress and evoked feelings of happiness in people who were craving carbs.[13] Another study showed that people who were dieting were more likely to give in to cravings when they were in a negative mood; their brains reacted more strongly to images of appetizing food,[14] suggesting that cravings are an attempt to feel better. (As you now know, frequently responding to emotions with food is a habit—and one you can change!)

- **Sleep deprivation causes cravings.**[15] We know this one is true, especially when it comes to carb cravings. A 2019 study published in the journal *Nutrients* showed that, for women, one night with 33 percent less sleep resulted in increased hunger, more food cravings, more chocolate consumption, and larger portions at lunch.[16] Another study showed that, for young men, acute sleep deprivation increased portion sizes and impacted food choices.[17]

- **Seeing is craving.** "I'm on a see-food diet. I see food and I eat it!" While that may be a cringe-y dad joke, there is some truth to it. People tend to be responsive to food cues. It's probably a basic instinct that helped us survive, but when we see (or smell) food, it can make us suddenly crave it, even if we weren't thinking about food at all.

  One study looked at how cravings showed up in the visual cortex of the brain.[18] This study showed that people who tested higher on a "power of food scale" (indicating they were generally more susceptible to cravings) were more likely to report increased hunger when asked to visualize foods they were craving. Another study from 2017 showed that images of chocolate significantly induced cravings.[19] In fact, most people who experience food cravings say that sensory exposure to food (seeing it, smelling it, tasting it) makes cravings more intense; just imagining the look, smell, and taste of a desired food can intensify cravings.[20]

- **Cravings are habits.** As you may recall from Chapter 3, habits are automatic repeated behaviors. If you are in the habit of eating something sweet after dinner, and then you decide to stop eating something sweet after dinner, your brain will resist the change at first; you may experience cravings for the thing you were in the habit of eating. But the more times you don't eat something sweet after dinner, the easier it gets and the more the craving loses power and eventually disappears.

- **We live in a world that makes it hard to be healthy.**
An obesogenic environment is an environment in which calorically dense foods are widely and easily available, and people are constantly exposed to cues encouraging them to eat those foods.[21] Hello, US of A! Unfortunately, this constant exposure and societal pressure to eat all these foods engineered to be irresistible can trigger irresistible cravings.[22] It's easy to resist a food you can't get, but when you can get just about any food easily, in any amount, at any time, it's not so easy to say no.

Using Metacognition to Deconstruct Cravings

Many things cause cravings, but cravings don't have to be the boss of you. Here are some of our favorite psych tricks that use brain power—specifically, metacognition (thinking about thinking), to outsmart the cravings. No matter their cause, you don't have to let them derail your progress.

- **Decenter your craving.** A 2017 study published in *Current Addiction Reports* looked at how a mindfulness-based intervention called *decentering* can interrupt an unwanted craving.[23] Decentering is a type of metacognition involving a very particular thought process; it's the notion that a craving is not something within you, but something outside of you. When you dis-identify with your craving, you can perceive that it has no power over you. According to a Canadian study out of McGill University in Montreal comparing various mindfulness skills for craving control, this technique was more effective than distraction.[24] To use this technique, visualize the craving as a thing separate from you—maybe it's in a bubble—that's moving through or past you and then moving away. Understanding that cravings are in motion and are a thing apart from yourself that is already on its way out, can make it easier to ride them out.

- **Break the behavior chain.** In Chapter 3, you learned how habits are formed and how you can break the behavior chain to break a habit. This can work for cravings you have that are based on habits. Maybe you always eat potato chips when you watch TV. By identifying your trigger (like the TV being on), noticing your thoughts ("TV on . . . must . . . have . . . chips . . ."), recalling your actions ("This is the point where I usually go into the kitchen in search of chips"), imagining the consequences ("What do all that salt, fat, and all those calories do to my health goals when I eat chips every night?"), then choosing an alternative action ("Tonight I'll try some peppermint tea instead and see how that goes"),[25] you can interrupt the habit and, in doing so, interrupt the craving.

- **Argue with your craving.** This is another type of metacognition: You don't just think about your thoughts, you argue with them! When you have a craving, notice your thoughts (such as: "I'm sad and I want chocolate because it will make me feel better"), then argue with the logic of your thoughts (such as: "Really, you know perfectly well that chocolate won't fix anything. But what would?"). Be careful not to lapse into self-criticism—*that's not helpful*. Instead, talk yourself out of your craving by using logic and reason, and encourage yourself with motivational thoughts: *I've got this!*[26]

- **Eat the food less often, not necessarily in smaller amounts.** Although sometimes a few bites of a craved food can take the edge off, one 2017 study showed that over the course of a two-year weight-loss trial, eating a food less often decreased cravings for that food, but eating less of the food at the same frequency did *not* decrease cravings.[27] So, let's say you always have a sweet coffee drink at 3:00 p.m. Cutting the size down from a large to a small probably won't reduce your cravings (although it will reduce your calories), but having the larger drink only once a week probably will reduce the frequency of your cravings. You may soon feel like you don't need one every day.

How Much Is Enough? The Noom Satiety Scale

If you are often grappling with cravings, habits, and eating for reasons other than hunger, you may find that you can lose touch with what it feels like to actually be hungry and actually be full. That's why we developed the Noom Satiety Scale.[28] This scale can help you figure out how hungry you really are. It can help you determine whether it's really time to eat yet, how much you really need to eat, and whether you need to eat more than you already ate. Use this tool when you aren't sure whether you are hungry, or you aren't sure how hungry you are, before you start eating. Also, use the Noom Satiety Scale as you eat to help you pay attention to your fullness cues, so you know when you really have had enough.

There are eleven levels to the scale:

1. **Dabbling with delusion.** You're so hungry that you're delusional. Or maybe not delusional, but it's hard to think about anything else.

2. **Horribly hangry.** Nobody better get between you and dinner!

3. **Nosh-ready.** You're definitely ready to eat, but you're not going to lose your temper or anything.

4. **You could eat.** You're thinking about having a meal or a snack and your stomach may be growling a bit, but it doesn't feel like an emergency.

5. **Flirting with hunger.** The thought of food has crossed your mind, but you can wait until the next meal, no problem.

6. **Nothing but neutral.** You're neither hungry nor full. You don't feel like you have to eat but you don't feel full, either. You're in neutral, appetite-wise.

7. **Simply satisfied.** You're not hungry because you've eaten and it was enough.

8. **Fueled and fulfilled.** That was a great meal, and you're definitely full but also ready to take on the world.

9. **Beginning to unbuckle.** You ate a lot, and it was awesome, but now you're feeling a little too full. You might need to take a walk or something.

10. **Going overboard.** You feel extremely full and are now regretting that you ate so much because your fullness is uncomfortable.

11. **Fighting a food coma.** You're so full that you're about to doze off. Moving doesn't seem like an option right now. In retrospect, you can feel that you definitely ate a lot more than you needed. Now, you're eyeing the antacid and anticipating an unpleasant aftermath.

We've determined that the best time to eat is when you are between numbers 3 and 5, and the best time to stop eating is when you are between numbers 6 and 8. If you wait to eat until you're overly hungry or you eat until you're overly full, well, it happens to all of us. But it's also likely a sign that you weren't paying attention to, or heeding the signals from, your body.

To get into those zones where you eat when you are reasonably hungry and you stop when you are reasonably satisfied, pay attention to how you feel before and after eating. Be mindful of your body and what it's telling you. Your body knows when it's time to eat and when you've had enough, but thoughts and feelings can sometimes cloud that awareness. Practice makes it easier. Hunger and satiety awareness can help you figure out the amount of food that keeps you feeling good and gets you to the next meal comfortably without ever having to count a single calorie. What that looks like in terms of timing and food choices will be different for everyone, so zero in on what keeps *you* in your satiety zone of choice.

Noom's Seven Keystone Habits

Everyone's relationship with food is different, but we have discovered that there are seven habits that can assist almost everyone who is working on improving that relationship. We think of these seven keystone habits as a sort of food relationship checkup. Every one of these has been clinically proven to help people improve their relationship with food and get to a healthy weight. You can choose to use any of them, or all of them (or none of them—we're not telling you what to do!). Are you ready for some inspiration and guidance on healthy eating habit formation? Here we go:

Keystone Habit #1: Befriend Breakfast

To eat or not to eat breakfast—it's a hotly debated question. If you hang with the intermittent-fasting set, you may know a lot of breakfast skippers, and if you aren't hungry in the morning, we don't necessarily think you should be forcing yourself to eat. But what if you *are* hungry in the morning? In that case, eating breakfast may be a useful strategy, for multiple reasons:

1. **Carb control.** First, remember that *carbs aren't bad!* Portion control is likely more influential than carb control. However, a recent study indicated that people may process carbs best in the morning and not as well in the evening.[29] You could eat the same thing at 7:00 a.m. and 7:00 p.m. (say, two slices of toast), and your blood sugar is likely to rise higher in the evening than in the morning. There are many likely reasons for this, including the fact that most people are more active in the morning and more sedentary in the evening. Also, people generally seem to have better insulin responses in the morning than in the evening, when insulin becomes less sensitive and blood sugar goes higher. (Insulin is the hormone that helps blood sugar get into the cells where it can be used, rather than hanging out in the bloodstream.[30]) This isn't some justification to load up on doughnuts every morning, but it is a good reason to eat breakfast when your body typically expects some fuel after not getting any all night long. If you wait until noon to break the fast, your body may run out of usable energy, leaving you groggy or unfocused by the time 10:00 a.m. rolls around. That being said, note that some people do need to eat small amounts of carb-rich food in the evening,[31] if they have certain types of blood-sugar issues like diabetes or low blood sugar at night—remember, people don't all process food the same.

    But what if you really aren't hungry in the morning? You may have a natural drive not to eat in the morning, according to an article in the

American Journal of Clinical Nutrition,[32] because of your circadian rhythm and the ebb and flow of hunger and satiety hormones (ghrelin and leptin— the hormones that make you feel hungry and the hormones that suppress hunger).[33] If that's you, and skipping breakfast really does feel like the right thing for your body, listen to your body.

2. **Better diet quality.** Studies show that people who eat breakfast tend to get more nutrition throughout the day than those who skip breakfast.[34] A 2021 study of over thirty thousand adults, which examined data from the National Health and Nutrition Examination Survey, and which was published in the *Proceedings of the Nutrition Society*, showed that adults living in the United States who eat breakfast have greater micronutrient intakes, including of folate, calcium, iron, phosphorus, and vitamins A, B_1, B_2, B_3, C, and D.[35] Also, it showed that people who skipped breakfast consumed significantly more calories, carbohydrates, fat, and added sugars throughout the rest of the day, and were much less likely to meet the recommended intake of folate, calcium, iron, vitamins A, B_1, B_2, B_3, C, and D on the days they skipped breakfast. The study concluded that breakfast provides a "unique opportunity to consume important micronutrients that may be less present in subsequent meals."[36]

3. **Better metabolism, blood sugar, and hunger control.** Eating breakfast increases metabolism and contributes to more energy and more physical activity throughout the day. People who eat breakfast tend to be leaner and have more stable blood sugar,

including during the evening, compared to those who fast in the morning.[37] A study out of the University of Tel Aviv showed that eating a breakfast high in protein and carbohydrates (compared to a low-carb breakfast) lowered ghrelin levels throughout the day, which naturally reduced hunger.[38] Breakfast eaters also burn more calories; a 2020 study by the Endocrine Society showed that eating a big breakfast rather than a big dinner increased diet-induced thermogenesis[39] (the additional amount of energy your body burns after eating[40]). No matter the calorie count, thermogenesis was double the rate after breakfast as it was after dinner.

So, yes—we here at Noom are bullish on breakfast! If you are into intermittent fasting, the healthiest fasting window might just be in the evening rather than in the morning. You may get better metabolic benefits by skipping dinner rather than breakfast.

Keystone Habit #2: Eat Regularly

How many meals *should* you eat each day? There are a lot of opinions on this one. A comprehensive article published in *Nutrients* reviewing a wide body of scientific literature on meal timing and composition showed that, generally, those who ate two or three meals a day—including eating breakfast and having dinner on the earlier side—ate plenty of protein, and didn't eat for between twelve and sixteen hours each day (including overnight) tended to have lower cholesterol, lower inflammation, better insulin sensitivity, and a more even and healthy circadian rhythm, including better sleep.[41]

The general (science-supported) consensus in our well-credentialed team is that opting for three nutritious, substantial daily meals with limited snacks based on hunger level just makes sense. It works for blood-sugar control, keeps hunger hormones steadier, helps you feel fuller after meals, and, it's worth noting, allows you to comfortably fit into the culturally accepted eating schedule. That being said, of course you should adhere to whatever kind of eating feels best for you—the kind that leaves you feeling healthy. But keeping a regular eating schedule will teach your body when to expect meals. That way, you will be less likely to think about food all the time, and you might be less easily swayed by food cues if your body knows it's not always time to eat.

Keystone Habit #3: Control Your Portions

Oh, portion control—such a nice idea, and so hard to execute! But mastering portion control is a great skill that can help you regulate your food intake without counting and measuring everything—and what a time saver that is! Portion control can help you avoid overdoing it without having to put a lot of thought into every single thing you're eating. [42]

Portions are something people don't necessarily pay attention to—they tend to automatically eat what's in front of them. This can easily lead to overeating when people don't pay attention to the subtle signals of hunger and fullness. According to an article in the *American Journal of Clinical Nutrition*, when both adults and children were given larger portions, they didn't report any difference in fullness. [43] One solution is to serve yourself smaller portions, knowing you can always get more if you're still hungry. If you have a large portion on your plate (hello, giant restaurant servings!), it's easy to eat it all without noticing, even though it's more than you wanted.

Since we here at Noom think portion control is cool, but are not so hot on the idea of counting and weighing and measuring your food for the rest of your life, we've developed some handy psych tricks for learning how to control your own portions in a sensible but not-obsessive way:

1. **Put it on a plate.** Instead of noshing out of the bag or grabbing food off a platter, make a decision about what you want to eat and put it on a plate. Take a look at it so you know what you're eating. This gives your stomach and your brain a chance to confer and fully, consciously register that you are eating something. It also helps you decide if the amount of food on your plate matches your hunger level. If you poured a whole bag of chips onto a plate and the chips were piled high in a mountain and falling off onto the floor, you might be less likely to eat the whole thing than if you were fog eating directly from the chip bag, with no visual cue to your portion size.

2. **Make that plate a side plate . . . maybe.** A dinner plate can be pretty big, but a side plate or salad plate is a good size for smaller meals, and especially for more calorically dense foods. (We encourage you to go large when it's veggies!) The beauty of the side plate is that it creates a sort of optical illusion, technically called the Delboeuf illusion.[44] The white space around an object (in this case, your food) makes the object look smaller than if there were no "border" around it. That translates to a full-to-brimming side plate looking like a lot of food, compared to how that same amount of food looks when dwarfed by a large dinner plate. Using a small plate can make a sufficient portion look like what it is—enough food. Taking large portion sizes may just be a habit, and you may find that you are perfectly and comfortably satisfied with the amount of food on a side plate.

   The small-plate trick isn't just a Noom thing. A study compared two groups of people eating the same amount of food. One group ate from a small plate, and the other ate from a regular dinner plate.[45] The people eating from the small plate reported feeling fuller and more satisfied after the meal than the people eating from the large plate. However, this effect was less pronounced in people who were technically considered "overweight" in the study, suggesting that this doesn't work for everyone.

It especially doesn't work for people who are undereating and are feeling hungry. Studies have shown that people who are hungry owing to food deprivation won't be filled (or fooled) by a small plate if there's not enough food, according to a study published in the journal *Appetite*.[46] The small-plate technique is for helping to normalize portion sizes; it's not a technique to trick you into not eating enough! Many of our Noomers really like this trick, but we suggest you use it only if you like it and it works for you.

3. **Use caloric and nutritional density to make food decisions.** We introduced you to these concepts in the last chapter, but here's a refresher: Foods that are calorically dense have a lot of calories for their weight, and foods that are nutritionally dense have a lot of nutrients for their calories. Vegetables are nutritionally dense but not calorically dense, so you can eat more of them and get full faster. Foods like lean meats and low-fat dairy products are moderately calorie dense but nutritionally dense, so they are good for eating in moderate amounts. High-fat, high-sugar foods like avocados, nuts, and sweets, though delicious and often quite nutritious, are calorie dense and may or may not be nutritionally dense. For balance, these are best eaten in smaller quantities.

4. **Learn to eyeball portions.** Measuring everything is tiring, and although some people find it useful, it's not necessary for portion control. There are easy ways to eyeball portions based on things you can compare them to. No measuring cups are required, or use them once or twice just to get a sense of the basic size. Here are some standards to keep in mind as you navigate the wonderful world of portion control:

- **Vegetables and fruits:** You can eat vegetables and fruits in large or small bowls, but a standard portion is typically 2 cups of raw or 1 cup of cooked veggies, or one piece of whole fruit or 1 cup of chopped raw fruit. Don't hold back if you want more!

- **Starchy vegetables (like sweet potatoes) and whole grains (like brown rice or oatmeal):** A standard portion is about a serving spoon or ladleful, or approximately 1/2 cup.

- **Lean proteins (like chicken, fish, tofu):** The standard measure is the size of a dollar bill, a deck of cards, or about the size of your palm. This usually translates to approximately 4 to 6 ounces.

- **Healthy fats, sauces, spreads, and oils:** These are typically measured in large or small spoonfuls, or the size of a thumb or a thumb tip. A standard serving of olive oil or salad dressing or peanut butter is 2 tablespoons.

- **Dairy products:** About a fistful, or 1 cup of milk, is a standard serving size; more concentrated dairy products, like yogurt and cheese, are more calorically dense and, therefore, the portion size is typically smaller. Yogurt might be 4 to 6 ounces, while shredded cheese would be a small handful, or about 1/4 cup.

Don't forget that the purpose of measuring is to be able to stop measuring as soon as you get used to what a standard-sized portion really is. Once you start seeing more standard portions as normal, restaurant portions are going to look *huge*; seeing this can be a revelation (and a big help in realizing how much of that giant plate of spaghetti or that 16-ounce steak and massive baked potato you actually want to eat).

5. **Log your food *at first*.** Just like measuring, keeping a log of your food (like in a food diary or on an app) is a temporary practice to get you more mindfully tuned in to what food choices you're making. Logging can help you see if you're defaulting to foods that aren't very nutritious, or if you're eating more sugar than you intend, or anything else. Logging works for a lot of people, and our own experiments have shown that imprecise logging doesn't work as well as precise and accurate logging. Multiple research studies have also shown that people who track their daily food consumption lose more weight.[47] One study showed that keeping a food diary doubled weight loss,[48] and another showed that just using a smartphone app to track meals without any additional in-person professional guidance resulted in significant amounts of lost weight.[49] One study we conducted here at Noom showed that logging what people ate for dinner was the most important factor in their successful weight loss.[50] In another of our studies, we showed that the more frequently people logged their meals, the more weight they lost.[51]

    Knowledge is power, and logging provides knowledge for you about your own eating habits; that's the first step in setting goals and making healthy changes where you want to make them.

NOOM COACH Q&A

Logging is too hard and overwhelming. I don't like logging, so why does Noom ask me to do this?

Calorie counting can never be 100 percent accurate, so it's okay to leave some wiggle room and log alternatives or substitutions. Go easy on yourself and do the best you can. It sounds like you're starting to become more aware of those choices already, which is the goal of logging. That being said, we generally recommend logging as a learning tool, not something to do forever. For some people it's not useful, so while we encourage it, we don't require it.

Keystone Habit #4: Unprocess Your Diet

Processed foods contain a lot of highly refined ingredients, and even food chemicals. They are engineered to be so delicious that they are hard to resist, and while they are fine some of the time (fun foods!), they are a lot less nutritious, less filling, and the way they are formulated can actually make people hungrier after eating them. By contrast, when you eat whole, unprocessed food, you can eat bigger portions for the same number of calories. Unprocessed foods (fresh vegetables, fresh fruits, whole grains) also tend to be much higher in micronutrients and fiber, so you get more nutritious bang for your buck.

Nutrition experts generally agree that the healthiest dietary patterns are those that are primarily whole-food based[52] (fresh meat and fish are also whole foods, by the way): the Mediterranean diet, vegetarian diets, and so-called Paleolithic/ancestral diets.

CONTENDING WITH "ADDICTIVE" FOODS[53]

What do you do when there is a food you can't resist, that makes you want to eat more and more, and that you have a very hard time moderating? Here are three strategies:

1. **Substitute.** A whole-food swap may not feel quite as satisfying as your junk-food darling (a baked potato isn't the same as a potato chip, but it *is* a lot more nutritious and filling). However, it's likely to make you *feel* much better after you eat it, and it can help to reset your taste buds. You'll soon come to appreciate the taste of food the way nature made it.

2. **Moderate.** Can you eat just a little of the food or (even better) eat it less often? Can you have just one square of chocolate or have chocolate only on the weekends? If the food is too tempting for you to moderate, consider number 3:

3. **Avoid.** This is a temporary measure to help loosen the grip of an addictive food. You and doughnuts (for example) can be "on a break" for a while. That doesn't mean you can never have it again, but this might be a good time to flirt with other breakfast choices.

Keystone Habit #5: Lose the Labels

Imagine a chocolate chip cookie. Now, what are three words that come to mind when you think about that cookie? Delicious? Sinful? Indulgent? Evil? Heavenly? Fattening? These are all labels.

People like to classify and categorize things—it helps us understand the world. But when we start putting value judgments on foods (or anything else), like "desserts are bad," "vegetables are good," "sugar is evil," or "whole food is virtuous," we distort our perception of these foods. If you think a food is "bad" or "off-limits," but you also want it, that can become a trigger, not just to eat it but also to eat it without discretion. If you "give in to the sin," that can cause guilt and shame, and none of this is productive.[54]

This can apply to labeling foods as "good" as well. If you think you have to eat something because it's healthy, you may begin to eat things you don't want, which can disrupt your natural hunger and food preference cues. That, too, can distort your relationship with food. There is nothing wrong with eating healthy food because you know it's good for you even if you don't particularly love it, but forcing yourself to eat food you don't like while denying yourself pleasurable food because it isn't "good" can distance you even more from your natural instincts about what to eat.

But what if the cookie isn't evil? What if eating kale isn't virtuous? What if (get ready because this is a big one) *you can eat anything you want?* What?

Base your food decisions on facts about food like caloric and nutrient density, and factor in your individual food preferences (you like sweet potato fries better than baked potatoes). Remember that it's great to fuel-eat, but it's also just fine to fun-eat. It's all about finding your equilibrium. Rather than good and evil, should and shouldn't, can and can't, you will have a much easier time achieving balance, and eventually, food freedom.

Keystone Habit #6: Ditch the Drinks

Sweetened drinks go down easy and contain a lot of calories for very little nutritional payoff. By some estimates, soft drinks, fruit drinks, sports drinks, and energy drinks make up nearly 40 percent of the added sugar in peoples' diets. Many of these drinks also contain a lot of chemicals, like monopotassium phosphate, pyridoxine hydrochloride, caramel color, and of course, sugar, often in the form of high-fructose corn syrup. What they don't have is protein, fiber, or healthy fats.

One twelve-ounce can of soda is about 150 calories, and you get basically nothing but a sugar rush and, in the case of caffeinated drinks, a slight temporary buzz. Many scientific studies, including an overview of a large body of research conducted by researchers publishing in the *American Journal of Clinical Nutrition*,[55] have associated consumption of sugar-sweetened beverages with weight gain and metabolic problems in adults, adolescents, and children.

Artificial sweeteners probably aren't much better. Although they don't contain any calories, many large, well-controlled scientific studies show that they cause people to eat more and gain more weight. One, the San Antonio Heart Study, looked at 3,682 adults over a period of seven to eight years in the 1980s, and found that those who drank artificially sweetened beverages consistently weighed more at the end of the study than at the beginning.[56] Researchers theorize that this may have to do with the brain circuitry related to food rewards: When we taste something sweet, the brain expects calories, and when they don't come in, we don't feel satisfied, so we eat more. There's also the issue that artificial sweeteners may encourage continued sugar cravings and the dependence on sweet things.[57]

A more recent study looked at erythritol, which is in many "naturally sweetened" products containing sweeteners like stevia and monk fruit, showing that even these naturally low-calorie sweeteners can cause weight gain in young adults.[58]

Another theory is that artificial sweeteners change the gut microbiome (those bacteria and fungi in our intestines that help us digest food and do other good things for us) in a way that leads to a decreased feeling of fullness after eating and alters blood sugar in ways that make people eat more and gain more weight.[59]

Remember how we told you that drinking more water is associated with lower body weight? Nothing beats it. Swapping some (or all) of your sweetened drinks for water could help you feel better and reach your goals more easily.

Keystone Habit #7: Mindful Eating

Mindful eating is eating with self-awareness. It's not fog eating or storm eating. It's purposeful. We'll talk a lot more about mindfulness, including mindful eating, in Chapter 9. For now, here are three ways you can start eating more mindfully today:

1. **Eat with intention,** rather than out of habit. Think about whether you really want that food before you decide to eat it. You may still decide to eat it, but you will be eating it on purpose, and that makes all the difference.

2. **Eat with attention,** rather than while doing something else. Pay attention to the experience of eating and the sensory experience of your food. Chew slowly, savor, and enjoy (or notice if you don't like the food), and you'll be eating mindfully—and potentially less.

3. **Practice makes perfect.** The more you do it, the easier it gets, until finally mindful eating becomes your very own healthy habit.

Is Mindful Eating Really Possible?

The goal of everything Noom does is to help people learn how to eat mindfully—without counting, without measuring, without labeling, and without distress. Your body is wise. It knows what you need, and it knows what you want. Tuning in to your body to discover what it's telling you about what to eat is a skill, but anyone can learn it.[60]

It starts with mindfulness, which evolves into honoring this one body you have to carry you through life. You can learn to trust that what your body communicates to you is true and meaningful. Set that guiding star in your sky and know that, yes, you can achieve mindful eating. You are already on the path.

◆

And that's all we have to say about food—for now. We all know there are many things that influence your health besides food. In the next chapter, we're going to dip into some other influencers—namely, genetics, exercise, sleep, stress, hormones, relationships, environment . . . basically, the whole rest of your life beyond what you eat.

6

Beyond Food

Life is but a collection of habits.

—Ida Tarbell

When you are trying to feel better, be healthier, and enjoy your life more, food matters—but it's not the only thing that matters. Life is complex, and balancing all the parts in a way that feels right—and not like you're missing, neglecting, or overemphasizing anything—is the work of, well . . . life itself. No book about health, or weight management, or behavior, for that matter, would be truly complete without its own balance, because there are so many things that contribute to all of these. In this chapter, we're going to talk about Noom's Four Pillars of Health, but before we get there, let's take a look at you and your own personal sense of balance.

How you feel about how balanced your life is makes a difference in your self-efficacy—that is, how much control you think you have over your own life and how much you believe in yourself and your ability to make positive changes. If you feel like you're neglecting parts of your life and spending too much time on other parts, it can affect your happiness, confidence, and ability to do things like change habits and get motivated.

How's your balance? We have an exercise for you that can help you answer that question in a detailed way that can help you. It's called the Wheel of Life.

Your Wheel of Life

To get an idea of how all the parts of your life are influencing your health and the way you live (including how well you are able to set goals and form or change habits), it can be useful to *round* them all up (literally—see the circle that follows) and periodically assess how well you feel you are doing in each area. This Wheel of Life is adapted from a popular concept often used by life coaches that dates back to the 1960s and has many forms. This is the one we use.

This Wheel of Life, created in the 1960s by Paul J. Meyer at the Success Motivation Institute, exists today in many different forms, and it's frequently used as a life coaching tool. But you don't need a life coach to fill one out. Here's what it looks like:

Each of these categories represents a part of life, and most if not all of the areas take a little bit of effort. If the wheel is imbalanced—say, you spend all your time on career and money and hardly any on health or fun—then your life can feel as bumpy as a ride in a car with a flat tire.

To fill out your own version of the wheel, use the template that follows. For each piece of the pie, there are five levels. How satisfied are you with each area of your life? For example, consider the role family and friends play in your life. If you're a little satisfied, color in that first slice of pie, starting in the center of the circle, up to the first line. If you're totally satisfied and that part of your life is excellent, color in the whole wedge. If you are only partially satisfied, color the wedge up to the level that feels right to you. Coloring up to one is "a little satisfied" and coloring up to five is "totally satisfied."

Do each wedge of the pie, then take a look at how balanced the chart appears. Does this give you any insights into how you might want to rebalance your wheel? Are there areas where you feel stuck, or you realize you've simply been ignoring? Are there things you can do to balance your wheel a little bit better?

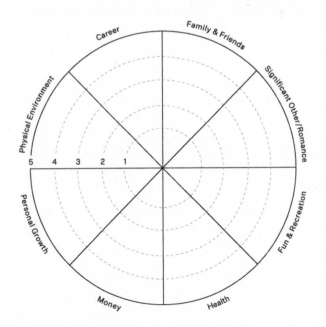

Most of us realize, when we map out the various parts of our lives, that we give a lot more attention to some areas of our life and hardly any attention to other areas. Filling out your own Wheel of Life can bring awareness to where you are expending your energy and how you might want to shift it, if you discover you aren't giving enough attention to some aspects of your life that are important to you.

If you find you do spend a lot more energy in some area than in others, that might be just fine—we all have our own sense of life balance, and Dr. Michaelides cautions people doing this exercise to recognize that your wheel doesn't have to be completely balanced in every way. "What's important is to put your energies where you want them to be—this is how you make your wheel harmonious in a way that makes sense for you," he says. "Getting overly concerned with perfectly balancing work and life, or whatever else people are trying to balance, can actually cause more distress. It paints a picture of 'supposed to' and 'have to,' and that's not realistic. Knowing mindfully that it's okay to spend less energy on things you care less about and more energy on things you care more about can be a realistic and more useful way to approach this exercise."

Keeping that in mind, here's an example of how a filled-out wheel might look.

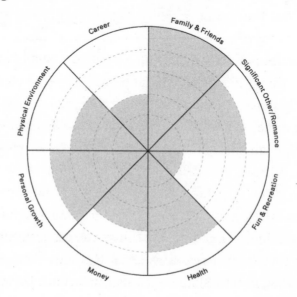

As you can see, this imaginary person is totally satisfied with family and friends, pretty satisfied with significant other/romance, health, and personal growth, and not very satisfied with career or fun and recreation. This person may decide that they could spend a little more energy on finding a job they love, or they may recognize that a career isn't that important to them in this stage of life but that they could use a little more fun. Balancing the wheel, not to make it perfect but to make it yours, can improve life satisfaction significantly, and better life satisfaction makes for a better sense of self-efficacy, personal power, and the importance of self-care.

What Else Influences Health?

Your personal life balance influences a lot about your life, but there are also some bigger-picture influences that come into play that can influence your health, weight, behavior, and even your personality.

Genetics, of course, plays a part in health, as well as weight, body type, height, hair color, and much, much more. "Genetics are important," explains Dr. Michaelides. "They are part of your destiny, but the extent to which they influence you varies, and genetics is not the dominant influence."

Genetics probably makes up a relatively small part when it comes to things like behavior and personality—no more than 50 percent in most cases, and in many cases, much less than that.[1] When it comes to health, genetics may have an even smaller effect,[2] although that effect depends on the issue. Most of what determines health as well as weight, according to researchers, has more to do with lifestyle,[3] environment, and even the composition of the gut microbiome[4] (those bacteria and fungi in your lower intestine)—and these are things you can influence.

But because genetics does affect the body—height, muscle composition, general shape—it's also important, Dr. Michaelides reminds us, to appreciate your unique body type. "You can't change your body type, bone structure, or the way that your muscles are formed. There are a lot of things that you can change and some things that you cannot change, and it's important to really distinguish those rather than letting outside influences like the media dictate what they allegedly should be. What you *can* do is create the healthiest version of your own unique body type possible, and that's significant."

Environment is another big influencer. "We think about 'nature versus nurture' a lot," says Dr. Michaelides. "The environment in which you were brought up has an effect on how your genes express themselves. The *diathesis stress response* is a theory that stress can activate a genetic predisposition. Just because you have the gene for something doesn't mean you're going to develop that thing or end up that way, because your environment can activate or not activate that gene. High stress can activate a gene for a health condition that might not have been otherwise activated. This is just one example of the complex interplay between genetics and environment."

Environment also influences behavior. "It's easier to, for example, maintain healthy habits if you can create a healthy environment, surrounding yourself with people who have shared goals or who have normalized the kind of lifestyle you're trying to maintain. Another example is setting up your environment to support your goals," Dr. Michaelides adds, using the example of living with someone (a roommate, a partner, children) who might not share your goals—they might keep tempting foods you are trying to avoid in the house, or they might not support your efforts to exercise. "If you can set limits with others and really stand up for and be vocal about those limits, and you can model behavior that others might imitate, you can maximize your chances of success," suggests Dr. Michaelides.

Other influencers on health, weight, and behavior include age, hormones, geography, social profile, food availability, what job you have, how supportive your relationships are, and self-efficacy—that is, how much power you think you have over your own health, weight, and behavior. Those are a lot of influences! Stepping back and looking at the big picture, however, we at Noom have discovered that, in the scheme of things, there are Four Pillars of Health that have the greatest influence on how you feel, how healthy you are, and how easily you will be able to achieve your health and healthy weight goals. These four pillars are:

1. Nutrition
2. Exercise
3. Sleep
4. Stress management

The previous two chapters of this book were all about nutrition, and it is indeed important and deserves its number-one spot. Every cell in your body consists of things that were made out of the food you ate. But if you only pay attention to what you eat and neglect the other three pillars, your roof is going to cave in (metaphorically, that is). Let's go through what you might want to know about the other Big Three: What are they, how do they work, and how can you use them to get healthier? How do they fit into the big picture that is You?

Extraordinary Exercise

Second in command is exercise. You may be what you eat, but you are also how you move. Your body is made for movement. Movement keeps your muscles strong, your heart pumping, your lungs working, and your joints mobile. It makes your bones denser, and it makes your brain work better.

Humans evolved to exercise; just imagine how our ancestors would have fared if they just sat around all day. In the modern world, it's much easier to get everything you need without moving very much, and that's all cool and high-tech, but it's not doing our bodies any good. "Our bodies are not calibrated for the world we live in today," Dr. Michaelides tells us. "If we want to thrive, we have to make some adjustments." One of those adjustments is moving more on purpose.

Exercise has extraordinary benefits—some of which will help with weight loss indirectly, but most of which will do so many good things for your body and your mind that you'll feel like a million dollars (if a million dollars was super-fit). Here are some of the amazing and wonderful things exercise can do for you:

- **Exercise boosts serotonin and dopamine.** Serotonin and dopamine are those feel-good, mood-lifting hormones that make you feel happier, more capable, and less stressed, and exercise will make sure you've got both on tap. Serotonin is the cause of the "runner's high"—that euphoric feeling you can get during vigorous exercise—and dopamine in particular seems to help people not feel so tired during exercise, according to a review of what happens in the brain with aerobic exercise, published in *Frontiers in Psychology*.[5]

- **Exercise reduces cortisol.** If serotonin is the feel-good hormone, cortisol is the feel-stressed hormone. When it's pumping through your bloodstream, you might feel anxious, nervous, irritable, and hangry (hungry + angry). Cortisol levels go up briefly during exercise (exercise is stressful, after all), but regular exercise reduces average circulating cortisol to take the edge off that stress.[6] In fact . . .

- **Exercise lowers stress.** It's not just cortisol reduction. Exercise improves the way the body handles stress, and research shows that exercise is a good intervention for helping people deal with stress.[7] Exercise can also protect against the bad feelings people get when stressed. A study published in *Frontiers in Physiology* compared how people who exercise regularly and people who don't exercise regularly each responded to a social stress test.[8] Exercise didn't appear to affect mood in either exercisers or non-exercisers before the test (although the exercisers had lower heart rates), but after the stress test, the non-exercisers had a much more rapid and dramatic decline in mood. The stress made them much grumpier! The exercisers were able to maintain a more positive mood after the stress.

- **Exercise helps you sleep better.** Studies show that exercise helps you stay more alert during the day, fall asleep more easily at night, wake up less during the night, and feel more rested in the morning. A systematic review of the relationship between sleep and exercise that analyzed thirty-four different studies on the subject determined that exercise promoted increased sleep efficiency and duration.[9] The study also concluded that exercised benefited sleep, and sleep benefited exercise. Reciprocity!

- **Exercise lowers your risk of all the major chronic diseases.** Heart disease, stroke, hypertension, diabetes, cancer, arthritis, osteoporosis, lung disease, restricted mobility, and frailty due to age—exercise improves your chances of avoiding them all, according to a comprehensive survey of the health benefits of physical activity published in the *Canadian Medical Association Journal*.[10]

- **Exercise resets cravings.** According to the science, exercise may be the single most important impact in your food and other health choices throughout the day, especially if you do it in the morning. A 2020 study published in *Medicine & Science in Sports & Exercise* showed that after twelve weeks of daily exercise on a treadmill, exercisers had a significantly reduced desire for high-fat junk food and were better at avoiding foods they didn't want to be eating, even if they were tempted.[11] They made healthier food choices, ate fewer calories overall, and were more active throughout the rest of the day than non-exercisers. Morning exercise sets the tone!

There is one area where exercise doesn't take center stage, and it's weight loss. But wait; before you go canceling your gym membership in a huff, rest assured that exercise helps with weight loss indirectly. Yes, exercise burns calories, but it also makes you hungrier, and people tend to up their food intake to match their effort. Exercise alone is more about breaking even in terms of calories in/calories out, but all the other good things it does for you can make you better at sticking with healthy habits that do help with weight loss.

If weight loss is your goal, your best bet is to combine healthy eating patterns with exercise. The Nutrition and Exercise in Women (NEW) study was a yearlong randomized controlled trial that compared the effects of a calorie-reduced diet, moderate-intensity aerobic exercise, or a combination of the two for weight loss.[12] After a year, the women who only exercised lost an average of 2.4 percent of their body weight. The women who only dieted lost an average of 8.5 percent of their body weight. The women who both dieted and exercised lost an average of 10.8 percent of their body weight.

Since weight loss happens when there is a calorie deficit—more energy going out than coming in—exercise can absolutely help tip that balance. But if you take in more energy when you burn more energy, or if you move less later in the day because you exercised, you can end up in the same place you started, weight-wise.

But not health-wise. Health-wise, exercise is a superstar.

NOOM COACH Q&A

I don't feel like exercising. Any tips to help me increase my motivation?

Staying motivated to work out isn't always easy. Here are two specific tips to kick-start your motivation:

1. **Never miss a Monday.** For most of us, Monday marks the beginning of our week. The weekend is over, and we go back to work. The more structured routine of home, office, school, or errands kicks back into full swing. Starting off on an active note can help keep things in motion for the rest of the week. Even if your Monday isn't actually on a Monday, the tone is now set for a week of movement and productivity!

2. **Buddy up!** Every now and then, it may feel like you're on this journey alone. We're here to tell you that you're not. (Seriously!) Finding a friend to go for walks, enjoy a class, or even challenge each other can feel encouraging and massively motivating. Not only does it feel amazing to be supported but it can be motivating to support others in their efforts toward being more physically active.

How to Exercise

You might be thinking, "All right, all right, you've convinced me. Now what do I do? Because I hope you're not going to tell me I have to . . ." Hold the phone—we aren't going to tell you that you have to do anything! The good news is that any and all types of movement are beneficial. Whether an exercise bike in the quiet of your own home, or a daily brisk walk through the park, or a rousing game of intramural soccer is more your speed, you will get the great benefits. It's all good! A variety of exercises will get you the most benefit, just like a variety of foods will get you the most nutrients, but anything you do is better than doing nothing. In fact, you will start benefiting just by sitting less, even if you never break a sweat.

Sit Less

Sitting all day appears to be even more harmful than not exercising, and it's associated with all kinds of physical ailments, like back, neck, and shoulder pain; high blood pressure; and high cholesterol.[13] But moving periodically throughout the day and never sitting for more than about thirty minutes or an hour max, can reverse the pretty serious health risks of sitting all day long. The modern world makes sitting easy, and many of us have jobs that involve a lot of time at a desk, but there are ways to pepper in more movement all day long, to counteract the health-damaging effects of a sedentary lifestyle. Some ideas:

- Try a standing or treadmill desk, so you can work while moving (or at least while not sitting).
- Take lots of short breaks to get up and stretch and walk around. It's not just good for you; it can make you more productive and put you in a better mood. If you can't manage a few minutes every half hour or even five minutes every hour, practice the 10:2 rule, moving for ten minutes every two hours.
- When you can, take the stairs, walk on your breaks, walk while talking on the phone, and set an alarm to get up and move around at least once an hour.
- Park farther away from your destination or get off the bus a stop or two early. Better yet, walk to and from places when possible.
- Move more in your free time (hike, bike, ski, skate, dance!), and try to have more active social time.

Do Cardio

In addition to moving more throughout the day, it's great for your health to get some cardio. Anything that gets your heart rate up counts! Cardio strengthens your heart and lungs, your brain, your mood, and your resolve. A 2019 study out of the University of Texas at Austin of 2,680 young adults who didn't regularly exercise or reduce their calories showed that several weeks of regular aerobic exercise improved food choices, tipping the participants' preferences more toward lean meats, fruits, and vegetables, and away from junk foods like fried food and soda, even though they were not asked to change their diet in any way.[14] The only change was the aerobic exercise! Examples of cardio:

- Brisk walking
- Jogging or running
- Cycling
- Gym machines: elliptical trainers, treadmills, stationary bikes, stair climbing machines, rowing machines
- Kickboxing
- Dancing and dance-fitness classes (like Zumba)
- Certain calisthenics, like jumping jacks, jogging in place, high knees, mountain climbers, and Burpees (especially Burpees!)
- Workout videos/online classes that get you moving

Lift Weights, aka Strength Training

Cardio benefits your heart muscle, and lifting weights benefits all your other muscles. Lifting weights will make you stronger, better able to pick things up (grocery bags, heavy packages, toddlers), and less likely to suffer a fall or get injured when you fall. Lifting weights also burns abdominal fat faster than cardio,[15] and helps burn off excess blood sugar.

Muscle tends to shrink with age; people who don't exercise can lose 3 to 8 percent of their muscle mass every decade! But lifting weights can prevent that loss and increase your resting metabolic rate by 7 percent.[16] That is the rate at which you burn energy when doing nothing at all. Studies also show it makes you better at sports, increases your walking speed, makes your bones stronger and denser, can help resolve chronic low back pain, helps your brain work better, and even increases your self-esteem and improves body image.[17,18] Those are some rockin' benefits for just lifting heavy things a few times a week! Lifting weights doesn't necessarily have to involve actual weights, either. Lifting your own body weight counts, too. Here are some examples of strength-training exercises:

- Machines at the gym with weights
- Free weights: barbells, dumbbells, kettle bells
- Weighted training balls (sometimes called medicine balls)
- Heavy battle ropes
- Resistance bands
- Yoga exercises during which you hold your own body weight, like plank, upward dog, downward dog, and some of the balance poses
- Certain body-weight–hefting calisthenics, like push-ups, crunches, leg raises, pull-ups/chin-ups, and wall sits

Stretch It Out

Flexibility is just as important as strength. It helps you move more gracefully and easily and can decrease the chances that you will be injured if you fall. If you can bend, you're less likely to break. Flexibility increases your range of motion so you can do things more easily, like touch your toes or scratch your own back (useful when nobody else is around). It reduces stiffness and keeps joints more mobile, and if you do some stretching after a cardio or weight-lifting workout, you may be less likely to feel sore later.

One way a lot of people like to stay flexible is through yoga, which contains many different movements that stretch all parts of the body. A study published in the *International Journal of Yoga* looked at the impact of ten weeks of yoga on college athletes and found that the athletes doing yoga significantly improved their flexibility and balance compared to a control group that didn't do yoga.[19] It can help you in your daily life, too, by increasing strength, coordination, balance, and mood; several studies have shown that yoga can improve depression, anxiety, stress, and insomnia.[20] Some forms of yoga could also be considered cardio.

The American College of Sports Medicine recommends doing a few minutes of cardio-type movement before stretching, then holding stretches for fifteen to thirty seconds and repeating two to four times. Do this two to three days a week to round out your regular cardio and weight-lifting workouts.[21] You could also have a professional show you the moves, at least at first, to be sure you are stretching in a beneficial way. Some great sources for instruction include:

- A trainer at the gym, who can give you a good basic stretching routine that works out all your major muscle groups
- An online stretching or flexibility class
- A yoga class, in person or online; there are hundreds out there to choose from

Go Hard with HIIT

Cardio, weight lifting, and stretching used to be considered a complete workout, but there is a new(ish) kid on the block: HIIT. HIIT stands for "high-intensity interval training." It's an intense but time-saving form of exercise in which you alternate short bursts of all-out effort with more moderate or low-intensity recovery effort.

For example, if you are walking or jogging, you might sprint as fast as you possibly can for fifteen seconds, then walk or jog for two minutes, or until you get your breath back and feel recovered. Then repeat. Over time, you can work up to a 1:1 ratio, such as a one-minute sprint followed by a one-minute walk or jog. (Note: Some HIIT trainers say you can work up to a 2:1 ratio, with your effort being twice as long as your recovery, but other trainers say the recovery period should be longer. We suggest you start slow and work up to a level that feels challenging and beneficial to you—you should feel fully recovered at the end of the recovery period.)

After just ten or fifteen minutes, you're done with your workout, and you will feel it! HIIT workouts torch calories and improve fitness fast,[22] so it's the perfect choice when you don't have much time.

HIIT may be quick, but it's not easy, so it's a good idea to start slow and work up to longer or more frequent speed bursts to prevent injury. The more you do this, the easier it will get and the longer you will be able to go at your highest intensity. You don't need to do HIIT for more than twenty minutes or so, even when you're good at it—that's all the time you need to benefit.

Those benefits are significant. A meta-analysis published in the *British Journal of Sports Medicine* showed that HIIT had significant cardio-metabolic benefits. In the short term (doing HIIT workouts for fewer than twelve weeks), it significantly improved blood oxygen levels (a measure of aerobic capacity), diastolic blood pressure (the bottom number on a blood pressure reading), and fasting glucose.[23] In the long term (doing HIIT workouts for longer than twelve weeks), it significantly improved waist circumference, body fat percentage, resting heart rate, and systolic blood pressure (the top number on a blood pressure reading).

You can do HIIT on a bike, a treadmill, an elliptical trainer, running/walking outside, or with any kind of cardio you like to do. Ways to try it:

- Follow a HIIT workout online, to get the hang of it.
- Try Tabata, a specific type of HIIT, or interval training that is like HIIT but works up to a 2:1 ratio of exertion and recovery, so it's more intensive than some other forms of HIIT. You can take a class or work on Tabata workouts with a trainer (in person or online), or try it yourself, working up to that 2:1 ratio.
- DIY your HIIT. Pick your favorite cardio. Warm up for two or three minutes, then go for twenty seconds at your highest intensity, then reduce for ten seconds while you catch your breath. Repeat a few times. Work up to a minute or two of high intensity with time in between to recover.

Making a Movement Plan

Inspired to get moving? Great! The most effective exercise is the one you will actually do on a regular basis over time, so set goals, yes! But remember to make them SMART: specific, measurable, attainable, relevant, and time-based. For example, instead of planning an hour a day at the gym every day, start where you are and calibrate up. Some beginner goals might include:

- Taking a ten-minute walk every day at lunchtime
- Going to the gym three mornings this week
- Sign up for a new dance class for later in the week
- Taking the stairs instead of the elevator every time you have the opportunity
- Trying one new form of exercise this week. Maybe HIIT?

As exercise becomes a habit, you can change your goals to match where you are, increasing the time and intensity. Choosing to commit to your exercise plan and remembering all the benefits can help keep you motivated.

And remember, even when you're time-pressed, a short workout is better than no workout at all. Fifteen minutes of fast walking, a few weight-training exercises or calisthenics, a couple of rounds of HIIT, or breaking up exercise into two or three ten-minute sessions are all ways to put you in a state of mind to make healthy decisions for the rest of your day. And that feels great, right?

Sweet, Sweet Sleep

The next of Noom's Four Pillars of Health is sleep. Ah, sleep! Sleep might seem like that isolated thing you do at the end of your day, but it's actually all tied up with the other pillars: How well you sleep influences how you eat, how you exercise, and how stressed you feel. It's that important.

Dr. Michaelides emphasizes the importance of sleep because if you are trying to change your behavior in some way on a day-to-day basis, you're going to need to use a lot more of the front part of your brain, which governs executive function. "Sleep deprivation basically turns that part of your brain off," he says. "So, it's like trying to run a race on one leg, when you have the option of running it on two."

To understand how sleep impacts how you eat, you should know about two very important hormones: the hunger hormone called *ghrelin* and the satiety hormone called *leptin*. Normally, these two hormones ebb and flow according to when you need food and when you don't. However, how you live can influence how these hormones balance each other out.

Sleep deprivation is one major way to upset this delicate balance. When you don't get enough sleep, ghrelin levels increase and leptin levels decrease,[24] so you feel hungrier than you would normally feel before eating and less full after eating. That often translates to eating a lot more than you would if you slept well. Research shows that sleep deprivation significantly increased desirability for calorie-dense foods,[25] and research published in the journal *Psychoneuroendrocrinology* showed that after a poor night's sleep, study subjects chose larger portions of food for breakfast and snacks than they did after sleeping well.[26]

Sleep deprivation can also interfere with your exercise intentions. When you don't get enough sleep, it's harder to exercise, according to multiple studies that show sleep deprivation reduces muscle strength,[27] and it puts exercisers in a worse mood and possibly at greater risk of injury.[28] It can also decrease energy for and motivation to exercise,[29] so you may be more likely to skip your workout—and when you are sleep deprived, a nap might be more important than a workout.

Sleep-deprived people also tend to move a lot less during the day, as the body tries to conserve energy. The amount people move around during the day really does add up to a significant calorie burn, even without exercise—this is called *non-exercise activity thermogenesis*, or NEAT.[30] When you move less, you use less energy, and that makes it harder to get into a calorie deficit, if that's your goal.

And it definitely worsens stress. A 2019 study that evaluated how medical residents performed their stressful jobs after being on call for twenty-four hours versus getting a good night's sleep showed that sleep deprivation significantly increased the stress hormone cortisol and significantly decreased mood, cognitive performance, and heart rate variability (a measure of how well your heart recovers from stress).[31]

All these effects can kick in if you periodically get less than seven hours of sleep per night. Turn in a bit earlier, and you could reset your appetite, your hormones, your motivation, your mood, and your stress level, which will make everything good you are trying to do for yourself a little bit easier and more enjoyable. Try to get seven to nine hours of sleep on most nights.

IMPROVING YOUR SLEEP HYGIENE

It's easy to say you're going to get a good sleep, but actually doing it can be a challenge. Whether it's that urge to watch just one more episode of your favorite show, the siren song of scrolling through social media, finishing off those lingering items on your to-do list, or some stressful situation that has your thoughts going in frantic circles, it can be tough to actually get into bed, turn off the light, and go to sleep.

But what you do in the hours before bed, and your sleeping environment, can impact how well you sleep. This is called *sleep hygiene*. How's yours? Here are some ways to improve it, with actions you can take to send your body and brain the signal that it's time to wind down, chill out, and get into a drowsy frame of mind.

- **Set a schedule.** Have a set time when you stop doing daytime things, like looking at a screen, working, or trying to solve problems. To help you put aside your daily concerns, make a to-do list for tomorrow, put it in a place you'll see it tomorrow, and then let it go.
- **Cue the relaxation response.** Take a warm bath or shower, get into your PJs, have a cup of tea, listen to relaxing music or read a book, have quiet, pleasant conversations—all those things can help you wind down, especially if you do them every day in the same order.
- **Set the scene.** A clean, quiet, dark bedroom is the best environment for sleeping. Turn off electronics and lights, and turn down the thermostat. Research shows that people tend to sleep better in cooler temperatures, and that too-warm temperatures can in-

terfere with sleep.[32] One study of people who have sleep apnea showed that people slept much better at 61ºF than at 75ºF.[33] Light exposure, especially to blue light from screens, can also suppress melatonin,[34] which is the hormone that helps you feel sleepy. That's a good reason to stop looking at screens for an hour or two before bedtime.

Mastering Stress Management

The fourth Pillar of Health is stress management, and it's a biggie. Stress—that response to pressure, adversity, danger, or just life overload—can make everything in life more difficult. Our bodies are designed to handle stress—short-term stress, that is. But when stress never lets up, it can break the body down.

"Stress isn't always a bad thing," says Dr. Michaelides. "People think of the word 'stress' as negative, but it's a physiological function and part of our internal radar for danger. It's when stress goes too far or goes on for too long that it becomes a problem."

The stress response has a purpose. When your brain senses a threat, it switches into sympathetic nervous system mode and you release stress hormones like cortisol and adrenaline. These hormones cause physical changes that help you either fight the threat or run away from it, which is why sympathetic nervous system mode is called *fight-or-flight*. When you are in fight-or-flight mode, your body diverts blood to muscles so you can be stronger and run faster. Your vision and hearing get sharper for maximum threat detection, and your heart rate, breathing rate, and blood pressure all increase. Your liver releases more glucose for energy, and all your reflexes get quicker. Basically, you temporarily turn into a superhero.

But here's the important part: When the threat is gone—you fought, or you fled, or you jumped out of the way of the speeding car, or you saved someone's life, or you finished your presentation or your test, or you had that tough conversation—your brain senses that the threat has passed and switches back into parasympathetic nervous system mode. Blood returns to your internal organs, your muscles relax, your heart rate and breathing slow down, and you get back to normal—and maybe take a nap. This is why parasympathetic mode is called "rest and digest."

What *isn't* supposed to happen, Dr. Michaelides explains, is that you stay in sympathetic nervous system mode, or fight-or-flight, *all the time*. Our bodies are made to be superheroes once in a while, for short periods of time, but then we need to recover from all that effort so we can get back to baseline and feel like ourselves again—not superheroes, but pretty awesome nonetheless because we are calm, cool, and collected.

If we don't get that recovery time, stress can become chronic, and the stress response system can become overly sensitive and hyper-reactive, mounting a stress response to all kinds of situations that aren't dangerous. That's not good for health. Or, as scientists say, this is maladaptive.[35] When stress hormones like cortisol hang out in the bloodstream for too long, metabolism can slow down,[36] which can cause the body to store more calories as fat rather than burning them off. It can increase blood sugar and insulin levels,[37] which should rise when you need more instant energy but which shouldn't stay high all the time. This can increase hunger, overeating, and can even damage organs over time. It can increase inflammation and interfere with a healthy immune response. It can cause mood issues like anxiety and depression, as well as other physical health issues like heart disease, hypertension, achy joints, headaches, and poor coordination. Chronic stress can even shrink parts of the brain![38]

One study found that women who were chronically stressed burned 104 fewer calories per day than women who were not stressed. This could add up to eleven pounds over the course of a year, even if you do nothing else differently.[39] Chronic stress also leads to more cravings for calorically dense, nutritionally sparse foods like those containing a lot of sugar, carbohydrates, or added fat (such as fried foods).[40] It can lead to more emotional eating in the presence of anxiety or depression, which could translate to regularly eating more than your body needs.[41]

There's no way to completely eliminate all stress in life, nor is that even a healthy goal. Remember, says Dr. Michaelides, "Stress is just part of being human. Imagine a world with no stress—nothing would get done!"

Dr. Michaelides explains that, rather than fighting stress, you can see stress as an alarm that something is going on that you need to address. "Sometimes stress is about showing you what you need to pay attention to and learn from. Take a step back and look at what is triggering your stress, and see what comes up," he suggests. "And if you find your warning system is activated all the time, that's a signal that you need to recover and let that parasympathetic nervous system kick in. Think about what you need to do to make that happen for yourself."

Need some ideas? You can reduce and manage chronic stress with these psych tricks:

- **Fake it 'til you make it.** If you smile and think positive thoughts, even if you aren't really feeling it, and if you do things that you know will make you smile in spite of yourself, like watching funny videos or comedy shows, or talking to kids or playing with pets, you may find you can relax more easily. Even just smiling can help to reverse the stress response.[42]

POSITIVE THOUGHTS

Positive thinking is a habit, like so many other things. The more you practice it, the better at it you'll get. Here are some examples of positive thoughts you can think on purpose, until they become more automatic—consult this list when you need a dose of positivity:

- I'm making a really great effort here!
- This is hard but I can do it.
- It's okay to take a rest.
- Everything's going to be okay.
- I'm just having some thoughts, but they don't have to control me.
- I didn't mean to do that, but it's okay. We all make mistakes.
- What matters is what I do *next*!
- It's perfectly okay to ask for help. That's what friends are for!
- Today is going to be a great day!
- I did my best today.
- I'm proud of myself.
- I. Am. Awesome! (We'll just interject here: Yes. You. Are!)

- **Visualize it away.** "Visualization is changing your mental environment to one that is less threatening," explains Dr. Michaelides. "If you're feeling really stressed, take a few deep breaths and let your body relax. Your body knows you can't be stressed if you are taking long, slow, deep breaths. Then take a minute out to imagine that you are sitting by a quiet stream relaxing. There is no threat. Everything is fine. When you visualize away the stress, your brain can get a break. You give it a chance to calm down and step away from the stress for a while." Consider these breaks mini vacations. When you feel calm again, open your eyes and get on with your day.

- **You don't have to say yes.** Yes is a choice, and it is okay to say no to things that aren't required. "Do you want to join this book club?" "Do you want to join our carpool?" "Come to happy hour!" "Can you volunteer?" "Can you bring three dozen cookies to the bake sale tomorrow?" "Do you want to take this extra class?" "Can my seven children sleep over at your house this weekend?" Practice with us. You can do it! "No, thank you." "No, thank you." "No, thank you!" Say it over and over until you're comfortable with it. Taking just one thankless task off your plate can be a profound relief. Try it!

- **Oh, well.** We here at Noom are big fans of the "Oh, well" statement. This isn't (as it may sound) a statement of resignation. Quite the contrary! "Oh, well" means total acknowledgment and acceptance of how you feel in the moment, and then, with a shrug, persevering nevertheless.

  For example: "I'm feeling so stressed right now! Oh, well. Stress happens to us all. If I finish my work, I can go home and relax." Or, "I'm feeling anxious and I want to gorge on cookies and forget my troubles! Oh, well. That's an understandable reaction, but maybe I can do something else instead. I could probably use a good walk right now." Or, just to give you one more, since sometimes acknowledging your feelings means changing your plan, "I'm exhausted. I don't know if I can make it to the gym tonight. Oh, well. Sometimes a body needs rest more than exercise and the gym can wait. I think I'll go home and turn in early."

The "Oh, well" statement is a great way to redirect any feelings of guilt or being overwhelmed by simply accepting the situation and dealing with what's really going on, instead of what you wish was going on (like, not being stressed!).

- **Single-tasking is a skill.** Stress and being overwhelmed are often about having too much to do and trying to do it all at once. While multitasking is sometimes necessary, in times of great stress, we've found that switching to single-tasking can help stress to dissipate.

  Single-tasking is just like it sounds: doing one thing at a time. Let's say you're at work and your attention is split in ten different directions. Multiple people want things from you, or you've got projects open on multiple computer monitors, or you're trying to knock out a bunch of things at once. Instead, try taking a beat, prioritizing briefly, then putting everything but one task aside. Devote all your attention to this one task. When it's done, take another beat, then move on to priority number two.

  Studies show that single-tasking is actually more efficient because of the switch cost. That's the time you spend constantly switching from one task to another while multitasking, as your brain adjusts to changing gears.[43] There are always a few seconds, or a few minutes, of adjustment as you switch from one thing to another, and the more switching, the more time is wasted. Add up all those transition moments, and it turns out that multitasking actually takes 40 percent longer than single-tasking to complete the same amount of work.[44]

When you single-task, there is no switch cost. It can also feel more relaxing and afterward, you will have a better sense of what you really accomplished.

- **Boost your mood with food.** Certain foods can actually help to calm the body and relieve stress. Taking a break to enjoy a snack of mood-boosting foods can help to lower cortisol and adjust your biochemistry in favor of relaxation.

MOOD-BOOSTING FOODS

Food really can change your mood. Some of the foods scientists have found contain nutrients that improve mood are:[45]

- Nuts and seeds
- Soy products
- Mushrooms
- Green tea
- Yogurt
- Olive oil
- Oats
- Legumes, like white beans and lentils
- Oysters
- Oily fish, like salmon, mackerel, and tuna
- Leafy greens, like baby spinach and kale

Put them together for a happier day: A snack consisting of yogurt with walnuts or cashews, or oatmeal with flax seeds, or a light lunch of a spinach salad with salmon and an olive oil drizzle, or a cup of lentil soup could ease stress and make you feel better.

Life is a balancing act, and even if you are prioritizing health right now (or want to be), all the other parts of your life can support or undermine that goal. Balance makes people feel good. It can help you take a calmer, more controlled approach to what you eat, it can give you more energy for exercise, it can help you sleep better and manage stress, and it can generally increase your quality of life.

The Wheel of Life—and working on the Four Pillars of Health—can remind you that you are a whole person. You're not just someone on a health journey, not just someone dedicated to fitness, not just someone trying to sleep better or learn to meditate; rather, you are someone with many different parts to their complicated and interesting personality. When you let all those parts shine, everything gets a little bit easier.

Of course, it's all very exciting at first—changes, progress, big plans, habit changes, dietary changes, exercise changes, life changes! But what happens when the honeymoon is over? When all those changes start to feel difficult, and the old habits start calling to you again? How do you keep your motivation strong? Read on to find out.

7

Mastering Motivation

Champions keep playing until they get it right.

—Billie Jean King

You might have noticed something by now, and we think it's time that we spotlight it, because it's very important to remember: *Motivation is not constant.* If you started this book with great excitement and have already been implementing some of the techniques, maybe your motivation was sky-high and then you started making progress and it shot even higher. Hooray! Maybe you have already lost a few pounds or have cleaned up your snacks or have started an exercise program. And then . . .

At some point, and this is just reality, your motivation isn't going to be quite what it was when you first started making changes in your life. It might happen sooner, or it might happen later, but it's going to happen. Does that mean you are doomed? Is that why so many people give up on habit change, diet change, exercise resolutions, and more?

It's true that motivation can seem downright elusive sometimes. That can be frustrating to people who think they are supposed to be motivated all the time. But, as much as we all wished we were gung ho and rah-rah-rah 24/7/365, our brains just don't work that way.

There will always be days that feel harder. There will always be times when you feel defeated by your lofty goals. But guess what? That doesn't mean you've failed. It doesn't mean you have done anything wrong. And it *certainly* doesn't mean you should give up. ("Never give up!" said every motivational speaker ever, including us.)

As Dr. Michaelides tells us: "The biggest thing to remember about motivation is that it is always changing. You're not always supposed to be motivated all the time to do everything. That would be exhausting. It's natural and normal for motivation to ebb and flow."

We think of motivation as being like waves in the ocean. The water comes to shore in a series of waves. Sometimes the waves have a high crest, and sometimes it's a low one. Sometimes there's a raging hurricane, causing high winds to stir up the waves, and sometimes the weather is in the doldrums so there is no wind at all. But that never lasts forever. The ocean is ever changing, and if there's one thing you can depend on, it's that there will always be another wave.

And isn't that motivating? Especially if you are a surfer riding those waves. There will always be another wave, another crest to ride and another plummet after the wave passes. This is such a steadily unsteady phenomenon that we have a name for it: We call it the Motivation Model.

Meet the Noom Motivation Model

Noom's Motivation Model is a kind of map showing how motivation works. There are three phases to this model, and if you've ever tried to do anything difficult, we bet you'll relate to this model. First, here's how it looks:

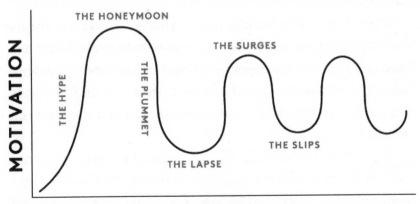

Now, here's how it works:

Phase 1

The hype: Motivation begins with the hype. This is that stage when you decide you want to accomplish something. You're thinking about starting and you're making a plan. You're nervous. You might feel slightly skeptical, but you're gathering information and starting to get excited, even exhilarated. The more you plan, the more you think: "Hey, I think this is really possible!" This time, you're going to *make it happen*! You can see it and you can feel it—it's fun and frightening and a little thrilling to imagine your goal completed. You, crossing the finish line. You, cooking up healthy food and loving it. You, with a calm, clear mind, meditating on the daily. You, feeling energetic and full of a new zest for life. You, *rocking it*, whatever it is. You think about what you need to do to reach your goal, and your general feeling is: "I've got this!"

The honeymoon: When your motivation is riding that first wave, you are in the honeymoon part of phase 1. You've probably started working on your goal and you're already seeing positive results, and that is super-motivating! Maybe you lost two pounds in the first week, or you made serious gains at the gym, or your nature walks are making you feel fitter, more energetic, and giddy with joy, like, "Why haven't I ever noticed how amazing *trees are*!" You may be so pleased with yourself that you might consider making your goal more ambitious. You are starry-eyed and optimistic, and your motivation is through the roof. Off the hook. Sky-high. Woo-hoo! But . . . not necessarily 100 percent realistic.

Phase 2

The plummet: After the honeymoon comes phase 2, and with it the dreaded plummet following that first wave of motivation. This is when your starry eyes begin to see straight because the honeymoon is over. Suddenly your goals are feeling more difficult. Suddenly you realize that to reach your goal, you have to keep working hard, even though you really *want* ice cream tonight or you don't *feel like* working out today. Your exciting goal is starting to look awfully far away, and you begin to think that you're never going to make it . . . and then you're wondering if sweats could possibly be considered casual business attire. (They can't see your pants on Zoom.) Maybe you can't achieve your dream after all. Maybe you should just give up. You are feeling supremely disillusioned because the honeymoon was *so awesome* and now all you've got is a lot of work to do.

The lapse: With the plummet comes a lapse in motivation. This is when you really start skipping the gym or giving up on your eating plan; whatever you were doing starts to feel too hard, so you stop doing it. Or, you stop doing it as consistently as you did when your motivation was high. You may still intend to work toward your goal, but suddenly it's not very fun anymore, and you're not as confident as you were that you can really get there. You may start making compromises. "Maybe I can just start a running program. I don't need to actually do the 5K." "Maybe five pounds is enough to lose because . . . what is life without cookies?" When that lapse in motivation comes, you get the troubling feeling that you have failed. You think: "I always fail. I failed before, and I've failed again."

But here's the thing about that lapse: It's followed by another wave. The lapse can feel defeating and permanent, but it is absolutely a natural and normal part of the process of behavior change. *Normal!* It happens to everyone, no matter what it looks like on social media. It even happens to celebrities and health gurus. The important thing about lapses in motivation is that they teach you things about yourself, about your goals, about what's working and what's not working. They give you a chance to reassess, check in, and regroup.

Nobody goes hard on achieving their goals all the time. A lapse is not the end. *Au contraire*—a lapse is just part of the process, and the exciting thing is that a lapse can be followed by a surge, another wave perhaps stronger than the first. How long your lapse lasts will vary and is mostly up to you. It could last a day, a week, or months, until you feel like you have to start all over again. But that, too, is normal. Everyone is different, and every time you go for a new goal, that will be different, too. When will you decide that your goal is worth pursuing after all? When you see a lapse for what it really is (temporary), all you have to do is hang on to your surfboard and wait for the next wave.

Phase 3

Slips and surges: Experiencing that first lapse can bruise the ego and cause you to pause a bit, but when you catch that next wave, you'll be riding high again. From that vantage, as the wave crests, you can have a look around. Check out the ocean around you: There are waves everywhere. Big ones. Little ones. Swells and dips. And that is how it will go for, well, forever.

We call this phase "slips and surges" because sometimes you'll slip and not do what you meant to do, and sometimes you'll be riding high on a wave, sticking with all your great new habits and feeling awesome. The slips and surges of phase 3 are forever. This is what motivation does. One day, you may slip; the next day, you may surge. You don't stay in a lapse, especially when you are intrinsically motivated, meaning you are deeply, personally motivated for reasons that aren't just about getting a reward but, rather, are about something very personal to you. Intrinsic motivation keeps you going because it is important and valuable to *you*, and it can be a continual source of new surges that follow the slips. As one researcher from the Australia-based Institute of Positive Psychology and Education put it: "Intrinsic motivation refers to people's spontaneous tendencies to be curious and interested, to seek out challenges and to exercise and develop their skills and knowledge, even in the absence of . . . rewards."[1] Keep your intrinsic motivations close by, and even if it doesn't always feel like it will happen, know that another surge is just over the horizon.

The Transtheoretical Model of Health Behavior Change

We think the Motivation Model is pretty easy to understand, which is why we like it so much. It's our way of translating the science into information that you can use in your life. But the science that's behind our Motivation Model is called the transtheoretical model of health behavior change.[2] To go a little deeper into motivation theory, let's take a look at this model and what it can teach us about the process of motivation in the context of behavior change.

According to this model, there are six stages you will go through to make a change in your life:

1. **Precontemplation:** Dr. Michaelides says, "This is the stage when someone thinks that whatever they are doing is fine. They aren't thinking about changing. This is, for example, the person who has a desk job,

sits most of the day, doesn't exercise, and thinks that this is no problem, even if they know, at some deep level, that it's not healthy. At this stage, they have no conscious intention of changing their habit."

2. **Contemplation:** This is the stage when any subconscious misgivings you may have about your behavior begin to rise to the surface and you get the idea that maybe, just maybe, you do want to make a change. Maybe you've had a health scare, or haven't been feeling energetic lately, or you've gained some unwanted weight over the holidays and it's making you feel uncomfortable. You start to think: "Hmm, maybe I can do something about this," and then you start thinking about what kind of change you might want to make. Dr. Michaelides notes, "A hallmark of this stage is ambivalence. You are in that 'maybe I should, maybe I shouldn't' frame of mind."

3. **Preparation:** This next stage is what Dr. Michaelides calls the "Okay, I've decided to make a change so I'm going to get ready to do it" point. This is when you go beyond just thinking and you actually start doing something to make the change, like buying healthy food at the grocery store, getting a nicotine patch, joining a gym, or signing up for the Noom app (shameless plug!). You haven't actually started your plan, but things are happening.

4. **Action:** This is the stage during which you're actually making the change. You're exercising. You're wearing the patch. You're eating better food. You're going to sleep earlier, or actively managing your stress. Whatever it is you decided you wanted to do, you're actually doing it.

5. **Maintenance:** This stage is when you maintain the change. Maybe you've broken your nicotine habit but you're still vigilant, or you've become fitter or lost weight, but you're maintaining your healthy habits.

6. **Termination:** This is the final stage, and although it sounds ominous (is the Terminator going to be involved?!), this is actually a point of achievement when the person has no desire to fall back to the original, unhealthy behavior. Their new behavior has become automatic and is just a normal part of their life. There is no "I'll be back" with those old behaviors. They are gone for good.

Dr. Michaelides explains: "A lot of people think that you start from one end and you work through to the other end, everything in order, and it's beautiful and a straight line; but in reality, most people go back and forth through the stages at different times." You can cycle through them all over and over, and that is totally normal. Sometimes you backslide out of the maintenance stage and you have to go back to the preparation stage. In fact, sometimes you have to go back to the preparation stage a few times before you ever make it to the maintenance stage. Sometimes you will spend a long time cycling through contemplation, preparation, and action, and you may not reach the maintenance stage for a long time. Some people never reach the termination phase. And that's okay, too! Life is a process, not a result.

What really matters more than anything—more than any model or theory—is understanding that slips and surges, progress and backsliding, are all part of the process. They are not signs of failure. They are 100 percent normal. Inevitable, even. And never, ever permanent.

Phew, right?

Conscious Decoupling

Just knowing that slips are a natural part of the process might be heartening to you, but you also might be thinking: "How am I going to make the kind of progress I want to make if I keep having slips?" "What if I never reach termination?" If that's your concern, you might like to get in on another little secret psychologists know: Motivation is not the boss of you.

Dr. Michaelides tells us that it really is possible to do something even if you aren't motivated to do it. He says, "You can decouple action from motivation by building in actions as separate from motivation. Then those ebbs and flows, slips and surges, won't derail you so much. You could call it conscious decoupling." (Not an official psychology term, by the way.)

Dr. Michaelides uses the analogy (to continue our wave theme) of a surfer versus a submarine. "When you separate motivation from action, you can move steadily forward beneath the waves like a submarine. A surfer has to ride those waves of motivation, but a submarine just keeps on with its steady progress, even when the waves on the surface are going crazy. A submarine is deep down in still water, undeterred by surface waves—in other words, not subject to the ebb and flow of motivation."

To do this, Dr. Michaelides suggests making sustainable, realistic decisions and routines about what you are going to do in various situations that are already tied to other habits you have. (Remember habit bundling?) This separates these decisions from motivation.

Let's say you're motivated to exercise every morning—until you're not. If you put a routine into place, such as laying out your exercise clothes and shoes the night before in a conspicuous area, getting your gym bag together, or having your workout playlist cued up on your phone, and you always do this, then in the morning, whether you feel like it or not, you'll be much less likely to skip the exercise. Everything is right there, ready to go, in your line of sight, so you might as well just go ahead, whether you're motivated or not.

Decisions in the moment that require work will be likely to ebb and flow along with motivation, but if you've already prepped for it you won't have any decisions to make when it feels difficult. Everything is already decided.

Motivation SOS Plan

Another concept we use in the app, because our experiments with coaches showed how well it works, is the Motivation SOS Plan. This is a plan you make before your motivation drops so you can take action before you derail your goal progress. This concept is based on a psychological strategy called *implementation intentions*.[3] There is a lot of science showing that implementation intentions work really well. Basically, they're "if . . . then" plans. The strategy is to identify your usual pattern surrounding a behavior you are trying to change, such as: "After I have a bad day at work, I get stressed and reach for snacks." Then you create an "if . . . then" plan: "*If* I've had a bad day at work and I'm stressed, *then* I will call a friend/watch a comedy/go for a walk outside." This helps create desired habits that people maintain without needing to feel consciously motivated.

A Motivation SOS Plan has three parts:

1. The warning sign
2. The danger zone
3. The reaction

The warning sign is what you do, or don't do, when your motivation starts to recede a bit. Let's say you have a goal of logging all your meals. You know that people who log their meals tend to be more successful in reaching their weight goals.

Knowing that research supports this habit, you've decided to do it, and you are motivated! (Looking at the supportive research is a great way to stay motivated, by the way.) But then, after a really hard week at work, you wake up on a Saturday morning realizing you didn't track that pizza and beer you had last night, and, well . . . you just really don't want to know what that would do to your day's calorie count. So, you skip it. You'll get back to it today. Won't you?

You're in **the danger zone** when you realize that your warning sign is becoming a problem. It's a red flag. That one meal you didn't log has turned into a whole weekend of not logging your food. You've also noticed that, knowing you aren't going to log your food, you've made some dietary decisions that you wouldn't have made if you had been accountable to your food log. Maybe you ate more than you wanted to, or you chose some foods that aren't in line with your healthy weight goal instead of the foods you intended to eat. Because who's looking, right? When you are in the danger zone, it probably means something else is going on that's interfering with your goal pursuit, and you have an opportunity to dig a little deeper and see what it is.

The reaction is what you will do when you recognize that you are in the danger zone. This is the SOS part of your SOS Plan, and this is when you can pull out your implementation intentions. In the app, this is where coaches can intervene by contacting people to alert them that they're in their danger zone. You can do this for yourself, too. First, you recognize what you've been doing: "When I get stressed, I don't log my meals." Then you can make an "if . . . then" plan, recognizing that it's totally fine not to log your meals once in a while; but if logging meals regularly really is your goal, then not doing it for more than a few days probably means you are going in a direction you don't want to go. Your "if . . . then" plan might look something like: "*If* I don't log my meals for more than two days in a row, *then* I will . . ." Maybe it's contacting your accountability partner to help you get back on track, or it's taking five minutes to think in detail about YBP, or it's writing in your journal for five minutes about why logging is important to you, or it's spending fifteen minutes reading research studies showing how effective meal logging is for weight loss.

Think about what *your* Motivation SOS Plan will be, enlist help if you need someone to help you monitor your warning signs and danger zone, and commit to what your reaction will be when you get into that dangerous territory. Your Motivation SOS Plan can act as a lifeboat that's stocked and prepped for rescue. The next time you find yourself unmotivated, all you'll have to do is jump into that lifeboat and be saved.

Everybody Loves a Reward

Let's be honest: Sometimes all we humans (and dogs and cats and rats and everybody) really want is a reward. You may have heard that people shouldn't get rewarded for everything they do, but are rewards really so wrong?

Actually, rewards are all kinds of right. According to Dr. Michaelides, the anticipation of a reward gives us a hit of dopamine, which is a neurotransmitter in the brain that causes a rush of pleasure. You can use this information to your advantage. If you're going to reward yourself with something fun (like a dinner date) if you do something you have set out to do (like work out today), then just thinking about the date while you work out can cause a rush of dopamine, which your body will then associate with exercise. That makes exercise *itself* feel rewarding. Cool, right?

Do this habitually, and you can associate that reward-cued dopamine rush with any activity you're trying to establish as a new habit. It feels good to feel good and to celebrate accomplishments, and that can make you want to achieve even more.

While there is some research showing that too many rewards can reduce intrinsic motivation—if you get praised every time you do the slightest good thing at work, it stops being meaningful after a while—generally, rewards help you get things done. And more recent research says that rewards may even increase intrinsic motivation.[4] Rewards also increase creativity, innovation, and the willingness to work hard.[5] Yay, rewards!

When you're working on your health, it's rewarding when people notice your glow, and it's rewarding to feel it for yourself.[6] When you can feel that you're fitter, that you tire less easily, that you can move better, that you're in a better mood, or that you just feel better overall, that's super-motivating.

It's also rewarding to achieve hard things. This is called *learned industriousness*, which is something amazing that happens when you have been rewarded previously for trying hard, so that trying hard becomes rewarding in itself. This feels great and raises your self-efficacy: You can *achieve things*!

In the app, we employ many different rewards, like earning Noom Coin for completing certain tasks like finishing minicourses or achieving learning goals. It can also be useful to reorient your goal toward learning rather than performance; that makes it more motivating. Performance goals are oriented toward results, such as losing five pounds, which may or may not happen, even if you work as hard as you can. Learning goals are oriented toward growth, such as learning to make healthy food. Learning goals, also called mastery goals, lead to more success than performance goals, especially for complex tasks like behavior change.

MAKING PEACE WITH THE SCALE

Measuring, tracking, and logging your progress are all helpful ways to achieve your goals, according to the science of goal-setting.[7] But should that include weighing yourself on that dreaded scale?

Scales are funny things. For some people, they are extremely motivating. They represent a way to monitor progress, catch weight gain in the early stages, and provide hard numbers to celebrate on a healthy weight journey. For others, scales are the stuff of nightmares. That number in the morning haunts them all day long, affects their self-esteem, spoils their fun, or even makes them feel depressed. You probably already know which one you are. Which one *should* you be? There is no right or wrong.

If weighing yourself daily, or every other day, or weekly, is motivating to you and helps you achieve your goals, then great! You've got a tool you can use that tracks a biometric that is useful to you. Research shows that people who weigh themselves regularly while trying to lose weight tend to be more successful at weight loss, fat loss, sticking with behaviors that help with weight control, and weight maintenance.[8] The science supports self-weighing, and it has worked for many people, which is why we have weight tracking as an option in the app. It's part exposure therapy; some people who have not weighed themselves for a long time because they are afraid of what the scale will say may find that weighing regularly helps lessen the anxiety concerning the scale. It's also, of course, a great way to track progress toward your goal.

If you aren't sure about weighing yourself, you find it's a little scary, but you are feeling motivated to lose weight and you think it might help you, it might be useful to spend some time exploring why the scale is so discouraging or scary for you. You could do this through self-awareness, sitting with your thoughts and feelings non-judgmentally, and asking "Why?" questions to uncover why you might be feeling this way.

On the other hand, if weighing yourself is too overwhelming, discouraging, or you know you'll get thrown for a loop if you gain weight, even if you know it's because you ate something salty or it was "that time of the month," then there is absolutely no reason why you have to use a scale. It's just a tool that's not for you. You don't have to explore your feelings about it if you really don't want to. You don't even have to own a scale.

Use a scale if it's motivating. Don't use it if it's not. We think you are amazing and capable, either way. The only thing that matters is that you are taking steps to meet your goal.

Whenever you reach a sub goal, it's fine to treat yourself, knowing that this will reinforce your accomplishment. Science says it will help you reach more goals in the future.

One study gamified exercise by giving study subjects points they could use toward rewards when they met exercise goals.[9] The researchers found that rewards significantly increased exercise levels, and the effect was largest for the advanced users who redeemed their rewards multiple times and were able to earn more and more valuable rewards.

Noom does this in the app using Noom Coin, a fun way to get coins for completing certain tasks that helps people see and measure their progress objectively in a rewarding way. "When your pursuit of your goal feels like a game, it's more fun," says our cofounder Artem. "To be fun and interesting, games have to have an appropriate challenge level so they aren't too hard or too easy, which builds self-efficacy. They have to have a variety of things to do, be entertaining, and operate on the principle of positive reinforcement. You can't just give people points for no reason. That's not rewarding. But when you complete tasks and get something for it, that becomes motivating. It's what we try to do with Noom Coin, and it's what you can do for yourself as a way to help you reach your own goals."

Not all rewards are created equal, of course. Rewards that help you build intrinsic motivation (doing something because you're deeply, personally motivated to do it, like get healthier so you feel better) will generally sustain motivation more than rewards that help you build extrinsic motivation (motivation based on an external reward, like the approval of others). Considering this, seek out rewards that make you really want to partake in that behavior. This is why gamification done in the right way really works.[10]

Your sub goal can be anything you want. (You lost a pound! You ran a mile! You had an indulgent meal and didn't feel bad about it!) Whatever it is, celebrate your success. Your reward could be simple—some small trinket or privilege for every sub goal achieved, something bigger (a vacation? a spa day? that sweater you've had your eye on?) for more significant goals.

You don't have to spend money to reward yourself. Self-care is a great reward. Take a nap, watch your favorite movie, take a drive or a day trip. Give yourself a DIY mani-pedi, draw or paint something, or watch a new (or your favorite old) sitcom; laughing is great for your health! It reduces stress, improves mood and pain tolerance, and even increases a healthy immune response.[11] Rewarding!

Rewards can also be things that are obviously healthy, so you can reward yourself for healthy behavior with more healthy behavior. Twofer! You could sign up for a class in Pilates, or Zumba, or ballet. Finally join that gym or hire that personal trainer. You are ready! Buy a new kitchen gadget you've been wishing you had, or a new cookbook (maybe even a Noom cookbook . . . hint, hint!). Kick back and create a playlist that's just the right speed for your walk/runs, try a new healthy-meal delivery service, sample that new healthy restaurant, or give that healthy recipe a spin.

ARE FOOD REWARDS "ALLOWED"?

What—food? As a reward? Isn't that taboo? People who are working on their health often think they can't have food rewards, but we don't agree. If you are working on your relationship with food, that doesn't mean you give food the cold shoulder. It means you have a goal of being able to eat what you really want, in balance and in a healthy way, rather than letting "shoulds" and "shouldn'ts" drive your choices. It also means you can decide when to have a treat and when you don't need one. Food is one pleasurable part of your life, and it's meant to be enjoyed, not feared or unnaturally restricted.

So, food *can* be a reward, and in fact, we think special food items that you don't want to eat every day (like sweets) are nice rewards for special occasions, when you can really savor and enjoy them. There's nothing wrong with enjoying a food treat now and then—when you've decided to do so.

We do think food treats should be *worth it*. Maybe you'll split a piece of that amazing chocolate cake at that trendy café, or treat yourself to a slice of pizza, or indulge in that beautiful strawberry cupcake in the window. But there is nothing special or rewarding, for that matter, when you mindlessly eat a whole bag of chips while watching TV. Treat rewards are deliberate and special, which we think makes them taste even better! And when you make them yourself with high-quality ingredients *you choose*? Better still! (To refresh your food philosophy, refer back to Chapter 4.)

Making Rewards More Rewarding

If rewards aren't really working for you, it might be that your rewards aren't rewarding enough. You may be used to them because you use the same rewards all the time and, eventually, that dopamine hit isn't as strong anymore. Or, they just might not be something you care enough about.

You may have heard of Maslow's Hierarchy of Needs. This is a theory, first developed by psychologist Abraham Maslow in 1943,[12] and expanded upon throughout the 1960s and 1970s,[13] that shows the order in which people are motivated to get things they need. The bottom part of the pyramid shows the most basic human needs, and Maslow says we are motivated first and foremost to get those. As we meet the needs at each level, we will be motivated to seek out the needs at the next level.

Not everyone agrees that people are motivated by these needs in order. A so-called starving artist may not have their basic needs met but may still be most motivated by aesthetic or self-actualization needs. Others argue that this is nonsense, and if an artist is truly starving, food will be more of a motivator than art.[14] (Eating less than you need is never a good thing, if you can possibly help it.) Others quibble about other parts of this pyramid—what should go where, what's missing, and so on.

Being lovers, not fighters, we at Noom don't feel the need to get into the middle of these arguments, and while we agree that progress up Maslow's pyramid probably is never really a straight line from bottom to top, what's interesting to us is how our higher pursuits really can get derailed by physiological needs. We think this is particularly interesting when it comes to health.

Or, to get straight to the point: If you are truly hungry, can you really focus very well on anything else?

In our opinion, what diet culture gets all wrong is trying to encourage people to eat less by appealing to higher needs like aesthetics (looking good), or self-esteem (you'll feel better about yourself), or even self-actualization (be the "real you," reach your potential). How can you really, genuinely work with those levels of need if you're hungry all the time? We think Maslow would agree with us that this really isn't tenable.

Maslow says that motivation to achieve your basic needs is strongest when those needs aren't currently being met, so we say that before you can move up that pyramid and get motivated by things like improving your self-esteem, nurturing your relationships, pursuing your interests, or appreciating beauty, first—seriously—you need to eat enough to fuel your body, and you need to take care of your health.

So, to answer our very first question: How do you make rewards more rewarding? First, eat. Get the motivation to eat off your plate (so to speak), and then you can start moving up that pyramid and working on more subtle aspects of your lifestyle, your habits, even your *relationship* to food and exercise, which we would say is more about self-actualization than basic needs.

Wherever you are on the pyramid, that's where your greatest motivation will be. Don't get stuck on the ground floor. Love, self-worth, curiosity, and the pursuit of joy are a lot more interesting than food, once you're not hungry anymore. Have a good meal, then get out there and get inspired by all the world has to offer!

Call in the Reinforcements!

Rewards are a form of positive reinforcement, which in psychology is just one of two types of reinforcement, according to the psychology theory of operant conditioning:

◆ **Positive reinforcement** makes you do something more often because you get something good when you do it. For example, if every time you go to the gym you see friends and have a fun social time, you're more likely to keep going to the gym. This is what most people think of when they think of rewards.

◆ **Negative reinforcement** makes you do something more often because it stops something you don't like from happening. For example, maybe a friend is constantly hounding you to go to the gym and you're really tired of it. You go to the gym with them, and they stop bugging you about it. You are, essentially, rewarded by the cessation of the thing you don't like.

Research on positive and negative reinforcement shows that combining the two is an effective way to stick with a new behavior.[15] However, when pitted against each other, positive reinforcement wins out. In several studies, a food treat (positive reinforcement) was a more effective reinforcer of a behavior than a break from work (negative reinforcement).[16] However, negative reinforcement may also work for you. Depending on what you are trying to do, one or the other, or both, might work best for you personally. If you can manage both, you'll get the most power out of the strategy of reinforcement.

QMTs

The last tool we want to give you in this chapter is a list of our absolute favorite QMTs, or quick motivational tips. These are small things you can do to boost your motivation in the moment. They are handy to have up your sleeve. Stash these in your (metaphorical) Noom toolbox.

QMT #1: Let. It. Go.

Life doesn't always go the way you want it to go. *You* don't always go the way you want yourself to go. Even though you know now that slips and surges are all part of the process, it can still be frustrating when you have an intention and then you don't stick with it. But, hey: reality. Sometimes you're going to overeat. Sometimes you're going to skip your workout. Sometimes you're going to get triggered. *It's okay.* Give yourself a little kindness. Instead of stressing about it, ruminating constantly about it, getting all full of regret or whatever, let it go and move on. Guilt and shame will only hold you back. What matters more than what you did is what you'll do next. Focus on what's ahead of you, not what's behind you, and be gentle on yourself. Nobody is perfect, and we all act against our intentions sometimes. If you are compassionate with yourself, you'll probably be able to get back on track with your goals a lot faster, and maybe even achieve them more easily.[17]

QMT #2: Put your feet up

We all need a break sometimes. If you've been going hard, good for you! A certain amount of effort and stress is motivating, but if you overdo it, it can become defeating. Take a break and put your feet up at least once a day, for at least fifteen minutes. Relax. Take some deep breaths. Unwind. Listen to your favorite music or go outside and take a short walk and breathe the fresh air. Chat with a friend about something frivolous and fun. Heck, play a game on your phone or watch funny videos and get in some good, healthy belly laughs. All work and no play makes *anyone* dull.

QMT #3: Share your goals

Guess who wants to hear about your success? Your friends! One of the things we like best about people is how supportive they can be of each other. When you meet a sub goal, or slay a Super Goal, or basically do anything awesome (and we know you can do awesome things), don't be afraid to tell people about it. You don't have to be braggy, or even humble-braggy, to share your successes. Just be honest: "I did it! I ran the 5K! I lost the ten pounds! My doctor says I'm healthy! High five!"

Whether you have an accountability buddy or you just post on social media when you did that thing you've been trying so hard to do, you're going to feel really motivated when the "Congratulations, my friend!" and "You rock!" comments start rolling in. You'll also feel more accountable, once you have let people know about your success, to keep up the good work, so sharing can keep you motivated long-term.[18]

QMT #4: Picture success

Remember in Chapter 2 when we had you visualize how your life will be different when you achieve your goals? Well, guess what: That is super-motivating! Whenever you feel your motivation lagging, take a beat, close your eyes, remember YBP, and picture yourself succeeding. Feel the glory, the satisfaction, the energy, and the surge of confidence.

You can also use other visual cues to help motivate you. You can snap photos of your healthy meals, or even the things you chose *not* to eat, or only had a few bites of, that you might have overeaten before but have learned to moderate now. Take workout selfies, photos of plummeting scale numbers (if weighing motivates you), progress photos of you getting fitter and fitter, or just photos of beautiful nature scenes or fun times with friends to remind you what's really important in your life.

NOOM COACH Q&A

I hate weighing in every day. Why does Noom make us do this?

Noom doesn't make you do it—all parts of our program are optional, and we advise that you do what works for you—but we offer and encourage it as a useful tool for monitoring your progress. Weighing in every day gives you a small view of the big picture of your weight loss. It can be hard to see that big picture in the moment! Your weight will fluctuate from day to day based on factors that can be unrelated to true fat loss.

QMT #5: Ask questions

Part of changing behavior is awareness, mindfulness, and switching off automatic behaviors so they become more purposeful and conscious. One great way to do that is to ask yourself questions, especially when you're tempted to go back to those old ways that weren't working so well for you, but which may feel good in the moment. We've got a handy-dandy set of five things to ask yourself before you jump in and do, or don't do, that thing you may feel triggered to do. Stop, take a breath, then answer these questions before you make a final decision:

1. **Why** am I doing this right now? Try to think of the real reasons, your feelings, how your day went, anything that is influencing you in the moment.
2. **What** else could I do instead of this thing I want to do now but won't want to have done later? Could I

take a walk? Call someone? Listen to some music? Do a crossword puzzle? Just say no? What are my options here?

3. **Who** is telling me to do this thing? A friend? A food-pusher? My anxiety? My fear? My boredom? My anger?

4. **When** do I feel I need to do, or not do, this thing? Right now, or can I wait and decide later?

5. **How** will I feel later if I do, or don't do, this thing? How will I feel later if I resist this temptation right now?

After this inner interrogation, you may still decide to do, or not do, the thing, whatever it is. You may choose the cupcake, skip the workout, have the outburst, or take the nap, and that is *totally fine*. The point is that you didn't do it automatically. You went through a process and made a conscious decision. Yay, you!

◆

We hope, here at the end of this chapter, that you are feeling motivated, or at least feeling like you know how to get motivated when you need it the most. But we have even more wisdom for you! First up, let's talk about what happens when your thinking gets skewed and turns against you. When you see these goal-thwarting thoughts for what they really are—thought distortions—you'll be in a better position to tackle them and get your head back in the game.

8

Thought Distortions

Thoughts are acrobats, agile and quite often untrustworthy.

—Bess Streeter Aldrich

Sometimes, even with the best of intentions and the most effective psych tricks (ahem, you're welcome), you will face an adversary that convinces you that your goals are unachievable. That adversary, the one that is seemingly so strong and so intimidating is . . . your own mind. It may seem dark in there sometimes—scary, even—but we think it's worth doing a little mental spelunking at this point because sometimes, when it comes to thoughts, all is not what it seems.

Your brain is a complex and impressive organ that puts the most advanced computer to shame. But just as a computer can get a virus that interferes with its programming, brains can (and often do) become subject to something psychologists call *cognitive distortions*. Cognitive distortions, or what we here at Noom call *thought distortions*, are progress-foiling irrational thoughts. They influence your emotions in a way that makes what you're trying to do for yourself harder.

Dr. Michaelides says, "Thought distortions are thinking patterns that prevent you from behaving in the way you want to behave. They are beliefs that limit your ability to reach your goals." Thought distortions are patterns that may be biased, exaggerated, or otherwise inaccurate, but that influence you to draw conclusions that aren't based in reality.

Thought distortions are very common. "I think we can all relate to a thought distortion in some way, shape, or form because we've all experienced them," notes Dr. Michaelides. "The tricky thing about thought distortions is that they don't feel like thought distortions in the moment. They feel true."

Dr. Michaelides explains that thought distortions are all tied up with emotions, which can prevent us from being objective. "Imagine you are trying to read a book. You hold it up right in front of your face, against your nose, an inch from your eyes. It's right there in front of you, it's all you see, it's blocking out everything else, but you can't make out the actual words." This, he says, is like a thought distortion. "You're too close to the thought, so you can't see it for what it is. Only when you get a bit of distance can you observe it and see that it's a thought distortion."

Thought distortions are often unhelpful and hindering, and yet, we often can't see that. So, how do we push back that metaphorical book and take a good, hard look at the actual words?

Learning to recognize thought distortions is the first step to unpacking their content and assessing them realistically. As Dr. Michaelides tells us, everyone has thought distortions once in a while. It's natural and human. However, since thought distortions can also derail your progress, interfere with your self-efficacy, and douse your motivation, let's look at some examples. You might recognize that you occasionally have some of these thoughts. Seeing this can help you begin to tease out the differences between something you know is true (like a fact) and something you only feel is true in the moment:

- "Oh no! I ate candy! Candy is *bad*!"
- "Everybody is looking at me and judging me!"

- "I have to finish all the food on my plate."
- "I finished all the food on my plate and got seconds— I'll never be able to control my eating!"
- "I bet that fit person on the stair climber is thinking how out-of-shape I look."
- "If I go back to the buffet, everyone will notice and judge me."
- "I'm such a lazy person."
- "I have zero willpower."
- "I'm destined to be overweight."
- "I can't eat that."
- "I'm so virtuous for working out this morning."
- "If I eat ice cream while standing in front of the freezer, it has no calories." (Wait, that's not true?)
- "I gained two pounds overnight! My goals are futile."

Have you had any of these thoughts? Or similar ones? See if you can remember having a thought distortion of your own. Some of these familiar thought distortions might also feel obviously untrue to you when you read them on the page, but think about how real and true they felt in the moment. Maybe later you realized they weren't true or recognized that you couldn't know for sure whether they were true. That can help in retrospect, but it's even more helpful to recognize thought distortions as they happen. This can help you analyze them more objectively.

Types of Thought Distortions

To help you begin to identify your own thought distortions more systematically, let's group them into categories. These are all pretty common types of thought distortions that psychology has identified. See if these are familiar territory for you.

All-or-Nothing Thinking

"It's good!" "It's bad!" "I can never do this!" "I'm a success!" "I'm a failure!" "This is always true!" "This is never true!" These are thought distortions that stubbornly cling to all-or-nothing, binary thinking. They consider no shades of gray, no nuance, no middle ground. That may make the world (and problems) easier to understand, but this kind of thinking blatantly ignores the subtle and complex nature of reality.

"All-or-nothing, black-and-white thinking is probably one of the most common types of thought distortion," says Dr. Michaelides. "It's that idea that you are either going to be this person who does it all, eating the perfect diet, working out every day, and doing twenty things at the same time, or you're that person who can't do any of it, so you might as well not try." To recognize all-or-nothing thought distortions, look for words like *good*, *bad*, *always*, *never*, *success*, *failure*, and *I* [something you did] . . . *so I might as well* . . . or *I* [something you didn't do] . . . *so I might as well* . . .

Some specific, health-related examples of these kinds of thought distortions are:

- "Carbs are bad, so I should never eat them."
- "Vegetables are good, so I should eat them at every meal."
- "If I don't get eight hours of sleep, my day is ruined."
- "If I sleep too much, I'm lazy."
- "I have to count every calorie (or carb gram or fat gram) or I'll fail on my diet."
- "I should never eat after 7:00 p.m. or I'll gain weight."
- "I must fast every day for sixteen hours."
- "I must eat every four hours during the day."
- "If I don't do HIIT/cardio/strength training, I'm not exercising enough."
- "I sit at my desk all day, so I'll never be able to lose weight."

- "I have to work out every day for one hour or I'll gain weight."
- "I skipped dessert, so I'm a success."
- "I ate dessert, so I'm a failure."
- "I ordered a pizza, so I might as well give up on this diet."
- "That meal I made was terrible, so I obviously can't cook."
- "I didn't go to the gym all last month, so I might as well quit."

As you begin to recognize all-or-nothing thoughts, see if you can formulate a middle-ground thought. For instance, you could counter the thought: "Carbs are bad" with the thought: "Refined carbs are calorically dense without much nutritional value, so it's a good idea to limit them in my diet as I'm working toward my healthy weight goal." Instead of "bad," which is an oversimplified opinion, you are assessing the actual facts about carbs. Doesn't that seem a lot more reality based?

Negatively Biased Thinking

This is a type of thought distortion in which someone notices the negative more than the positive, even when there is more positive than negative to notice. It's like when you get a performance review from your boss that's full of glowing praise, with one thing that "needs improvement." Instead of celebrating the praise, you obsess about that one "needs improvement" part.

Scientists say humans—even as infants—tend to register the negative more easily than the positive. This is called *negativity bias*, and it may have once been useful for survival;[1] in fact, there's a theory that negative stimuli are more informative than positive stimuli. For instance, touching a hot stove and discovering that it burns your hand is more informative than, say, discovering that it's pleasant to pet a fluffy dog. Sure, petting a dog is nice, but it's not a matter of personal injury. If you don't want to get burned, it's more important to remember not to touch a hot stove.

While negativity bias has its purposes, it can also be debilitating. It's a type of thought distortion that can interfere with progress, goal achievement, and happiness. It has even been associated with depressive symptoms.[2]

A good way to counter negativity bias is simply to, as the song goes, "accentuate the positive." There's *always* a bright side, and if you notice yourself being negatively biased, it is important to deliberately practice looking at the other side of the story. Because there's always another side to the story. In this way you can begin to practice optimism, which, science says, significantly influences physical and mental health and well-being and can even make healthy habits easier to achieve.[3]

TOXIC POSITIVITY

It's great to practice optimism, and research has shown that there is a link between positive thinking and high self-esteem, and that these qualities can make people more resilient to hard times.[4] However, when it's applied indiscriminately, positivity can become toxic. *Toxic positivity* is a term for putting a positive spin on everything, even when it is irrational or unkind to do so. If someone undermines the validity of your grief or trauma by telling you to "look on the bright side" or "at least you still have blah blah blah," that is toxic positivity. It doesn't acknowledge the deep feelings of another person, and that can be hurtful.

You can also do it to yourself by forcing yourself to act cheerful or happy to hide your sadness or other negative feelings. This isn't helpful. It's suppressive. Instead of suppressing negative emotions, it's often more helpful to let yourself feel them and to talk about them with supportive people so you can process them, rather than pretending everything is fine.[5] It can even be harmful if someone stays in a dangerous situation because they are trying to see it in a good light.[6] Another study showed that trying to make the best of a bad situation only works when that situation is something you can't actually control.[7] When you *can* control it, you may be better off changing it than enduring it with a fake smile. So, be positive, yes! But don't let positivity stand in the way of action.

Irrationally Comparative Thinking

In a time when so many people are comparing their real lives to what they see on social media, this thought distortion runs rampant. People constantly see the curated, filtered versions of others' lives, and it's hard not to compare. But comparison is the thief of joy, as they say, and comparing oneself to someone else can distort self-perception and destroy confidence.

Imagine you are feeling great about yourself and decide to check your social media. Then you see someone else's feed full of impossibly attractive photos ("Is that a filter?" you wonder, nervously glancing at yourself in the mirror), or a travelogue to exotic places you only dream of going, or professional successes that seem so much bigger and better than your own. Or maybe you walk into a classroom, or a party, or some other event and see someone who (in your opinion) looks better dressed, or acts happier, or seems more popular, or has nicer things, or is in some way "better" than you.

Maybe you go out for a walk, feeling great, feeling fit, enjoying the fresh air, proud of yourself for getting outside and moving . . . and then you see that runner, in amazing shape, barely breaking a sweat. "They probably compete in triathlons," you think. "They probably have virtually no body fat," you think. "Look at those muscles," you think. And suddenly you feel completely inadequate, like your walk is a joke. How could you even call it exercise? All those good feelings drain away.

In reality, of course, you were feeling perfectly fine about yourself before the social media, or the party, or the encounter with that person who, for all you know, might be a professional athlete under great pressure to be so fit. Even though nothing about you has changed physically, your inner critic has interrupted your pleasant day and made you feel badly about yourself.

But since you really don't know much about that other person's life, why not put aside the comparison, which is based largely on your assumptions rather than on facts? You can't know how someone feels on the inside even if they look great on the outside or have a lot of things you don't have. And as for that runner, maybe they were right where you were a year ago, and that could be you in a year. Maybe you're comparing your pit stop to their finish line. And for that matter, other people may be looking at you and feeling worse about themselves.

The next time you notice yourself doing it, see if you can shift your perspective back to *your* successes. All you can do is know yourself and work on *you*. The only valid comparison is you in the past versus you in the present. That is something you can realistically assess, and it's also something you can actually do something about.

Mind Reading

Sometimes we really can guess what other people are thinking by correctly interpreting facial expressions or body language. However, when you assume that people are judging you or have a bad opinion of you without any real evidence, mind reading becomes a thought distortion.

If you think you know what someone is thinking, ask yourself if you really have any evidence, and whether that thought benefits or harms your own self-esteem or progress. If it's a harmful assumption, it can be useful to remind yourself that you don't actually know, so why waste energy with unnecessary negativity?

A common example of mind reading is assuming you know what people are thinking about how you look or what you are doing. For instance, you might think that you'll be judged for being diet-obsessed if you order a salad, or that if you get something like fries or a burger, people will be thinking that you really shouldn't be eating foods like that. Other examples might be thinking that the people at the gym are secretly laughing at you, or your being sure your friend is going to notice and judge you for your weight gain.

Mind reading is often a form of *projection*, a psychological term for projecting your own feelings onto someone else. The next time you think you know what others are thinking, consider whether what you think they're thinking is really what *you* are thinking about yourself. If you think someone is judging you for ordering dessert, maybe you're actually being self-critical about your choices. If you think people at the gym are laughing at you, maybe it's really that you are feeling self-conscious about your fitness level.

The next time you find yourself supposedly reading someone else's mind, test out this theory. If it rings true, then consider whether that thought you are having about yourself is actually helpful or not (and if it's self-critical, it's not helpful!).

Fortune-Telling

It's human nature, and an important survival mechanism, to try to predict the future based on the past. Sometimes this can help us protect ourselves or avoid danger. However, constantly assuming you know what's going to happen when you couldn't possibly know isn't helpful. People don't like uncertainty, but when you combine fortune-telling with negativity bias, you've got a maladaptive thought distortion. Some examples of fortune-telling:

- "I won't be able to run a ten-minute mile, even if I practice."
- "I won't be able to stop after one piece of pizza."
- "If I eat this piece of cake, I'll gain weight by tomorrow."
- "If I have a salad for dinner, I'll lose weight by tomorrow."

Of course, not only could you not know these things, but fortune-telling can become a self-fulfilling prophecy. You might be perfectly capable of running a ten-minute mile with practice, working up to it, but if you tell yourself that it's impossible, then you might make it impossible because you won't believe you can do it and you'll stop trying.

One good way to counteract this type of thought distortion is to bring yourself back to the here-and-now and think of three possible ways the future could turn out. This can free your mind from your assumption that there is only one possible outcome. If you think you won't be able to stop after one piece of pizza, you could decide that:

A. You won't be able to stop after one piece of pizza.
B. You will be able to stop after one piece of pizza.
C. You will have two pieces of pizza and feel satisfied.

Wow, options! Now you get to choose one, rather than feeling like a victim of fate.

Justification

This is a thought distortion that enables you to get out of doing something you don't feel like doing in the moment. It's a derailer because it's basically you talking yourself out of working toward your goals or putting off work you could be doing now. You can recognize justification because it often includes words like *but* and *because*, such as "I was going to work out, **but** I just didn't have time" or "I'm going to have second helpings **because** I worked out today."

Justification is self-sabotage, plain and simple. Remember in Chapter 3, when we told you all about how, every time you do something difficult, like riding out a craving or practicing a new habit, it gets a little easier the next time? The opposite is also true. Every time you make an excuse *not* to do something hard, like riding out a craving or practicing a new habit, it gets easier to skip it again next time. Your brain is a creature of habit, so what you do now becomes what you are more likely to do later.

Remember this: Every time you do the hard thing, it becomes an easier thing to do. Instead of making excuses, make informed decisions, and you'll be exercising more power over your own behavior.

Rumination Nation

Thought distortions are often the subject of rumination, which is the process of thinking the same thoughts over and over or obsessively going back and replaying the same scenarios again and again. Rumination is incredibly common and incredibly nonproductive. There isn't anything wrong with thinking back over the past to see what you might want to do differently next time, or recognizing mistakes and learning from them, but rumination doesn't actually involve any reflection or change. It's your thoughts going in circles, like a dog chasing its tail.

Ruminating may take the form of worrying about something when you are trying to focus on something else (like falling asleep), or it might be replaying a conversation in your head over and over, like, "If only I had said . . ." It's an unproductive way to try to deal with stress because it makes stress worse. People often believe they can think their way out of a problem, but rumination only *feels* like thinking. It's actually more like obsessing. Research has linked rumination with depressive symptoms, negativity bias, social anxiety, and unhealthy habits like binge eating or drinking.[8]

So, what can you do to disempower rumination, not just when it comes to health-related goals but also anything else? Try out some of these techniques, to break out of a rumination pattern:

◆ **Give yourself ten minutes.** Set a timer if you need to, but put a time limit on your ruminating. Ruminate all you want for ten minutes, then stop and do something unrelated to the subject of your rumination.

◆ **Do something.** You know that saying, "Don't just sit there, do something!" and the humorous turnaround: "Don't just do something, sit there!"? Rumination is a bit like sitting there instead of doing something, whereas doing something can actually disperse ruminating thoughts. Instead of going over and over the same thing, make an actual plan of something you can do that could help the problem you're ruminating about. If you're ruminating about what you should have said to someone, you could write a letter to that person expressing everything you wish you would have said. Whether you actually send it is up to you—you might find that writing out your responses is enough, and that allows you to let it go.

◆ **Create a distraction.** Do something that won't allow you to ruminate because you need to concentrate, like watching a movie, or reading an article, or doing a dance fitness video, or playing a game on your phone that requires focus.

◆ **Ruminate out loud to a friend.** If you say what you're thinking out loud in front of someone you trust, you may realize that you've blown things out of proportion. A friend can also sympathize with you, which might make you feel better, and could help you work through what's bothering you or see solutions you didn't see because you were too close to the problem. Sometimes just telling someone about what's bothering you can take all the energy out of the rumination, and you won't need to do it anymore.

◆ **Observe the thoughts without engaging.** Try stepping back from your rumination and emotionally disengaging from it. Observe it neutrally, as if you were someone else. Imagine you can see those thoughts swirling around in your head. What do they look like? Notice how you feel as you observe them. See them as outside of yourself, rather than letting yourself get caught up in them. This is a mindfulness technique. A review of nineteen studies on the effectiveness of cognitive behavioral therapy and mindfulness techniques demonstrated that emotionally disengaging from repetitive thoughts so you can see them more objectively was an effective way to break the rumination cycle.[9] (For more specifics, read on to learn more about cognitive fusion and defusion. We'll also talk more about how to do this in the next chapter, on mindfulness.)

NOOM COACH Q&A

What are some ways I can decrease stress? Any tips?
The best approach to avoiding the negative effects of stress is to prevent unnecessary stress whenever you can. Here are two tips to help you keep stress at bay.

1. **Practice saying no.** Saying no can be hard, but it's important to think ahead about the consequences of saying yes and whether it will cause you unwanted stress. Try coming up with a few phrases that you can use when you feel pressured to do something you don't want to do, and remind yourself: "My heart says yes, but my health says no."

2. **Set small, realistic goals.** Setting a goal that you perceive as being far from where you are now can be a big source of stress. Setting smaller, more realistic goals that you're confident you can achieve is less stressful, and can elicit the short-term positive reinforcement you need to keep going.

Cognitive Fusion and Defusion

Cognitive fusion is a term for what happens when your thoughts trigger such strong emotions that you fuse with the thoughts and believe they are inner truths. *Cognitive defusion* is a method for disconnecting the thought from the feeling or emotion so you can see it more clearly and separate yourself from it.

Dealing with the emotion behind a thought distortion as something separate from the thought itself takes the energy out of the thought and also validates the reason for the thought. Dr. Michaelides elaborates: "Arguing with a thought gives that thought energy. Instead, you can fully acknowledge the thought, and instead of taking it literally, consider the feeling attached to it, confirm the feeling behind the thought as valid, and consider where that feeling might be coming from."

For example, if you're thinking, "Everyone is judging me," that can feel very personal. But rather than accept as a fact the thought that everyone is judging you, try to determine how you *feel* when you have that thought. Anxious? Insecure? Angry? "The feeling that thought has engendered is valid," says Dr. Michaelides. "Only by listening to it and letting yourself experience it can you allow it to change your situation. Only by acknowledging it can you let it go." Cognitive defusion allows you to see the thought as false but the feeling behind the thought as true.

Once you contend with the feeling behind the thought, you can see the thought as something apart from yourself. This will quiet the thought. Let it be there, as a messenger of your emotions, but don't mistake it for truth. It's just a thought. Indeed, Dr. Michaelides suggests using the word *just* to put the thought in its place: "It's *just* a thought."

It's not always easy to separate a thought from its accompanying emotion, but we have a psych trick for that! For this trick, which you might call the "Say it again" psych trick, you will repeat the thought so many times that you wear out the emotion you've attached to the thought until only the words remain, and you don't feel so attached to them.

When you are having a thought distortion with a lot of emotion behind it, find a mirror, close the door, look in the mirror, and say the thought out loud. Say it again and again. The more you say the thought, the more you drain the thought of its power. The more you say the thought, the more unreal it begins to sound, and the more you can see it for what it really is: just a thought.

For example, maybe you're thinking, "If I haven't lost weight at this point in my life, I never will." Go to a mirror and say that to yourself. Then say it again and again. Listen to yourself as you say it. How does that thought make you feel? Is that something you would tell a beloved friend? Is that what you really believe? Is there any evidence that it's true? Are you just fortune-telling?

If you keep repeating it and keep feeling the emotion that goes with it, the power of the emotion will begin to wane, and then the thought can begin to seem a little ridiculous—and honestly, something that you can't possibly prove is true. In fact, it's just as likely that the opposite is true.

"If I haven't lost weight at this point in my life, I never will" doesn't indicate anything other than that you are feeling frustrated or a little overwhelmed right now. When the emotion has fallen away from the thought, you can consider it officially defused. Because the real truth is: Even if you haven't lost weight yet, you can still do it.

CALL YOU BY YOUR NAME

Another strategy for helping you to separate yourself from a thought distortion is to place it verbally outside of you by playing the part of the third-person narrator. Dr. Michaelides says, "To help you see the thought as something outside of yourself, attach your name to it. Like, I might say, 'Andreas is having the thought that he's nervous about giving a speech.'" Naming yourself as a third party having the thought can help you to become the observer of yourself thinking the thought. "This distances you from the thought and the emotions attached to it, so you can view them more objectively," Dr. Michaelides adds.

More Techniques for Managing Thought Distortions

If we had to pick just one litmus test for determining whether a thought is actually a thought distortion, it would be this: What effect is it having on you? Dr. Michaelides explains, "If a thought you are having is holding you back from something you are trying to do, such as by making you feel bad about yourself, then it's probably a thought distortion." Once you know you're dealing with a thought distortion, there are even more things you can do to keep it from interfering with your progress. Here are some more of our favorite thought-distortion–busting psych tricks.

Walk It Back

When you recognize a thought distortion entering your mind, metacognition (thinking about thinking) can help you step back from a thought distortion and see it in context. "Using metacognition, walk yourself back through the chain of events that led to the thought," suggests Dr. Michaelides. "What was the initial trigger for the emotional response that created this thought? What did you think after the trigger? What did you do? What did you do after that?" Retrospectively examining the chain of events can help you identify patterns of behavior. When you have discovered that exposure to a certain trigger always leads to a pattern of thoughts that become thought distortions, you can go back to the initial trigger and work on formulating a new response that won't lead to a thought distortion.

For example, try this exercise:

1. What did you do that is causing you to feel bad or ruminate? You might say, "I ate a big piece of cake."

2. What was the thought that led you to eat the cake? You might say, "I was thinking that I shouldn't eat the cake because it's not healthy and has too many calories, but everyone else was eating it so I did it anyway."

3. What was the emotion that made you have that thought that led to the action of eating the cake? You might say, "Rebellion. I didn't like that I had a rule that I couldn't eat cake, and I felt deprived since everyone else was eating it. This made me feel rebellious, so I ate it anyway."

4. What triggered that emotion of rebellion? You might then recognize that having a rule that cake is bad and you can't eat it is all-or-nothing thinking, and that is a thought distortion that was your trigger.

5. How could you respond differently to this trigger? You might say, "I won't make all-or-nothing rules about food. Instead, I'll stop and assess my hunger and situation and make a more conscious decision about whether or not I really want to have some cake." You might even recognize that, had you done that, you might have eaten less cake, or even chosen not to have cake on that occasion. If it's not forbidden, you might not want it so much.

Your process might look completely different from this, but you can see how you can work your way back from action to thought, to emotion, to trigger, then determine why you reacted to that trigger the way you did and how you might do it differently next time. This can help you to see your thought distortions, such as "Cake is bad and I am not allowed to eat it," as distortions rather than rational thoughts—you can see them as something you have, but not something that controls you.

Reframe It

Another useful way to take a step back and get real about the thoughts you're having that threaten to derail your progress is *cognitive reframing*, also sometimes called *cognitive restructuring* or *cognitive reappraisal*. This is a process of changing the context around a thought, like you might change the frame around a photograph. Applying different facts to the same situation can completely alter the outcome. According to one study, people who used reframing (in the study they called it cognitive reappraisal) were less likely to default to negative perceptions when under stress.[10]

Since you are more likely to see the negative side of things when you are stressed, cognitive reframing can be a great intervention to counteract this tendency. One effective way to do this is to use the "Yes, but" psych trick. Here's how it works.

Let's say you're thinking: "This has been a terrible week. I'm just way too stressed out to eat well right now. I need my comfort food and I need it now!" That is an understandable reaction to stress, for sure. However, you can use the "Yes, but" psych trick to completely change the context of the facts. To reframe your stress-requires-comfort-food thought, you might think: "This has been a terrible week and I need my comfort food, yes, but I know super sugary/salty/prepackaged food will make me feel worse. I need healthy, nutrient-dense food to feed my brain and I need it now!" Same scenario, completely different frame.

If this feels hard to do in the moment, get some literal distance. Take a break from what you're doing or about to do. Take a few deep breaths, think it through, even take a quick walk. Reframing takes a minute, and this time-out can help you reassess rather than acting on the first stressful food-related thought you have.

Separate Thoughts and Feelings from Facts

Thoughts are not necessarily facts. You might think: "The grass is green." That is a thought, and it's also a fact. You could think, "I'm experiencing stress right now." Also, a fact. But thinking, "That green grass is gorgeous!" or "I'm so stressed that I can't possibly exercise today!" are expressions of opinion—and opinions can change!

To help separate thoughts and feelings from facts, try the "Is it true?" psych trick.

So, you're too stressed to exercise. Is that really true, even though exercise is a proven and effective stress reliever? If you think about it, you might realize that what's actually true is that the circumstances around you are making you think that you don't *want* to exercise. If you recognize that your thought isn't a fact, you have options. Yes, you're stressed, but the feeling of stress does not automatically dictate that you should go home to sit on the couch. Maybe you'll choose not to work out that day because, when you think about it, you realize that you really do need some rest, and that is fine! But you might also decide exercise is likely to make you feel better. It's hard to see these options until you can recognize that your thought isn't a fact. That gives you control over how you choose to respond to the thought, rather than feeling railroaded into an action by the illusion that you didn't have a choice.

Reinforce Your Self-Efficacy

Remember self-efficacy, from Chapter 2? When thought distortions are rising up, self-efficacy can be a huge help in putting them in their place. As you may recall, self-efficacy is the belief that you can accomplish things—it's confidence in your ability to reach your goals. But we all have the occasional crisis of confidence, especially when we are tired, had a stressful day, or have faced some setbacks and our executive function is exhausted.

When you're not feeling confident in your abilities—maybe you're having fortune-telling or all-or-nothing or negativity bias thought distortions like "I can't do it," "I'll never succeed," "I might as well quit"—you can try the affirmation psych trick. Instead of "I can't do it," form the opposite thought, which emphasizes your strength and capability: "I *can* do it!" Basically, you are giving yourself a pep talk and that's a great way to reverse the negative emotion around a thought distortion.

Say them until you believe them:

- I know how to do this.
- I'm good at this!
- I am strong and powerful.
- I've succeeded before and I can succeed again.
- This is a no-fail zone.
- No failure, only feedback.
- Frankly, I'm pretty awesome. (Yes, you are!)

Radical Acceptance

The last technique we want to talk about is a pretty radical one (hence the name): *Radical acceptance* is totally accepting your current reality as your current reality. *Not* your future reality, but your current reality. This can be difficult for people who are afraid of losing confidence or momentum, or who think it will be too scary or depressing, but let's get real: The present moment is what it is.

In psychology, there is a concept that suffering comes not from pain itself but from fighting against the pain. Radical acceptance is used in dialectical behavioral therapy (DBT) to help people deal with chronic pain and trauma, such as with post-traumatic stress disorder. Studies show it could help people reduce their negative experiences by accepting their situation rather than fighting against it.[11] Without the fight, pain becomes just pain, without so much suffering.

You don't have to be in chronic pain or have trauma to try radical acceptance. You can also use it to help contend with thought distortions, or any strong negative feelings, which so often are the result of fighting against reality. There is an aspect of cognitive defusion here: With radical acceptance, you accept any emotion you are having. Our complicated brains are full of excuses and reasons not to face or deal with, or believe or feel anything about, what's right in front of us. Radically accepting who you are and what your current situation is and how you feel about it doesn't mean you can't change, grow, evolve, or reframe your feelings. Not at all. It simply means that what exists now is *totally okay*.

You can love yourself no matter what shape you are in right now, no matter what situation you are in, no matter how much money you have, no matter what job you have, or what friends you have, or how healthy you are. And you can also love yourself enough to have big plans for yourself—goals and dreams, and plans for the future. Accepting the reality of now can make all those goals feel more grounded in reality.

The first step is to totally accept yourself, your pain, your circumstances. The second step is to have compassion for yourself. Imagine you are comforting a child in pain. You can be both the comforter and the child. Compassion can dissolve feelings of conflict and the fear and anxiety of unsuccessfully trying to avoid what's real and true in this moment.

At first it sounds scary, but once you radically accept who you are and what's happening in your life right now, it can feel like a huge relief. No more thought distortions. Just you, having thoughts, having feelings, having experiences, living your life, making plans, and being your amazing, beautiful, imperfect self. Just like everyone else.

That's a picture with no distortion.

◆

Many of the concepts in this chapter (and other chapters) have dipped into mindfulness techniques, so let's take the next step and dive headfirst into mindfulness itself.

9

Miraculous Mindfulness

Remember that there is only one important time and that is now.
The present moment is the only time over which we have dominion.

—Thich Nhat Hanh

Of all the behavioral strategies and psych tricks out there, mindfulness might just be the most powerful. To be mindful is to be aware
of yourself in the present moment. It's the aware part that's important.
You aren't just living your life. You're paying attention to living your
life, right here, right now. To do this isn't easy, but it can benefit you in
many ways, physically and mentally, because it puts you right smack in
the middle of your actual reality, where you can see what's real and get
things done—or not get things done. Mindfulness isn't about doing.
It's about being.

But thinking makes this difficult. To live in the present moment
is to just be, without lingering in the past or dwelling on the future.
That's no easy task, but metacognition, which you may remember from
Chapter 3 is a process of thinking about thinking, can make this easier.
When you see that you are not your thoughts, and you can watch them

without getting carried away by them, you can stay mindful of where you are right now, It's very easy to feel like you are your thoughts and that they control you, but as we have mentioned already in this book, it is possible to take a step back and separate yourself from your thoughts and your feelings (cognitive defusion). You can be the watcher of your thoughts rather than the passenger of your thoughts.

Basic reminder: You are not your thoughts! To make that sound a little less esoteric, let's talk about socks. Your thoughts and your feelings are like your socks. You wear your socks for a while, then take them off and wash them at some point (we hope). They are something you have with you sometimes, and not at other times. At some point, they get old and worn out, and you throw them away and get new socks. You may own your socks, but you are not your socks. You're not controlled by your socks (that would be weird). People probably don't judge you by your socks—unless, perhaps, you wear outrageously loud socks (in which case, you're probably making a specific choice). But even if people do judge you by your socks now and again, we will repeat: You are not your socks!

Now, the rational part of you knows that you are not your socks—no more than you are your thoughts or your emotions. You are not your weight or your height, your eye color or skin tone. You are something much too complicated and wonderful to be reduced to a thought—or a sock.

The you who knows this is the you who can observe your thoughts and feelings and see them as fleeting states of being that come and go (like that sock that never showed back up in the laundry basket . . . did the dryer eat it?). This is the part of you that knows how to be mindful, that is always mindful. That part is always inside of you, watching (but not in a creepy way). Not judging. Not hating. Not negative self-talking. Just seeing and feeling benevolent about all you go through, feeling proud about how you keep trying and eventually prevail. You could call it your higher self. We call it your Observer, and it exists in the here and now. It doesn't ruminate on the past or dwell on the future; rather, it observes that *part* of you might ruminate on the past and dwell on the future. Tap into that part of you—your Observer—and you'll get to experience the miracle of mindfulness.

Let's say you're lying on the couch thinking about exercise. Your thoughts might be spinning around and arguing with each other, like:

> **you:** "I should be exercising! Get up and go for a walk!"
>
> **also you:** "But I don't want to, I'm tired!"
>
> **also you:** "You'd have more energy if you'd just get up and do it."
>
> **also you:** "But I said I don't want to do it! I'm comfortable! Stop messing with my downtime!"
>
> **also you:** "Lazy!"
>
> **also you:** "Tired!"

Wow, it's like a playground brawl in there! (We know the feeling—we all have our inner playgrounds.) But let's go with that metaphor. Remember back in school when you used to have recess (ahh, recess! Good times . . .)? Remember how there was a teacher or some other recess monitoring-type person who would stand out there and watch everybody, and intervene in case something happened that required an adult to step in and say, "Hold up! It's everybody's kickball!" or "It's okay, just a skinned knee, you're going to be okay, let's go visit the school nurse."

That playground attendant wasn't intervening in every single playground interaction because otherwise who would ever sign up for that job? No, they stood back and watched and didn't step in unless it was really urgent. And that is your Observer—that playground attendant. As you lie there thinking all those thoughts, you can learn to call upon your playground attendant, aka your Observer, neutrally observing: "Look at me having all those conflicting thoughts about exercising. Interesting."

Your Observer doesn't necessarily step in and try to solve the problem, but your Observer is powerful because it stands outside of the push and pull of those thoughts, putting you into a position where you can be calm and grounded and see more clearly what you're really doing. Eventually, your Observer (aka you!) may discover that the conflict isn't such a conflict. Why are you arguing with yourself like that? Why aren't you either (1) peacefully resting or (2) getting up and doing something? All that internal conflict isn't accomplishing the benefits of either rest or exercise. Deliberately taking on the Observer role can help you cut through all the thought distortions and mindfully make a choice: Let go and rest, or get up and exercise.

How do you do actually do that? It's not that easy, when you really try to do it. "Mindfulness is one of those things that's a lot harder than it sounds, to really get down and feel and embrace. It wasn't until years of teaching it and practicing it that I really had a moment of truly understanding what it is," says Dr. Michaelides. "Mindfulness sounds simple and obvious, but humans are distractible. You can tell someone to be present in the moment, but what does that really mean? It's a difficult thing to explain in a way that helps people actually do it."

If you're like most people, you can try being present in the moment for, well . . . a moment. But before you know it, your mind is wandering back to the past, or forward to the future, or thinking about your to-do list, or just randomly thinking: "What was that person's name who was in that show about that thing?" And in a flash, you are out of the here and now. As Dr. Michaelides explains it, "Sometimes you only realize you're not present when you decide to notice whether you're present."

Every mindful moment you take makes you better at taking mindful moments, and it's a skill worth practicing because knowing how to dip into mindfulness when you need it can change your life, not to mention your mind and your behavior.

The Supreme Benefits of Mindfulness

Mindfulness is a worthwhile practice. Science says so! The practice of mindfulness can greatly benefit psychological health by improving your own subjective sense of well-being (more good days!), reducing that knee-jerk tendency to react to strong emotions without thinking first ("Why oh why did I say *that*?"), and generally helping you feel and be more in control of your behavior ("I'm going to go exercise even though I don't really feel like it").[1]

A 2021 study from the *International Journal of Environmental Research and Public Health* demonstrated that more mindfulness was associated with greater happiness (and less anxiety and depression), as well as with a greater sense of purpose in life and more engagement in activities.[2] Paying attention to where you are and what you're doing, in other words, can make your life better.

Mindfulness is the antidote to autopilot, and it's the most direct path to breaking habits that are not serving Your Big Picture (YBP). Remember thought distortions, from Chapter 8? Mindfulness can put all that worry and rumination, the blaming, avoiding, suppressing, and obsessing, into perspective. It doesn't take away the thoughts, but it takes *you* away from the unpleasant *pull* of the thoughts. It unhooks you from the emotional reactivity that thoughts can cause (again, cognitive defusion).

Doesn't that sound nice?

We think so, too!

That may be why mindfulness has become a major focus of the newest wave of cognitive behavioral therapy (CBT), through such CBT sub-practices as dialectical behavioral therapy (DBT) and acceptance and commitment therapy (ACT). Mindfulness has become an influential and powerful psych trick, and that's why we love it!

So, let's get to practicing, and you can start enjoying the many benefits mindfulness can offer you. Fortunately, mindfulness is one of those things that, although it may take a lifetime to master, is easy to practice in your everyday life—you could even do it right now. Let's look at some ways to do that.

Mindful Moments

We don't expect you to become a Zen master in an hour. But what you can do right now is practice mindfulness in small bites, which we like to call *mindful moments*.

Mindful moments are brief snippets of your day—a minute or two, or even just a few seconds—during which you stop what you're doing to tune in to how you feel and what's going on around you. Or, you don't stop what you're doing, but you make a point to notice and pay full attention to what you're doing. "The first step," says Dr. Michaelides, "is about understanding what mindfulness is and trying it on for size. Taking mindful moments can build curiosity about mindfulness. Once you build that curiosity, you can start applying it to different situations. Plant the seed and let it grow—but planting the seed has to come first, and mindful moments are about planting the seed."

Taking periodic mindful moments throughout the day trains your brain to pay attention. Even when the moments are brief, doing it regularly will make it easier—because remember, the more you do something, the more your brain gets used to doing it and the easier it gets. Here are some beginner techniques to try; you can do any of these for as long as ten minutes or as briefly as ten seconds:

- Sit down, close your eyes, and focus on how you feel internally. Notice how your breath feels, moving in and out. Notice any sensations, such as a sore neck, a stiff shoulder, or hunger in your belly.
- Stand up, do some simple stretches, and pay attention to how your body feels as you move it gently.
- Look around the room. Notice everything your senses can take in—what do you see, hear, feel, smell?

- Eat a snack and try to pay attention to the entire sensory experience of eating. How does the food look before you eat it? How does it smell? As you eat, notice how it tastes and feels going down, and how your body feels afterward.
- Take a short walk and pay close attention to everything around you—the weather, the people, the buildings, the trees, whatever you can see, hear, smell.
- Tune in deliberately to the sounds, textures, and smells of the entire process of brushing your teeth or taking a shower. It's harder than it sounds! Being mindful during chores that are routine, habitual, or boring is harder than paying attention to something interesting or new, but give it a try. It's like weight lifting for your brain.
- Notice everything in your environment when you stop at a stoplight (don't get distracted by the trees or the sky while actually driving, please!).
- Squeeze your hands together. Sometimes just using your own muscles can ground you in the present moment, as if it reminds you that you have a body and you know how to use it! Squats, push-ups against a wall, or jumping up and down also work.

MINDFULNESS CHALLENGES

As you get better at mindful moments, Dr. Michaelides suggests three challenges you can try:

1. "Go somewhere chaotic. Maybe it's out on the street with a lot of people walking around, or in a busy area with a lot

of traffic. Step back and take it all in, moment to moment. Disengage and just observe. What's going on around you? Connect with the chaos." Dr. Michaelides says this is a way to challenge your conception of mindfulness as something you only do in a quiet or serene setting. "Mindfulness isn't about closing your eyes and shutting out all the stimuli. It's observing the stimuli. This exercise is an experiment with a different way of thinking about mindfulness, to put yourself in a situation that is opposite of what you think of when you think of mindfulness, as meditative or peaceful. It can remind you that mindfulness is always possible. Doing this might even be the catalyst for that moment when you experience real mindfulness for the first time."

2. An opposite challenge is to be mindful about something that is overly familiar, even boring, that you hardly notice or see anymore. Pick any object you always see—a plant, a chair, a light fixture, a coffee mug—and really look at it like you've never seen it before.

3. Be mindful about something stressful. "I've literally got a big computer screen in front of me with two smaller screens over it. I'm bombarded with a lot, but that's an opportunity to take moments to mentally step back and just observe those things that usually keep me from being mindful," Dr. Michaelides says. If your computer screen, your work papers, your to-do list, or your bills trigger the stress response, you can even be mindful about that! Neutrally observe the stressful feelings—observe how they rise up, what they're connected to, and how they eventually fade.

This practice isn't about solving the stress. It's about separating from it and seeing it as something apart from you, that doesn't have to affect you. You may recognize what's causing it, and setting yourself apart may even dissolve the stress, but the point is to see those things that are causing stress apart from you and apart from the stress—as things you have or have to do, but not things you are or things that control you. It helps to put it all—stress triggers and the stress itself—into perspective.

More Mindfulness Techniques

Maybe you've already noted that there's a lot to pay attention to. How do you know what to focus on? You can't take everything in at once, internally and externally. But you can divide up your focus and practice mindfulness in different ways, at different times. As you practice your mindful moments, or longer sessions of mindfulness as you get better at sustaining your focus, here are some ways to vary your focus and keep it interesting.

Mindfulness Technique #1:
Physical Awareness

Your physical body is the container for your mind, and it has a lot going on all the time. Most of the time, you probably don't notice it much, unless something hurts, or you need to use your body to do something like exercise, or run fast, or lift something heavy. But even then, many of us, especially if our jobs involve a lot of mental effort but not much physical effort, can get a bit disconnected from our bodies—and then we get surprised when they don't work the way we expect! Yet, our bodies have much to tell us about how what we do (what we eat, how we move, how we behave) is affecting us, physically. Mindfulness is the key to getting those messages.

Take, for example, how your body responds to what you eat.

You might notice that eating a few big slices of pizza right before bed gave you heartburn, but maybe you didn't really notice that your stomach was bloated after that bowl of sugary cold cereal for breakfast because you were too busy getting on with your day. You can also notice when you have positive reactions to food, like how good and energetic you felt after having that salmon salad or when you tried a vegetarian dinner, for example. Being mindful as you eat, and checking in with a mindful moment after you eat to see how your body is responding, can help you pick up these more subtle messages from your body.

Your body has other messages for you, too, not just about how you eat but also about how you move. A twisted ankle will call your attention to the pain in a way you can't ignore, but that dull lower backache after yoga class might not get more than a passing notice. Taking a mindful minute after exercise helps you feel how your body responds to different kinds of movement, and that can guide you going forward. You might get the message that something you did felt really great, or that you overstretched a bit and need to heal.

What about that argument that gave you a stomachache, or that headache you got after watching four episodes of your favorite show in one sitting, or those butterflies you felt in your stomach when a special someone looked your way? Your body is always talking to you. "Listening" by being mindful of your physical body can help you understand your body better and be instructive about how to adjust what you do (eat, move, interact, rest) in ways that can make you feel better and get healthier.

To get you back in touch with your body again, so you can start paying more attention to what it's trying to tell you, try a simple exercise called the Body Scan:

1. Stand comfortably, sit in a chair with your feet flat on the ground or cross-legged on the floor, or lie down on a yoga mat or the bed. Get comfortable and close your eyes.

2. Take a deep breath, to the count of 4. Hold for a count of 4. Exhale for a count of 4. Feel your body relaxing. Notice how that feels.

3. Bring your attention to your head and face. How does your head feel? What is your face doing? Are your brows furrowed? Are you squeezing your eyes shut? Are your lips pursed? Is your jaw clenched? Does your face feel hot? Is your nose cold or runny? Does your head feel heavy, or are you feeling light-headed? Are you dizzy? Do you have a headache?

4. Exhale and relax the muscles of your face, and try to let go of any tension in your head and face.

5. Bring your attention to your neck. Is there a lump in your throat? Tightness in your muscles? Any pain? Exhale and let go of neck tension.

6. Move to your upper shoulders and back. Are you hunched? Are your shoulders forward or back? How is your posture (if you are sitting or standing)? Are your shoulders tight and pulled up to your ears, or are they relaxed? Do you have any pain in your shoulders? Exhale and relax the muscles in your shoulders and upper back.

7. Bring your attention to your arms, one at a time. Feel the upper arm, the elbow joint, the forearm. How does each arm feel? Heavy, tight, tingly, numb, relaxed? Take a deep breath and let the tension out of each arm.

8. Now, notice your hands. Are they tight, clenched, relaxed? Are your hands cold, hot, sweaty? Notice how each finger feels. Wiggle them if you are having trouble feeling them. Does anything hurt? Breathe deeply and relax your arms and hands.

9. Move your attention to your chest. Does your chest feel tight or relaxed? Can you feel your heart beating? Is it racing or slow? Exhale and let tension go.

10. Now, feel your stomach. How does it feel? Empty? Full? Satisfied? Does anything hurt? Are you bloated? Are you hungry? Do you feel queasy or nervous? Any knots or tightness? Breathe in, letting your stomach expand, and exhale, letting your belly soften.

11. Make your way to your hips. Is anything painful or tight? Do you feel open and flexible? Imagine breathing into your hips: let them sink down, relaxed and supported.

12. Bring your attention to your legs, one at a time. Do they feel heavy or light? How do your muscles feel? Do your legs feel shaky, or strong and firm? If you're lying down, are your feet pointing up or falling to the sides? What about your knees? Your ankles?

13. Move your feet and wiggle your toes. Does anything hurt or is anything tingly? Itching? Numb? Breathe to release any tension and pain from your legs and feet.

14. Now, slowly pull back your awareness and try to feel your whole body at the same time. Stay there for a few moments, breathing and feeling your body as a unit with many parts.

15. Take a deep breath in to a count of 4. Hold your breath to a count of 4, then exhale to a count of 4.

16. When you feel ready, open your eyes and slowly move, getting up or stretching. Mindful moment mastered!

Mindfulness Technique #2: Environmental Awareness

What's going on around you? When you're all up in your own head, it's easy not to notice. That could be dangerous (watch out for that bus!), but even when you aren't in a potentially hazardous situation, an awareness of your environment can help you feel more grounded in the present moment.

Your environment includes where you are—walking down the street, riding a bus or train, sitting in a park—as well as the things and people around you. It's different from physical awareness, which requires an inward focus. Environmental awareness requires an external focus. Take mindful moments to look around and observe.

So much happens around us that we don't notice. In part, that's because we often need to compartmentalize our attention, to do something like drive a car, or cross a street, or have a conversation with someone. But even when we have the opportunity to really notice and be present in our environment, we often don't. We're too busy thinking about the past or the future, ruminating, worrying, going over things we need to do or should have done.

To shift your focus to your immediate environment can be a refreshing and surprising break from your thoughts. You might begin to notice things you never noticed before—things that bring you joy. It's easy to forget how interesting and beautiful the world can be! It can also help you notice things you want to change—like, "Wow, I should really clean my room better," or "I never realized how much trash is on the street." Environmental mindfulness can wake you up, give you a new perspective, and improve your quality of life as you recognize what you like and appreciate about your environment, and what you don't.

To help you get more grounded in your current here and now, try these grounding techniques, which can help you feel your own body existing in the present moment, rather than drifting away on a cloud of thought distortions. Some of these may feel a little bit out there, but curiously, they have the exact opposite effect: They can make you feel right here.

◆ **Cover the crown of your head.** For some reason, this simple movement can have an extremely calming effect, almost like you're shutting off the thought valve so you can bring yourself back to reality. Just put your hands on the top of your head and notice how that feels. Look around; can you see the external world better now?

◆ **Go outside and plant your feet in the grass.** Take your shoes off for best results. Standing on grass (or dirt or sand) is also called *earthing* because you're directly connecting your body to the earth. It's worth a try!

◆ **Move your hands through water or sand.** Or grass. Or flower petals. Or gravel. The act of touching and really paying attention to the feeling of things in your immediate environment can help you feel more present wherever you are. This can also work inside, with anything in your immediate environment—water from the faucet, your jingling car keys, clothes in your closet, even your computer keyboard. Stop typing and run your fingers over the keys for a minute. Feel the individual component parts that make the texture.

◆ **Find a calming smell.** Identify something with a distinct scent that you associate with something positive—it could be soap, cut grass, essential oils, your cat. The sense of smell is known to impact mood, stress level, how you relate to other people, and even how well your brain works.[3] Use that to your advantage, to place yourself firmly into your environment and feel more present and engaged.

Mindfulness Technique #3: Thought and Feeling Awareness

We put thoughts and feelings together here because they are often intertwined. Channel your inner Observer to practice watching your thoughts and feelings. Sit quietly and notice what you're thinking and feeling, but instead of getting caught up in those thoughts and feelings, try labeling them as something you are having, rather than something that you are.

For example, instead of thinking, "I'm hungry," label that feeling as, "I'm having the feeling of hunger." Instead of thinking, "I forgot to buy apples," label that thought as, "I'm having the thought that I forgot to buy apples." Not "I'm so angry at my coworker" but, rather, "I'm having the feeling that I'm angry at my coworker." Not "I should have exercised today" but instead "I'm having the thought that I should have exercised today."

Practice doing this for a few minutes at a time. It might feel weird at first, but the more you do this, the easier it feels and the more easily you will be able to separate yourself from your thoughts and feelings so you aren't as controlled by them. This helps put things into perspective. For more on how to do this, see the section at the end of this chapter on mindfulness meditation.

Mindfulness Technique #4:
Behavioral Awareness

"What am I doing?" That's the question to ask yourself when practicing mindfulness of your behavior. Periodically throughout the day, take a moment to ask yourself: "What am I doing?" Is it something you need to be doing? Something you want to be doing? Or are you doing something that doesn't serve you well, like scrolling through social media when you have work to do, or putting yourself down to other people, or mindlessly polishing off the rest of the stale popcorn? Ask yourself if what you're doing is what you want to be doing. If you need a mental break, are you ruminating, or could you just take an actual mental break? If you are frustrated, are you getting angry, or could you instead try to parse out the problem? If you are hungry, are you depriving yourself because you're worried about calories, or could you just eat something satisfying?

Behavioral awareness can help you catch yourself in moments when you are not actively choosing a behavior so much as slipping into a habit that doesn't serve you. Taking a moment to ask, "What am I doing?" can help you stop doing something that isn't in line with your goals, and you can consciously, mindfully choose to do something else that lets you feel better faster.

Mindful Eating

Have you been waiting for this one? This is, after all, a book on health and weight, and since eating is so influential for both, eating mindfully is a great skill to learn. Eating mindfully can help you achieve your goals because when you eat mindfully:

1. You're more likely to notice when you're actually full, so you may end up eating less.
2. You're more likely to notice if food doesn't taste very good, so you may start to eat higher-quality food, or get better at stopping when you don't really like what you're eating.
3. You're more likely to notice whether you're actually hungry, or eating for other reasons, like boredom (fog eating) or stress (storm eating). This gives you the opportunity to take a beat and consciously choose whether or not you really want to eat.

Mindful eating increases the enjoyment of food, and it can help you respond to your own internal cues to eat, rather than to external cues to eat.[4] According to a 2017 review of sixty-eight different publications detailing studies of mindfulness and mindful eating,[5] mindful eating was demonstrated to be effective for addressing emotional eating, stress eating, binge eating, and eating in response to external cues. There are all those benefits, just from paying attention to what you're eating!

Yet it's difficult to mindfully eat in a high-stimulus and distracting world, and many of us are in the habit of eating while also looking at a screen (whether it's your phone, computer screen, or television), working through lunch (do you even remember eating that sandwich?), reading something, or just thinking about something other than eating.

To eat mindfully is to notice you are hungry, assess whether it's physical or emotional hunger, choose your food consciously, and then really see, smell, and taste your food, eating more slowly and noticing how you feel as you eat—the taste, the temperature, the texture, and the feel of swallowing and of having an increasingly satisfied stomach. To help you practice focusing more on the food you eat and the way you feel as you eat, here are some ways to make eating feel like an event you can savor:

◆ **Cook more.** When you cook your own food, you will be more tuned in to what's in your food and what it took to prepare it. Cooking puts you into more physical contact with your food. You get to make the decisions about ingredients and quality. Whether you love experimenting with new recipes or feel accomplished when you've successfully boiled water for pasta, cooking your own food can be an easy way to feel like you've achieved something.

◆ **Remove distractions.** We mean the aforementioned screens, books, or if you're old school, newspapers. Don't work while you eat or read while you eat. Eat while you eat.

◆ **Sit down.** Sounds simple, but people often don't do it. Even if you don't have the time or opportunity to make eating an event, at least take a seat before you eat! (Eating while driving doesn't count as sitting down to eat.)

◆ **Take a deep breath.** Taking a few deep breaths before you start eating can help you tune in to your food and calm yourself before eating, which could slow you down so you can notice and enjoy your meal more. It can also help you digest your food better. A review of current research on how mindfulness influenced stress and digestion showed that mindful eating can reduce chronic stress by restoring control to the parasympathetic nervous system.[6] This in turn helps to establish optimal digestive function.

◆ **Engage your senses.** Before you take a bite, really look at your food. Smell it. Then, when you do take a bite, take your time and really taste it. Notice how the food feels in your mouth—its temperature, its texture, and how it changes as you chew. Let each bite be an experience, and when you realize the food is no longer as satisfying and you aren't hungry anymore, take a pause and think about whether you've had enough. Is it time to stop, or do you really want more?

◆ **Put your fork down between bites.** A 2013 study published in the *Journal of the Academy of Nutrition and Dietetics* showed that people who chewed their food longer before swallowing ate significantly less, spent more time eating, and ate more slowly.[7] A good way to ensure that you give yourself enough time with each bite is to try putting your fork down as you chew and reflect. This can help slow you down even more and enhance your mindful experience, rather than loading up your fork as you chew so you can immediately eat more without any conscious reflection.

◆ **Swallow and reflect.** If swallowing is just a signal to eat another bite, you may not notice when you've had enough. Instead, after each bite, take a pause to reflect: How did that taste? Was it enjoyable? Do I need more? Even a second or two of reflection can help you slow down, experience your meal more fully, and notice when you've had enough versus mindlessly finishing everything in front of you.

◆ **Practice, practice, practice!** Will you eat every bite of every meal with total mindfulness all the time? Of course not. But mindful eating does get easier the more you do it, so practice eating mindfully for at least one meal per day, or for the first five minutes of every meal, or on any other regular basis. Consistency is key and can turn you into a mindful eater most of the time, rather than a mindful eater only every now and then when you happen to think about it.

Mindful Movement

Just as you can be mindful when you eat, you can be mindful when you exercise, and that can improve your exercise experience, making it more enjoyable, rewarding, and even more effective. When you focus on what you're doing, you might put in more effort, really feeling the muscles you're using, how hard you're breathing, and the awesome feeling when that runner's high kicks in. Mindfulness during exercise might also help you avoid injury, as you'll be more likely to notice when something starts to hurt or feel unstable.

It's easier to be mindful in an exercise class, when you have to pay attention to the instructor and follow the instructions. People who exercise solo, such as running or using cardio equipment at the gym, often like to listen to music or podcasts, or watch shows or movies while exercising, and if that gets you exercising more often, then we have no problem with it!

However, you might benefit more from exercise if you take just a couple of minutes without any media input. Whether you're doing cardio, lifting weights, or stretching, listen to and feel your breath moving in and out. Feel your joints moving, your muscles working. Feel your balance. This is all great feedback and can help you truly appreciate what exercise is doing for you, too. That could inspire you to do it more often!

Mindfulness Meditation

Let's wrap up this chapter by addressing what most people think of when they think of mindfulness: meditation. There are a million ways to meditate (we haven't actually counted), but one of the easiest just might be mindfulness meditation. People often think that meditation is about stilling, or quieting, or even completely eliminating thoughts, but since that's *impossible* (because of our brains), mindfulness meditation has as its goal the much more attainable goal of observing your thoughts. And you already know how to do that! But beyond mindful moments, mindfulness meditation gives you a regular opportunity to really commit to the practice of being mindful in a consistent and regular way. Consider it next-level mindfulness.

Mindfulness meditation is the process of taking some time out every day to channel your Observer, and it's not just good for your mental health. It can also help you reach your health goals. Mindfulness increases self-efficacy and reduces stress,[8] and both of these important benefits can make your goals easier to achieve. When it comes to weight, that can make a big difference—a 2021 study showed that a mindfulness-based stress-reduction program was more successful than a healthy-living course for helping people who had recently lost weight to maintain that loss.[9] After six months, the mindfulness group maintained their weight loss, while the healthy-living group increased their BMI by 3.4 percent.

Here's how to get started:

1. Set a timer for five minutes, in the morning or evening.
2. Sit or lie down, or take a walk (moving meditation), and commit to the process of observation.
3. Focus fully on your environment or on your internal state. Notice everything around you: what you see, hear, smell, feel. Or, notice everything inside you: how all the parts of your body feel, where you have tension, how your breath feels moving in and out. Or, just let yourself take it all in at once, noticing what you notice.
4. Every time your mind wanders (and it will) to the future or the past, or starts ruminating or going over your to-do list, or doing anything that isn't present-moment-focused, go back to your

mindful now. No judgment, no guilt, just practice.
Keep coming back to the now until it feels like a
comfortable place to be.

5. Watch yourself existing in the world, in all its
facets. See yourself with kindness, fondness, and
compassion.

6. Repeat daily—you will get the most benefit from a
consistent practice.

If you can work up to meditating mindfully for ten to twenty
minutes once or twice a day, you're practically guaranteed to feel
less stressed, more confident, more content, more productive—
and smarter! Brain researchers have shown that mindfulness
meditation can physically change your brain, increasing cortical
thickness,[10] which is associated with intelligence.[11]

Mindfulness can increase your self-awareness, self-regulation,
and even your ability to see beyond yourself and your own needs,
to consider the bigger picture and the needs of others—what
researchers call *self-transcendence*.[12] You'll see the path to your
goals more clearly, you'll be able to make goals with greater understanding of what's important, and you'll get to know yourself
better—and that's great, because you're someone worth getting
to know.

Bottom line: Mindfulness is good for you,[13] and it makes everything else you're trying to do, now and for the rest of your life,
a little bit easier. And speaking of the rest of your life, we're coming to the end of this book, so let's talk about where you might
want to go from here.

10

What's Next?

If it is to be, it is up to me.

—Shirley Hutton

We've come to the final chapter of this book (pardon us, we're getting a bit misty-eyed), and whether you're still setting goals or you've met them and are already making new ones, we have a question for you to consider:

How far have you come?

Think back to where you were when you started this book. What have you learned? What have you changed? What new habits have you adopted, and which old ones have you left by the wayside? Even if you still slip up sometimes (because that's life), it's motivating and important to celebrate the changes you've achieved. Sometimes it helps to look back, to see how far you've come. Ask yourself, what were some of your:

✓ Old eating habits?
✓ Old exercise patterns?

✓ Biggest triggers?

✓ Worst thought distortions?

✓ Most challenging obstacles?

✓ Most difficult setbacks?

Really take some time to think about a few of the things you used to do that you no longer do. After you've taken this walk down memory lane, compare then to now:

✓ What new eating habits have you acquired?

✓ What new activity patterns have you created for yourself?

✓ How have you overcome negative triggers you had?

✓ How have you established positive triggers?

✓ How have you changed your mindset?

✓ What obstacles have you made obsolete in your life?

✓ How are you feeling about your ability to achieve change?

✓ What changes make you the most excited, the most hopeful, the most confident?

When we survey our community about what's changed about their lives in the time that they've been using the Noom program, many of them mention a number on the scale, as we would expect. They came to Noom primarily to achieve weight-loss goals, after all. However, what surprised us at first—and now we expect it and love it—is how many people raved about their NSVs.

NSVs are non-scale victories. These are things you gain during your Noom journey that have nothing to do with a number on the scale. NSVs can include things like more energy, better sleep, better fitness, fewer aches and pains, more confidence, more of a feeling of self-control, better self-efficacy, pride in overcoming long-term bad habits, more mindfulness, fewer thought distortions, feelings of personal empowerment, a more active social life, and a good influence on the health behaviors of friends and family. Do you have a different attitude from that you had before? Do you think about health, or habit formation, or behavior change a little differently than you did before? Do you trust yourself more? Do you listen more to your brain, your body, and your intuition, because you know that, deep down, you know what you need?

All that progress almost makes a scale number seem . . . not all that important, at least in this context.

We hope you'll take some time to be proud of yourself for the progress you've made, no matter how big or how small. Even if the lasting impact of this book has been to change your mindset and nothing else, we're sure proud of you!

And now we've got another question for you: What's next?

Your Next Move

Just because you reached a goal that doesn't mean it's over. Health is a journey that lasts a lifetime. Most people are always working on goals, and when they achieve them (or even if they don't), they are out there forming new ones that coincide with wherever they are in their journey. Maybe you achieved your happy weight, or you ran your first 5K, or now you eat vegetables almost every day. Maybe you no longer eat in front of the TV or you're getting better sleep. Maybe you gained the confidence to go for that new job, make that new friend, or finally join that gym. Maybe you have a fresh and optimistic outlook on your future health and life.

Whatever it was that you planned, whatever it was that you tried, whatever Your Big Picture is, there is always more progress to be made, and that's the whole fun of it! Are we ever really "done" in this life? We hope not, because how boring! There is always a new horizon, a new adventure, and a way to become happier, healthier, and more fulfilled. As you progress, there may be things you stop doing, like weighing yourself or tracking your food. If you can keep up with your healthy habits and you've gotten to a weight you love, you may not need those tools anymore. Your lifestyle is evolving.

Or maybe you love the tools and plan to keep at it. "At the end of the day, the things you've done to incorporate a different kind of lifestyle throughout his program aren't meant to be abandoned," says Dr. Michaelides. "There might be things you don't need to do any longer as you progress, but the program is designed for you to get a better awareness of food and how that makes you feel, and to understand how to decode the different components of food using simple ways to think about it. Those are life lessons."

So, maybe weighing yourself periodically or tracking your food works for you and it's become a part of your life. Research does show that these techniques are effective, not just for weight loss but also for long-term weight-loss maintenance.[1] In that case, there's no reason to stop doing it. There's nothing wrong with tracking your progress for . . . ever! Some tools and tricks are meant to transition you to a new stage of awareness and behavior, like friends who come into your life, change you, and then move on. Others can be those tried-and-true old friends who stay with you for as long as you need them. How, and for how long, you use the tools that work is your call.

So, what is your next goal? Are you ticking your way through the sub goals that will get you to your Super Goal, and you're making steady progress but you're not there yet? Do you still want to eat a little better? Run a little longer? Be fitter? Lose a few more pounds? Get even better at stress management? Then stay the course; you are an experienced Noomer now and you've got this. Or is that Super Goal in the rearview mirror and you're looking for a new one? Great. You're a goal-achievement master now, too, so you know how to achieve goals.

What do you want for your life now?

WHAT'S YOUR MOONSHOT?

What is your greatest, biggest, baddest dream? What's your moonshot? *Moonshot* is a term coined by the top-secret research division at Google, and they define it as a "specific type of technology that very few brave entrepreneurs are interested in investing in, although it may have a significant amount of potential." To us at Noom, a moonshot is the goal you have that most people wouldn't dare to pursue but that could likely reap you a lot of benefits.

What's your moonshot? Even if you don't think you have one, if you think about it, you might realize that you do, buried way down deep at the bottom of your brain where you stashed it because you didn't think it was really possible. But you keep it there because it means something to you that it's there. A part of you still believes you can do it. Someday. Maybe.

What if you went for it? Because even if you don't end up actually achieving it full on, you might end up achieving something amazing just by trying. You know that old saying: "Shoot for the moon. Even if you miss, you'll land among the stars."

Chasing something that seems impossible is a great way to learn about yourself, including how you might get in your own way more often than not, out of fear, or a lack of confidence, or because you put everything else before your own needs. But if you pull out that dream and dust it off, and shoot for the moon anyway, you might just learn that you're stronger, tougher, and more powerful than you think.

An Evolving YBP

If you've found, after first creating a YPB, that your big picture has shifted a bit, or even changed completely, that's normal and natural. As you learn more, gain more confidence, and change some of your habits, it's only to be expected that your goals and priorities will evolve right along with you. We encourage you to reevaluate YBP periodically to keep it updated and in line with how you've been changing as you commit to taking care of your health. In fact, in the app, we periodically cue people to reevaluate and refresh their big picture. YBP should always be motivating, so if yours doesn't feel like that so much anymore, maybe it's time for a refresh. Maybe the things you prioritized before aren't priorities for you now. Maybe now you've got different priorities. Bigger priorities. Greater aspirations.

If you haven't thought about it for a while, give some thought to YBP. Remember:

YBP = Super Goal + your Ultimate Why +
how your life will be different

Once you have something in mind—a new YBP candidate—think about your Ultimate Why. Remember how we had you question your motivations for your Super Goal, and had you keep asking yourself "Why?" until you got to the real core, the real heart of why you want that Super Goal? Try that again.

Maybe you're ready to take another big step with your eating, your fitness, your weight loss, your stress management, or your confidence. Or, now you're working on radical self-acceptance, or mindfulness, or something else entirely. Whatever it is, ask yourself, "Why do I want this?" Then ask yourself "Why?" again. Then again. Sometimes the goal itself is in disguise, and it really represents something more. For instance, getting to a normal BMI might really represent wanting to feel relaxed and comfortable in your body. Getting healthier might really mean wanting to sidestep a family history of a certain health condition. Getting fit enough to join the intramural soccer league or tennis team might really be about a desire to find your people.

What's your deepest most passionate reason for wanting that

thing? If you can't come up with any reason, then maybe there's another more important, deeper Super Goal you're even more passionate about today. Take your time. Something as important as YBP deserves some contemplation and testing.

After you think you've got your Super Goal and your Ultimate Why, take a few moments to visualize how your life will be different once you've reached your new Big Picture. Even if you aren't sure, let your imagination run wild. What *could* your life be like? What do you want your life to be about, now that you know yourself better?

As you make progress, don't be surprised if your goals start to shift. Many people find that the number on the scale is no longer as important as it once was, and they start prioritizing other things that mean even more to them. That's great! Noom techniques work for any life change, not just weight loss, not just for health. But health underlies the whole purpose and mission of our company. We want to help everyone achieve greater mastery over their own health, because let's be honest: When you feel vibrantly healthy, everything else gets easier.

Or maybe that's not your plan today. Maybe for today, you're still sitting with this book and that's enough. And that's totally cool, too. We love hanging out with you here! Either way, we want to send you off with a few more thoughts, a little more inspiration, a handful of psych tricks as a good-bye gift, and one more big affirmation:

You are the *best*.

The Challenge of Maintaining Lost Weight

Whether you're still working on your healthy weight goals or achieved what you set out to achieve, you may be at a point where you're feeling a little nervous about gaining the weight back. It's a legitimate concern. People often lose weight on a diet, then gain it all back when they go off the diet.

But you haven't been on a diet. The healthy strategies and psych tricks you've learned are not diets. They're behavioral-change tools, so they're things you can use for life. We want you to eat what you love, with tools for balance. There's nothing to go back to but old bad habits, and why would you want to go back to those? Noom is all about making the changes you wanted to make for life; although they might feel hard sometimes, once you've given yourself the gift of a healthy lifestyle, nobody can ever take it away from you.

"I don't really know too many people who say they're in 'maintenance,' not because they didn't achieve goals but because they always want to do more," says Dr. Michaelides. "I think it's important to come up with checkpoints, where you can pause and be proud of what you've done. There will always be new challenges to meet, new goals to achieve. The idea that you'll reach perfection and just stay there is a fantasy, but it's certainly worth celebrating every new skill, every boost in self-efficacy, and every small achievement."

But, yes, there are some legitimate physiological challenges that come with weight loss. However long it took you to lose weight (whether that was three months or three years), that's a drop in the bucket compared to the rest of your life. So, what do you do after you've gotten to a weight you're comfortable with? How do you stay there?

You just keep on keepin' on. Because with Noom, you were never on a diet. Reaching a goal doesn't mean you stop doing everything that got you there. It means you stick with those healthy changes and keep experimenting with new habits because, obviously, they work for you.

Your body changes in many complex ways when you lose weight, but your lifestyle has changed, too. It's true that your basal metabolic rate, or the amount of energy you use just sitting there being alive, goes down after weight loss. That's because the less people weigh, the less energy they need to maintain their bodies. If you lose ten or twenty or fifty pounds or more, you can't go back to eating and living the way you did when you weighed more—that will lead to eventual weight gain. Your body takes in energy and uses what you need and stores what you don't, so when you take in more energy than you need, that's going to get stored as fat and result in weight gain.

You may also notice that you feel hungrier more often. That's because after weight loss, your body and brain try to get back to where they were by shifting your hormones a bit. Your body doesn't know that you lost weight on purpose. What it (your primitive body) thinks was that there was a famine and you need to get those fat stores back. So, it adjusts, at least temporarily. Levels of ghrelin (your hunger hormone) increase with weight loss,[2] and leptin (your fullness hormone) levels decrease.[3] Other hormones also shift somewhat, and so does your brain's reward system, making calorically dense foods seem even more rewarding. You may also notice that your emotional control and decision-making concerning food doesn't seem as strong as it used to be. Conditions like high blood sugar, insulin resistance, and microbiome composition may also lead to difficulties maintaining weight loss, although losing weight alone often improves these conditions significantly.

These physiological changes likely are primary contributors to the tendency for people who have lost weight to regain it. However, that doesn't have to be you. "Just knowing your body will react to weight loss this way gives you the advantage of self-awareness," explains Dr. Michaelides. "Your body is going to want to gain weight again, and you're going to want to go back to certain things you did before, but knowing that allows you to put safeguards in place and pull out all your tools and strategies. You are well equipped now."

Too often, we're granted permission to give up on our goals because of the old adage "Diets don't work." And, to be honest, the research supports that. People who adopt short-term, restrictive rules aren't usually able to maintain those regulations or keep off the weight they lost. But there are plenty of people who've lost weight and have kept it off for five years or longer—many of whom keep it off for life. The National Weight Control Registry, which is "the largest prospective investigation of long-term successful weight loss maintenance,"[4] keeps track of people who successfully lost weight and kept it off. Registry members have lost an average of sixty-six pounds and have kept it off for five and a half years, but individual weight losses on this registry range from thirty to three hundred pounds over a period of one to sixty-six years. Some lost rapidly and some lost slowly.

What are their secrets? Nothing that is going to surprise you: They didn't "go on a diet," and they didn't "go off a diet." They changed their lives. Ninety-eight percent of the Registry participants modified their food intake in some way, most commonly with an eating pattern that is lower in calories and fat,[5] and 94 percent increased their physical activity in some way (the most frequent way for Registry participants was walking). There are a few other interesting consistent new habits the majority of Registry participants practice:

- 78 percent eat breakfast every day.
- 75 percent weigh themselves at least once a week.
- 62 percent watch fewer than ten hours of TV per week.
- 90 percent exercise, on average, about one hour per day.

In other words, the healthy habits these successful maintainers developed in order to lose weight are the same heathy habits they keep doing to maintain that weight loss.

What these successes, and the many, many Noom success stories we track, tell us is that maintaining change is hard, but not impossible! "Whatever you've done the longest in your life is what your brain feels the most comfortable doing," Dr. Michaelides reports. "That's why it's very easy to give up those skills that you've learned, even if they're helping you. But, if you've had success in acquiring certain skills, it will be much easier for you to redefine that success again. Your self-efficacy is higher, you already have those pathways in your brain."

Dr. Michaelides adds that the best predictor of future behavior is past behavior, so even if you experience some slips-ups, you can always access the part of your brain that knows what to do and trigger another surge to counter that slip. "If you find yourself going back to whatever you were doing before, just remember that you have these new skills now, and these skills will continue to develop and grow over time. You know how to do this now!" he says.

Creating Your New SOS Plan

Part of being prepared and knowing that there are some physiological difficulties after weight loss is to have a plan. So, here's another psych trick for you: the Healthy Habits SOS Plan.

"Soon after weight loss, or any other change, like working out, or calling a friend for support, or weighing in once a week, you are in a transitional period. You've been practicing your new habit, but you don't have it down to the extent that it's completely automatic," explains Dr. Michaelides. "Even if you're getting great benefits from what you are doing, you might start to backslide. Before that happens, you can create an SOS Plan that can be a trigger for regrouping."

One really effective SOS Plan element is to make sure you stay accountable to someone. Let's use Dr. Michaelides's example of calling a friend for support. Maybe you check in with each other daily or weekly, or always meet up to work out together, but then life gets busy and you stop calling that person. This is a sign that you may be backtracking. "The solution," says Dr. Michaelides, "isn't necessarily to call that person. Maybe that isn't working in your life anymore. Instead, look at what calling that person did for you. It was accountability. We often rely on other people for accountability, and if you stop calling that person, you no longer have that accountability and that can cause a slip. So, maybe you need to find another method for accountability."

THE VALUE
OF AN ACCOUNTABILITY PARTNER

One of the most powerful weapons against weight-loss relapse, or relapsing after any difficult behavior change, is to have an accountability partner. This is a person who can support you, encourage you, motivate you, remind you of your goals, help you figure out what to do during a lapse, and can help you take action. Research from 2018 looked at 704 people who enrolled in a fifteen-week online weight-loss program.[6] About 54 percent of the participants chose an accountability buddy and the others did not. Those with the accountability partner lost more weight and waist inches and had the greatest decreases in BMI. In some cases, the buddy was a romantic partner, but the study found that support by non-romantic partners was just as effective. It seems that it's the accountability, not the relationship, that makes the difference.

An accountability partner should be someone:

- You interact with often, so they notice when you're having a hard time or experiencing a setback.
- Who's supportive and is a positive influence with your best interest in mind.
- You trust, so you can be honest and vulnerable with them and know they will treat you kindly and supportively.

It's also a great idea to have some method for remembering the lessons you've learned to keep motivation high. When you know you're defaulting to an unwanted habit, go back to what made you change that habit in the first place. Dr. Michaelides uses mindless eating as an example: "Let's say mindless eating is something you no longer want to be part of your life, and one of your new habits is no longer eating in front of the TV. You've been doing it for a while now and it feels sustainable to you. But then life gets stressful, and you start to eat in front of the TV again. When you recognize you're doing this, make an effort to figure out the 'why.' Go back to your original motivation. Just the fact that you know this stuff, and you made that original decision for a reason, and you know what that reason is, and you know what your triggers were that made you eat in front of the TV, and you know how you stopped doing it before, gives you the advantage. You can access all that to help you get back to what you want to be doing."

Remember the "if . . . then" pattern of habit bundling? Another way to create a Healthy Habit SOS Plan can be to create an "if . . . then" strategy for what you will do if you fall back into old patterns. An "if . . . then" SOS Plan is what you want to keep doing, and what you will do if you stop doing it. It might look like this:

✓ "I want to continue eating vegetables with dinner every day. *If* I stop eating vegetables, *then* I'll switch to having a big salad for lunch every day instead, or I'll explore store-prepped veggies so it's quicker to use them, or I'll try a new vegetable or recipe I've never tried to get me interested again. I'll call a friend to follow up with me for the next few days. If I can do this three days in a row, I'll be back on track."

✓ "I want to continue taking a walk after dinner every evening. *If* I stop taking a walk after dinner, *then* I'll try a new workout that's different and more interesting to me, or I'll try moving more throughout the day rather than scheduling something. I'll join a yoga class and pay for it so I'll have a teacher and classmates to keep me accountable. Once I've completed a full session, I'll know I've got a successful new movement habit."

✓ "I want to keep practicing deep breathing when I get stressed. *If* I stop practicing deep breathing when I get stressed, *then* I'll try doing a yoga pose when I get stressed, or go for a walk, or really dig into what's stressing me and see if I can change something. I'll schedule an anti-stress walk with my partner and ask them to agree to keep me accountable. Or I'll start working with a life coach to get to the bottom of my stress, and they can keep me accountable for my commitment to stress management."

You don't have to enact your plan if you skip something once or twice. Part of honing your intuition and listening to your body means that on some days, your healthy habits just aren't going to happen. If you really strongly feel one day that you just can't deal with vegetables, or a walk, or any kind of organized stress management, then honor that. You don't need to obsess about it.

But if you skip the next day, or three days in a row, it may be time to dig a little deeper. What are you feeling? Is there a reason why you've stopped temporarily? Are you still committed to that habit? Did you simply forget and you just need a reminder? Are you sleep deprived, or on deadline, or in the midst of a crisis, or have some other reason that's requiring you to need to take a break? Or, are you bored sick of that habit and you need to change it to something else?

If you discover that there is a temporary reason why you've backed off from a healthy habit that was working for you, then give yourself a little grace and make a plan for getting started. Prioritize the actions that will help you get a good night's sleep after your deadline, after the crisis, or whatever it is. But if your habit isn't working for you anymore, it is time to consult your Healthy Habit SOS Plan and make a change. Sometimes, a change is all you need to get motivated again.

If you're into a more intuitive, less structured approach, another thing you can do is to take a few minutes to really tune in to your body. Think about how you felt when you were practicing those healthy habits. Remember how light and energetic and positive you felt? Now tune in to how your body feels at this moment. If you feel less good, that can be a motivator to get back to what was making you feel so great before.

Sustained Weight-Loss Action Items

On top of all those tricks you've got under your belt, here is a list of concrete behaviors that science says really are correlated with maintaining weight loss. Continually doing these things over the long term, according to the research, can significantly increase your chance of successfully maintaining weight loss:

✓ **Maintaining the approximate level of caloric intake you practiced during weight loss.** Remember, your metabolism is paired with a lower weight and doesn't need as much energy to support you, although many do find that they can add a few more well-chosen calories while maintaining weight loss without gaining.

✓ **Eating a lot of vegetables and fruits.** You can always rely on these nutrition powerhouses with low calorie density to fill you up and keep you satisfied.

✓ **Watching your portions consistently.** Portion control is a big part of maintaining a reduced calorie intake while staying satisfied. Studies have shown that people who are steady in their dietary patterns over time and that keep portions consistent most days (instead of, say, stuffing themselves all weekend long) are most successful and better able to maintain weight over the long term.

✓ **Having a plan in place for weekends, vacations, holidays, and special events.** It's great to enjoy them, and you should! But a plan can help you indulge moderately without going off the rails.

✓ **Choosing minimally processed whole foods.** Processed foods will always have that addictive quality because of all the added salt, sugar, and unhealthy fat. Whole foods really will change your taste buds and teach you to crave real food, not fake food.

✓ **Treating yourself.** Even though staying away from processed foods and not stuffing yourself on the weekends are part of long-term success, so is treating yourself. Healthy eating isn't about deprivation; it's about moderation. A slice of cake once a week or a small square of dark chocolate every afternoon can certainly be part of a healthy diet and lifestyle—and if they make you happy, we're all for it! There's nothing like positive reinforcement to keep you going.

✓ **Moving your body throughout the day.** You don't have to spend an hour at the gym every single day, but people who have successfully kept off weight typically burn about three hundred to four hundred calories per day in physical activity. That does translate to about one hour of brisk walking or thirty minutes of more intense activity, like running or HIIT. Walk when you can, use a standing desk, bike to work, or just get up and walk around at least once an hour. It makes a difference.

✓ **Doing strength training.** Not only will this maintain muscle during weight loss but the increased muscle strength can increase your resting metabolic rate, countering to some extent the decrease in metabolism that happens with weight loss.

✓ **Continually setting manageable short-term goals.** Having short-term goals can build your confidence when you achieve them. Incrementally, you can make big changes. You know what they say: A journey of a thousand miles begins with a single step. And, step-by-step, you can get there.

✓ **Planning ahead.** Keeping one eye on the future can help you avoid regaining weight over the long term. If you start to notice you're gaining weight back, you can always reevaluate. Have you stopped doing something that was working? Can you pull back on your portion sizes a bit for a few weeks? Can you add a little more exercise? Or maybe you just need to get back to your regular routine and readjust your mindset to that mode where you are excited to take care of yourself because you remember how that feels.

✓ **Celebrating your successes.** Look back every so often. Reflect on how far you've come and celebrate the milestones, even the small ones. It's a great way to keep going!

✓ **Keeping YBP in the back of your mind.** This way, you always have a meaningful reason for doing what

you're doing when it gets hard. And never be afraid to
reevaluate and change YBP.

YOUR MANTRA

Sometimes, something as simple as a mantra you can repeat
when you start feeling stressed or negative can get you back
on track and feeling calmer and more positive, in just a minute
or two. Your mantra can change, but choose one today to take
with you. What speaks to you today?

- I am strong and smart and capable of change.
- I am in control of my life.
- I create my own reality.
- I can achieve my goals.
- I am worthy of health and happiness.
- I choose to see opportunity in every situation.
- I am transforming my health every day.
- I become stronger every day.
- I have full confidence in myself.
- I can do this!
- I will choose to look at difficult things differently.
- I will not let a setback slow me down.
- I will use my inner strength.
- Every day I am moving closer to glowing health.

Finally, never forget the importance of having support for accountability, motivation, inspiration, and advice. Having a strong
support system can give you an outlet to talk about your experience and feelings. It's a place to ask for advice, and a support
system—whether it's one friend or coach or supportive group—

can help guide you, cheer you on, share their own experiences with you, and support your decisions. Accountability is where it's at when you need someone to say, "Hey, where were you today? We missed you at walking club," or "Here's a picture of the healthy dinner I made tonight. Send me yours!"

◆

We hope that when we part, you are feeling bold. You are feeling equipped. You are feeling ready. And you are feeling inspired to shoot for the moon, keep pushing yourself just a little outside of your comfort zone, and live fully and freely as the person you are, moving steadily and with self-efficacy toward the person you know you were always meant to be.

We'll be there on the sidelines, cheering you on. And if you don't quite make it to the place you intended? Look where you are nevertheless! If there's one thing Dr. Michaelides wants you to take from this book, it's a transformed relationship to "failure." "Failure is just another opportunity to learn," he says. "If you fail to fail, you fail to learn. That's so important to remember. Because whatever you do in life, there will be surges, and there will be slips, and sometimes things won't work out the way you thought. If you can redefine your relationship with 'failure' and begin to treat failures as learning opportunities, then I would say that your so-called failure has been a success."

No matter what happens, as long as you are going somewhere, you're going to get somewhere new. You're going to gain experience, knowledge, and wisdom. That's progress. Sometimes you'll change course. Sometimes you'll realize something you thought you wanted isn't really what you want after all. But if you never try, then you'll never know what you can accomplish—and you may miss the chance to figure out what really matters to you even more than the goal you first started to pursue. If your goal is burning you out or it's too much, that's a lesson, too.

So, whether it's to finally find food freedom, to achieve fitness beyond your hopes, to live more mindfully every day, to radically accept yourself for exactly who you are, to achieve a tranquil mind, to find true love, or to change the world with your gifts, there is some version of that out there for you.

And now you know how to get there.

HAVE A NOOMY DAY!

Are you ready to have a Noomy Day? Or, wait—just what *is* a Noomy Day?

The way we see it, a Noomy Day is a day *you* drive, full of conscious decisions, good feelings, and positive reinforcement. But there are lots of ways to have a Noomy Day, TBH, and your day can be as unique as you are. We won't pretend to know what you do with your time.

What, you want details? We are at your service! Here is an example of how we see a Noomy Day. This is just an example, and if your day is quite different, we are confident that you can adapt the parts you like to fit what you do. Check it out, then think about what a Noomy Day could look like for *you* (borrow whatever you want from this list—what's ours is yours!):

- ◆ **Wake up.** Stretch. Smile. Think about something you like about yourself. Think about YPB. Maybe try out a positive affirmation. May we suggest: "I'm going to have a fantastic day!"
- ◆ **Meander to the bathroom.** Stretch again. Use the facilities.
- ◆ **Weigh yourself, if that's your thing.** Know that number (whether it sparked a "Yay!" or a "Boo!") is only feedback, not a label on you. Your bathroom is a no-judgment zone!
- ◆ **Take a few minutes with Noom.** Curl up in a comfy spot with a glass of water (or tea or coffee) and go through your Noom lessons for the day on the app. It's so quick, and so inspiring!
- ◆ **Mosey on into the kitchen.** You're feeling motivated. Thoughtfully consider how hungry you are while you pour yourself a glass of

water and drink some (or finish the one you already started).
What, and how much, you would like to eat for breakfast?

◆ **Add another food.** Choose something that's nutritionally
dense or not calorically dense (like a piece of fruit) to
whatever you have decided to have for breakfast. How about
some berries, or an apple on the go?

◆ **Go back to that Noom app.** Record what you ate. Look at
all those vegetables and fruits! And other good choices, too.
High five!

◆ **Exercise and/or shower.** That is, if you like to do those
things in the morning. So invigorating!

◆ **Get dressed.** Tell yourself that you look nice today. So far,
you are killing it!

◆ **Pack your lunch.** That is, if you do that sort of thing. Add
another vegetable or two while you've got that lunchbox
open. How about a handful of leafy greens to add to that
sandwich? Some celery sticks with hummus on the side?
Maybe some cherry tomatoes? Add a snack or two if you
think you might want one. An orange, a peach, some grapes,
or maybe some nuts or trail mix?

◆ **Head to work (even if it's just your home office).** Have some
more water on the way, or as soon as you get there. Consider
how much you enjoy your water bottle. Or, if you don't enjoy it,
contemplate how you might deserve a nicer one. Before you
head into the office (or the spare room where you keep your
computer), log how much water you've had so far.

◆ **Do that thing you do so well.** (You know . . . work.) That's
why they pay you! Sip on water while you're doing it. Your
brain will work better.

◆ **Temptation alert!** Someone brought doughnuts, or a
birthday cake, or cookies, or you're going to pass that candy
jar at some point. Time for a psych trick! Will you savor two
bites and move on? Practice exposing yourself (no, not like
that! We mean the exposure psych trick—are you trying to
get us in trouble?) to a treat without having any because you

really don't want it and it doesn't fit into your budget today? Or, notice whether grabbing junky treats is a habit. Will you choose not to engage in that habit today? Instead, have that mid-morning snack you planned—if you decide you need it.

◆ **Log it!** If you do choose the snack, don't forget to log it.

◆ **Drink it!** Keep sipping that refreshing water!

◆ **Take a lunch break.** Enjoy that nicely packed lunch or get your lunch at work. Thoughtfully consider how hungry you are. What sounds good? Consider what foods you'll choose and what calorically dense foods will be the cherry on top. (Literally, cherries are, of course, not calorically dense but very nutritionally dense.) Then, *stop working for a second, for goodness's sake!* Pay attention to your food. Eat slowly, savor, chew thoroughly, and really enjoy your meal and how your heathy choices make you feel.

◆ **Log it!** Take the last two minutes of your lunch break to record what you ate. Looking good—plenty of calorie budget remaining!

◆ **Back to work you go (if that's your schedule).** Seriously, you're really good at this! They should probably give you a raise. Or a promotion.

◆ **Afternoon slump alert.** Are you feeling drowsy? Bored? Or is it legit hunger? Take a moment to feel your feelings. Maybe you need a snack, or maybe you just need to refill that water bottle or take a bathroom break. Your choice—and yes, you have a choice (the vending machine isn't the boss of you).

◆ **Head home, via the gym (if that's your thing).** Aren't you glad you keep your gym bag in the car? Or maybe you'll take a walk, since it's a beautiful day, or do some yoga because it's your fave way to decompress. Feels. So. Good.

◆ **Home at last!** But . . . mindful moment! Are you starving? Stressed? Relieved? Anxious? Notice your feelings, especially if they are tempting you to nosh on a whole dinner's worth of food (or drinks) before you've actually made dinner. Do you want to do that, or is it a thought distortion, making you think that food will calm you or that you "deserve it" after your hard day at work? (We agree you deserve something great . . . but overstuffing may not be that great, when you really think about it.)

◆ **What's for dinner?** Green foods? Awesome. What else will satisfy you? Start putting it all together. Enjoy the process— cooking is fun! (If you say that enough times, you might start to believe it. "Cooking is fun." "Cooking is fun.")

◆ **Dinner is served!** Consider your eating environment. What if you actually ate at the table tonight, instead of in front of the TV? That could be fun. No pressure, though. Sometimes a healthy, filling dinner goes perfectly with a good movie.

◆ **Something sweet?** Is it a day to have a little something sweet after dinner, or nah? Do you have room in your calorie budget, or have you had enough food for today? Consider whether an after-dinner sweet or snack fits into your plan and feels balanced in your day, or if you are genuinely satisfied and don't need it.

◆ **Log it!** After dinner, log what you ate, including any afternoon snacks or dessert. Did you meet your calorie budget? If yes, go you! If no, don't yell at yourself. Just think about why. Is your budget too low? Or did you eat more than you really wanted to? If so, think about the situations surrounding when you did that. Was there one point during the day when you veered from your goals? Why? Be curious, not critical. This is information that you can use tomorrow.

◆ **Time to relax!** It's so nice to wind down after a busy day. Maybe it's time to stroll through the neighborhood with your pup, or maybe you'll dim the lights and chill with a good book or some soothing conversation. Or maybe it's family game night.

◆ **A bath might be nice (if desired, right about now).** With candles! Maybe you're more of a shower person. How about a few minutes of meditation? Om . . . You are *so* Zen.

- **Do a few sweet stretches (feels great before crawling into bed).** You know, to sleep. Or . . . whatever romantic activities you might decide to do first. (There are benefits to turning in early.)
- **Think about how awesome you are (as you drift off).** Think about how powerful you feel, and how well you've taken care of yourself today. Nobody's perfect and you might be thinking about ways you could have done better, but that's cool, too. Remember, no failure, only feedback! The truth is, you rock, and you're sneaking up on that YBP like a ninja.
- **Sweet dreams.** And we'll see you in the morning!

For more Noom in your life, daily fun lessons, a personal coach, inspirational group support, and technology for setting goals, tracking meals and water and exercise, and so much more, we would like to officially invite you to join us on the Noom app. You'll find inspiration, motivation, community, and personal guidance from your very own goal specialist coach. We think you're going to love it here!

Or, if you want to focus on stress reduction and taking care of your mental health, try our stress management app, Noom Mood. We've spent over a decade helping millions of people meet their health goals, from weight loss to managing diabetes. Now we want to help you tackle stress. Learning to manage your daily stress is a journey, and the first step is often the hardest. That's why we're here to guide you, step-by-step, to mental wellness—and to help you develop the techniques, emotional awareness, and resilience to reduce stress and live a happier life. We'll give you the knowledge and support you need to feel empowered to take on whatever comes next.

To sign up for a two-week free trial to either Noom or Noom Mood, go to the Noom Mindset website: www.noom.com/book.

Note that, similar to other paid apps, you must cancel before your free trial is over to avoid being charged.

HAVE A NOOMY DAY!

NOOM GLOSSARY

Trying to remember what that word or term meant?
Here's a handy guide to all the terminology we use in this book.

Acceptance and commitment therapy (ACT): A recent type of psychotherapy that has grown out of cognitive behavioral therapy (CBT) and dialectical behavior therapy (DBT). ACT helps people to acknowledge and accept their emotional responses as valid, rather than denying or suppressing them.

Adrenaline: A neurohormone specifically tied to the stress response, produced by the adrenal glands that stimulates the body's sympathetic nervous system, activating the fight-or-flight response to help prepare the body for dealing with an emergency. It is the same thing as *epinephrine*.

Affirmation: A psych trick for reversing negative thoughts and turning them into positive, motivational thoughts, such as recognizing that you're thinking "I won't be able to do this" and telling yourself "I *can* do this!"

All-or-nothing thinking: A common type of thought distortion that sees things in absolutes, with no middle ground or nuance. Examples are: "All sugar is bad." "I'll never be able to get healthy." "I skipped the gym so I'm a failure."

Autonomous motivation: A type of motivation that comes from the idea that a behavior or action is worth doing because it is in line with one's personal values and beliefs.

Behavior chain: A series of events that can lead to habits. The events begin with a trigger, which leads to thoughts, which leads to actions, which leads to outcomes (we call these *consequences* in the app, FYI), which, over time, can lead to the formation of habits.

BMI (Body Mass Index): A number calculated using height and weight, often used to define the categories of underweight, normal weight, overweight, and obese.

Brain-derived neurotrophic factor (BDNF): A protein generated in and regulated by the brain that helps the brain produce more brain cells (neurogenesis) and helps existing brain cells survive longer; increases the communication among neurons; and helps with learning, memory, and neuroplasticity. Things that encourage BDNF production include exercise, managing stress, sleeping enough, eating less processed foods and sugar, meditating, spending more time outside, drinking coffee, and doing intermittent fasting.

Calorie deficit: Expending more energy than you are taking in. This leads to weight loss over time.

Calorie density: The calories by weight in a food. Foods with a lot of calories for their weight, like cheese, are calorically dense, while foods with few calories for their weight, like lettuce, are not calorically dense; also termed *caloric density*.

Celiac disease: An autoimmune condition in which the body reacts to gluten in the diet by attacking the lining of the small intestine. People with celiac disease are advised not to eat any foods containing gluten to minimize this damage.

Cognitive behavioral therapy (CBT): A type of therapy that teaches people to use coping strategies, with the end goal of changing problematic behaviors and feelings. Many Noom techniques are grounded in CBT.

Cognitive defusion: A psychology technique for separating a thought from a feeling or emotion, so you can more clearly see that while the feeling is valid, the thought may not be true.

Cognitive distortion: See *Thought distortion*.

Cognitive fusion: A psychology term for the fusion of thoughts with strong emotions, which can make untrue thoughts feel true.

Cognitive reappraisal: See *Cognitive reframing*.

Cognitive reframing: Another term for *cognitive reappraisal* or *cognitive restructuring*, cognitive reframing is to change the context of a thought or feeling like you might change the frame around a picture, considering different sets of facts, or seeing something in a different light in a way that is helpful.

Conscious decoupling: Purposefully separating actions from motivation so that a dip in motivation won't stop you from continuing with your new health habits. (Note that this is not an official psychology term.)

Consequence: The result of an action or behavior. Also called an *outcome*.

Construal level theory (CLT): A theory that when people think about the big picture, the "why" behind their behavior, they are more successful at avoiding habits they are trying to change than when they look at the details of their present situation. For example, thinking that you want to get healthy to avoid your family history of diabetes, and thinking about the people in your family who suffer from that condition, can become more motivating and more powerful than the doughnuts on the plate in front of you.

Cortisol: A hormone released in the adrenal glands in response to stress that coincides with the body's switch into fight-or-flight, or sympathetic nervous system mode.

Craving: A strong desire or want for something, like feeling as if you need chocolate.

Creative visualization: A type of visualization strategy. See *Visualization*.

Danger zone: The time during which you realize you may be backsliding in your new habits. This can be a cue to intervene with a Motivation SOS Plan to get back on track.

Decentering: A metacognition technique in psychology of perceiving strong feelings (such as food cravings) as something outside of yourself rather than within you. When you dis-identify with the feeling in this way, it loses power over you.

Decision fatigue: A term describing how decision-making becomes much harder when you have been making decisions all day; it's a side effect of exhausted executive function.

Delayed gratification: The process of waiting to obtain a reward rather than giving in to instant gratification because of the urge to have the reward immediately. Sometimes this refers to choosing a better reward later rather than a smaller reward immediately.

Dialectical behavioral therapy (DBT): A type of psychotherapy that grew out of cognitive behavioral therapy (CBT),

DBT focuses on building resilience to distress, learning emotional regulation, and building up self-efficacy by validating rather than by suppressing one's feelings. It was originally used for people suffering from trauma, such as post-traumatic stress disorder, but has become useful in many different situations to help people deal with problematic behavior and disturbing emotions.

Diathesis stress response: A theory that health problems come from the combination of a genetic predisposition to that problem and stress that triggers the issue to actually develop.

Diet culture: A culture centered on particular body and beauty standards, as well as food rules and so-called health rules. It is often used to refer to the idea that people should adhere to current standards of thinness and attractiveness.

Disidentification: A psychology practice of separating thoughts and feelings from the self so they can't control you.

Dopamine: A hormone that makes people feel good, increasing feelings of happiness and reducing feelings of stress. It is also released in response to pleasurable things in a way that can feel addictive, such as getting a dopamine hit every time you get a "like" on social media or a taste of chocolate, making you want to keep getting that pleasurable feeling.

EMOTE (Explore, Meditate, Observe, Talk/Text, and Exercise): The five actions that Noom recommends when you're having strong feelings and are tempted to blunt them with food. These are strategies to use in the moment when you aren't quite ready to deal with your feelings directly.

Emotional eating: Eating in response to strong feelings rather than hunger, as a means to self-soothe.

Executive function: A higher brain function that allows you to override more instinctual responses by doing things like reasoning, remembering, prioritizing, ignoring distractions, and delaying gratification.

Exposure therapy: A technique psychologists use to help people deal with phobias, anxiety, and other uncomfortable feelings. They expose the patient to the unpleasant thing—the heights, the enclosed spaces, the spider—in small amounts in a safe environment, gradually increasing the time they are exposed to the thing and the intensity of the exposure, until those feelings get less intense.

Extrinsic motivation: Motivation that is conditional on outside factors, such as receiving a reward or avoiding a negative outcome.

Feedback loop: The process describing how the output of any system (like your brain) in the past or present becomes an input for that same system in the present or future. For example, if you get a craving to eat cake, and you give in to the craving and get a dopamine hit (a good feeling), then your brain will seek the pleasant feeling in the future, making you want to eat more cake.

Fixed mindset: A mental state in which you believe your abilities are fixed, no matter what effort you might take to improve. This is the opposite of a *growth mindset*.

Fog eating: A Noom-y term for eating mindlessly, without really noticing what or how much you are eating.

Food culture: The food environment we live in—in the current sense, a culture of processed, high-reward junk foods and pressure to eat them.

Food pusher: Someone who, usually with good intentions, attempts to get you to eat more food than you would like to.

Food restriction: The process of someone's limiting the amount or type of food they allow themselves to consume, for weight loss or health reasons that may or may not actually be health-based.

Fortune-telling: A type of maladaptive thought distortion in which people assume they know what is going to happen in the future, often leading to negative behaviors or thoughts.

Four Pillars of Health: Noom's four primary aspects of life that are key to health: nutrition, exercise, sleep, and stress management.

Fuel eating: Choosing and eating foods that are nourishing to the body, for the sole purpose of providing the body with energy and increasing health, rather than for emotional or other reasons.

Fun eating: Eating for pleasure, regardless of nutritional content of the food. There is nothing wrong with eating for fun! It is one of several types of eating that are natural and normal.

Gamification: Essentially, making any sort of task feel like a game in order to make it more enjoyable or rewarding. Noom Coin, in which Noomers earn coins on the app for achieving certain activities and goals, is an example of gamification.

Ghrelin: A hormone that signals the need for food via feelings of hunger.

Gluten-free: A way of eating that eliminates any foods that contain the protein gluten, which is found in wheat, rye, barley, spelt, and other wheat relatives. People may choose to go gluten-free due to illnesses such as celiac disease, or for other dietary reasons.

Growth mindset: Having the mindset that your efforts will increase your abilities and that you can change. This is the opposite of a *fixed mindset*.

Guided imagery: A type of meditation or mindfulness in which someone is given specific things to imagine or envision by a therapist or meditation instructor.

Habit bundling: Pairing a habit you already have with a new habit you want to have, such as bundling flossing (something you want to start doing) with brushing your teeth (something you already do regularly).

Hangry: A term for that feeling of being irritable and angry when you are hungry; hungry + angry = hangry.

HDL (high-density lipoprotein): A type of cholesterol that is beneficial to health and reduces the risk of heart disease; the so-called good cholesterol.

Heart rate variability: A measure of cardiovascular health based on how well your heart recovers from stress. When your heart rate goes up, such as with exercise, it should come back down quickly when you stop. Heart rate variability is also influenced by what your resting heart rate is. The lower your resting heart rate, and the faster your heart rate comes back down after going up, the higher (and better) your heart rate variability.

HIIT (High-Intensity Interval Training): This is an intense but time-saving form of exercise in which you alternate short bursts of all-out effort with more moderate or low-intensity recovery effort, allowing you to get all the cardiovascular benefits of a longer cardio workout in a fraction of the time.

Honeymoon: The second stage of phase 1 in the Noom Motivation Model. When your motivation peaks, you are in the honeymoon stage. You've probably started working on your goal and you're already seeing positive results, and that is super-motivating! You are starry-eyed and optimistic, and your motivation is through the roof.

Hype: The first stage in phase 1 of the Noom Motivation Model, when you decide to make a change or accomplish something. You're thinking about starting and you're making a plan. You're nervous. You might feel slightly skeptical, but you're gathering information and starting to get excited, even exhilarated.

Implementation intention: The process of setting an intention to change a behavior, such as through an "if . . . then" plan: "*If* I've had a stressful day and want to have a sugary snack, *then* I will first have a piece of fruit and reassess my hunger in twenty minutes."

Intermittent fasting: Eating during a set window of time and fasting, or not eating, during the rest of the day. For example, you might not eat for twelve hours overnight. If you finish dinner at 7:00 p.m., you would wait until 7:00 a.m. to have breakfast.

Intrinsic motivation: Motivation based on something personally relevant and meaningful to you, as opposed to extrinsic motivation, which is motivation based on an external reward. For example, an intrinsic motivation might be setting a good example for your family.

Irrationally comparative thinking: A type of thought distortion in which one compares themselves to others in a detrimental way, such as assuming they could never be as fit as someone else or achieve the career success someone else has achieved.

Justification: Rationalizing a behavior to excuse it, such as the thought: "I worked out today so I deserve to eat a big dessert."

Keto: Short for *ketogenic*, referring to a high-fat, low-carbohydrate diet that is currently trendy and often used for weight loss. It can be difficult and possibly unhealthy to sustain long term.

Keystone habits: Seven foundational habits Noom has identified that can help with health and getting to a healthy weight. The habits are: befriend breakfast, eat regularly, control your portions, unprocess your diet, lose the labels, ditch the (sweetened) drinks, and eat mindfully.

Lapse: The second stage of phase 2 in the Noom Motivation Model. This is when you really start skipping the gym or giving up on your eating plan; whatever you were doing starts to feel too hard, so you stop doing it, or you stop doing it as consistently as you did when your motivation was high. You may still intend to work toward your goal, but suddenly it's not very fun anymore and you're not as confident as you were that you can really get there. The important thing about lapses is that they teach you things about yourself, about your goals, about what's working and what's not working. They give you a chance to reassess, check in, and regroup.

LDL (low-density lipoprotein): A type of cholesterol that has been associated with increased risk of heart disease; the so-called bad cholesterol.

Learned industriousness: Motivation to continue to work hard and try difficult things in the future; a result of being rewarded by the outcome of your hard work.

Learning goal: A goal centered on learning something rather than an external reward. For example, a learning goal would be to train for a 5K in order to become a runner, rather than to win a prize.

Leptin: A hormone that signals being full, so you stop eating. Some people can become resistant to this effect.

Low-carb: A lifestyle in which one consumes a lower amount of carbohydrates than other macronutrients.

Macronutrients: Three primary nutrients in food: fat, carbohydrates, and protein.

Maladaptive: Not adapting well or appropriately to a situation or environmental condition, such as getting stressed out and releasing stress hormones in response to something that isn't actually a threat.

Maslow's Hierarchy of Needs: A theory developed by psychologist Abraham Maslow in 1943 and expanded upon in the 1960s and 1970s that shows, in pyramidal form, the order in which people are motivated to get things they need. The bottom of the pyramid represents the most basic human needs, and Maslow says we are motivated first and foremost to get those.

Mastery goal: See *Learning goal*

Meditation: An ancient practice with many different modern versions for learning to still the mind or sit in mindfulness. Research shows that meditation is associated with many physical and mental health benefits.

Mediterranean diet: A way of eating that is traditional to the countries situated around the Mediterranean Sea; it prioritizes eating largely a plant-based, unprocessed diet rich in vegetables, fruits, olive oil, nuts and seeds, and seafood, with or without small amounts of wine. It's also associated with a lot of natural movement, family and community support, and time outdoors.

Melatonin: A hormone released in response to circadian rhythms influenced by light and darkness, as well as cycles throughout the day, that contributes to feeling tired, preparing the body for sleep.

Metabolism: All the physical and biochemical processes in the body involved in converting food into energy, as well as using that energy.

Metacognition: An awareness of the separation between you and your thoughts, and the acknowledgment that you are the one observing your thoughts. Technically, metacognition means cognition about cognition, or thinking about thinking.

Micronutrient: A vitamin or mineral in food that the body needs to function and stay healthy.

Mind reading: A thought distortion in which someone assumes they know what other people are thinking, usually assuming the thoughts are negative.

Mindful eating: Eating with full consciousness and attention to the process and sensations.

Mindful moments: Chances to pause and exist solely in the moment; opportunities to notice your thoughts and feelings as you go through your day.

Mindful movement: Moving with self-awareness, such as noticing the sensations you feel while exercising.

Motivation Model: A Noom model of how motivation generally works, which includes the hype, the honeymoon, the plummet, the lapse, and slips and surges.

Motivation SOS Plan: A tool to help you become more conscious and aware of how your current level of motivation is affecting you. It consists of three parts—the warning sign, the danger zone, and the reaction—and includes strategies that will help you recover from a slip in motivation rather than backsliding.

Moving meditation: Meditating while walking or exercising. Traditionally, moving meditation is practiced while walking in slow, deliberate circles, but you can do it anywhere, like while walking through nature or even doing more structured exercise like lifting weights.

Multitasking: Doing multiple things at the same time. Multitasking feels productive, but it actually takes more time than doing one thing at a time, which is known as *single-tasking*.

Negative reinforcement: An outcome that makes you do something more often because it makes something you don't like stop happening. For example, getting time off work if you do a good job on a project is an example of negative reinforcement because the reward is a break from work.

Negativity bias: A type of thought distortion in which someone notices the negative more than the positive, even when there is more positive than negative to notice, such as hyper-focusing on one single criticism on a performance review full of glowing praise.

Neurogenesis: The generation of more neurons, the most common type of brain cells.

Neuroplasticity: The idea that your brain is capable of changing as an adaptation to changing circumstances, such as rerouting after a brain injury.

Neuroscience: A field of science that explores any processes related to the brain and the larger nervous system.

Non-exercise activity thermogenesis (NEAT): The energy or calorie burn you get by moving throughout the day, apart from intentional exercise. With a lot of daily movement, you can burn more calories than you can from a single exercise session, so moving a lot throughout the day is really important if you are working on weight loss. It's also good for your health and combats the negative effects of sedentary living.

Non-scale victory (NSV): All the benefits of healthy weight loss that have nothing to do with the number on the scale, like feeling more confident, feeling more physically comfortable, and having more energy.

Noom Motivation Model: See *Motivation Model*

Noom Satiety Scale: See *Satiety Scale*

Noom's Four Pillars of Health: See *Four Pillars of Health*

Norm matching: The idea that many of our behaviors are the result of our syncing with the behaviors of those around us. This is an outcome of the human desire to bond and be part of groups, and can also contribute to habit development.

Nutritional density: The amount of nutrients a food has relative to its number of calories. For example, a candy bar has a lot of calories but not many nutrients, so it's not nutritionally dense. Blueberries have few calories but a lot of nutrients, so they are nutritionally dense.

Obesogenic: Anything that promotes excessive weight gain or obesity, generally referring to environments with a lot of chemicals, or highly processed foods.

Observer: The part of you that observes your thoughts and feelings rather than identifying with them or getting carried away by them. It's always inside of you. The Observer is sometimes called the *higher self*.

Operant conditioning: A psychology concept that actions that are reinforced are more likely to be repeated.

Outcome: See *Consequence*

Paleo: A dietary pattern, and sometimes also a lifestyle, that centers on imitating as closely as possible the diet and habits of Paleolithic humans. This generally means a non-processed, whole-food diet of vegetables, fruit, meat, seafood, eggs, nuts, seeds, and anything else that could be acquired by hunter-gatherers. It's also used to refer to natural movements instead of structured exercise and living in more harmony with nature. Paleo diets generally don't include grains or legumes, which became more prominent in the human diet after the agricultural revolution; in some cases, the Paleo diet also excludes dairy products.

Parasympathetic nervous system: Meant to be our default nervous system mode, this is the "rest and digest" phase during which we recover from stress.

Performance goal: A type of goal that is focused on achieving a certain level of performance, such as running a half-marathon in under three hours or holding a handstand for two minutes, in contrast with learning goals, which are more intrinsically motivating.

Phytonutrient: An antioxidant and/or anti-inflammatory compound in plants that is beneficial to human health, reducing disease risk.

Plant-based: A dietary pattern of only or primarily consuming food that comes from plants.

Plummet: The first stage of phase 2 of the Noom Motivation Model, following the honeymoon phase, when behavior change begins to feel more difficult. Suddenly you realize that to reach your goal, you have to keep working hard even when you don't feel like it. Your exciting goal starts to feel less attainable.

Positive reinforcement: A reward for a behavior that makes you more likely to do something again because you got something good for doing it. For example, if you meet friends and have a good time when you all go on a walk together, you'll be more likely to want to keep doing that.

Positive thinking: A way of seeing things in a positive or optimistic light, even if they are unpleasant things; making the best of a bad situation.

Processed food: Food that's formulated by food scientists to be hyper-palatable, that tends to be unnaturally high in sugar, fat, and salt compared to whole foods. Processed foods tend to be calorically dense but not nutritionally dense.

Projection: A psychological term for projecting your own feelings onto someone else.

QMT (quick motivational tip): The Noom-y acronym for an easy strategy for increasing one's motivation.

Radical acceptance: Totally accepting your current reality as your current reality, including where you are, what you are doing, how you look, your health, your job, or anything else you try to hide from yourself. This is an act of compassion that can help you to love yourself no matter what your size or state of being, which can increase your self-efficacy and be motivating. If you fully accept yourself, you take a lot of stress and pressure off and that could open up room for self-care and making healthy changes.

Reframing: See *Cognitive reframing*

Reward: A good thing you get for doing something, like the nap you get to take after meeting a deadline or the new sweater you gift to yourself after meeting a goal. Rewards can also happen spontaneously, like the great feeling you get after going for a run. Rewards make you more likely to repeat the behavior you were rewarded for.

Rumination: The process of thinking the same thoughts over and over, or obsessively going back and replaying the same scenarios again and again.

Satiety Scale: A Noom scale for measuring hunger and fullness.

"Say it again": A psych trick involving repeating a thought distortion over and over again until it begins to sound ridiculous and the emotion you have attached to it loses power, so you can get some distance and realize that the thought isn't true.

Script: A routine that you repeat in response to a trigger, which can result in habit formation. For instance, you may have a script that whenever you have a hard day, you automatically reach for a glass of wine or get fast food.

Sedentary: Inactive; a sedentary lifestyle is a largely inactive lifestyle, such as spending most of the day sitting.

Self-awareness: Knowing yourself and being aware of what you are doing and why.

Self-determination theory (SDT): The idea that human beings exhibit behaviors because of both outside influences (see *Extrinsic motivation*) and internal desires or drives (see *Intrinsic motivation*). This theory suggests that people who have more intrinsic motivation tend to be more successful.

Self-efficacy: A quality of believing in your own ability to achieve things.

Self-experimentation: Using yourself for experiments. You might, for instance, do an experiment of systematically trying different kinds of diets or different kinds of exercises to see which ones work for you. This would generally involve keeping track of what you do and how well it works so you can make an assessment at the end of the experiment.

Self-regulation: Having the ability to evaluate and moderate your behavior in ways that benefit you and others. This is a goal of many types of psychotherapy, especially DBT.

Self-sabotage: Doing something that is destructive to your own mental, physical, or emotional growth or well-being.

Self-transcendence: One's ability to see beyond themself and their own needs, to consider the bigger picture and the needs of others.

Serotonin: A hormone in the human body that contributes to positive feelings, including euphoria during physical exercise and physical touch.

Single-tasking: Doing one thing at a time, in contrast to *multitasking*.

Sleep hygiene: Your before-bed routine and sleep environment, both of which impact how well you sleep.

Slips and surges: Phase 3 of the Noom Motivation Model; fluctuating levels of motivation, during which sometimes motivation is lower (slips) and other times it's higher (surges), like a series of waves.

SMART goal: A strategy for effective goal-setting, stating that the most achievable goals are Specific, Measurable, Attainable, Relevant, and Time-Based.

Storm eating: A type of eating characterized by a lack of feeling in control over the type or quantity of food being eaten; indicative of using food as a means of self-soothing in response to strong emotions.

Sub goal: Also known as a *subordinate goal*, this is a smaller, more immediate goal that helps you work toward a Super Goal.

Super Goal: Also known as a *superordinate goal*, this is a high-level goal with sub goals that can help you get there. For example, a Super Goal might be to get fit, while sub goals might be to start going to the gym, hire a trainer, and work up to regular exercising.

Supportive accountability theory: A theory that a knowledgeable and supportive coach greatly increases adherence to new habits.

Sympathetic nervous system: The nervous system mode that is a response to high stress and causes physiological changes that help the body deal with an emergency. This is also called the *fight-or-flight* response.

Temporal discounting: The very human tendency to care less about future outcomes than present ones, and probably originally a survival response.

Thought distortion: A thinking pattern, often fueled by strong emotions, that feels true but that is not actually factual and is psychologically discouraging or maladaptive in some way, such as "Cake is evil!" or "I'm a bad person because I don't exercise." In psychology, this is often called *cognitive distortion*.

Toxic positivity: The act of focusing only on positive feelings and emotions rather than attempting to get to the root of negative feelings or situations. This can often feel invalidating to people on the receiving end.

Transtheoretical model of health behavior change: The psychology theory behind Noom's Motivation Model. It's a more complex version of how motivation works, with six stages: pre-contemplation (not thinking about change), contemplation (thinking about change), preparation (getting ready to change), action (making changes), maintenance (integrating change into regular life), and termination (the change has become fully integrated into your regular life and you don't need to think about it anymore). People often cycle repeatedly through preparation, action, and maintenance before they get to termination.

Trigger: The event or action that kicks off the behavior chain. This may be mental, physical, emotional, or social. Examples might be a time of day when you always eat, seeing a picture of a desirable food, or stress. The trigger results in thoughts and feelings that lead to an action that leads to an outcome.

Ultimate Why: Your personal highest-level reason for wanting to reach your goals. It may take some work to figure out what this is.

Urge surfing: The process of riding the wave of discomfort that comes from changing a habit, such as trying not to respond to a sugar craving.

Vegan: A lifestyle in which people eat no animal products of any kind, including dairy products, eggs, and honey. Vegans also consider veganism to be more than a diet; it's an ethical position against using animals for personal pleasure or profit.

Vegetarian: A lifestyle in which people eat mostly plants, but often also eat dairy products and/or eggs.

Visualization: Imagining a scene, situation, or goal achievement—anything you imagine in your mind visually.

Warning sign: A thing you start doing, or stop doing, that signals you may be relapsing into a habit you are trying to change.

WFPB (whole-food, plant-based): An eating pattern in which people only eat whole foods that are not processed. The whole foods are entirely or mostly plant-based.

WFPBNO (whole-food, plant-based, no oil): An eating pattern in which people eat only whole foods, mostly or entirely plant-based, and also do not add any oil to their diet.

WFPBNONSNS (whole food, plant-based, no oil, no salt, no sugar): An eating pattern in which people only eat whole foods, mostly plant-based, with no added oil, salt, or sugar.

Wheel of Life: A visual representation of different aspects of one's life in the form of a pie chart that health coaches often use to show how much time and effort are dedicated to each one in order to assess life balance and life satisfaction.

Whole food: A food that has not been processed; food the way nature made it.

YBP (Your Big Picture): A culmination of your Super Goal, your Ultimate Why, and your vision for your future, representing the big picture for your goals.

"Yes, but": A psych trick for cognitive reframing, whereby you acknowledge a thought but then say, "Yes, but" and put it into a different, more positive or useful context.

ACKNOWLEDGMENTS

A book like *The Noom Mindset* is truly a collaboration. So many people contributed to making this book all that it is that it would be difficult to name them all . . . but we have a can-do spirit here at Noom, so we're going to try!

First and foremost, we must thank our founders, Artem Petakov and Saeju Jeong, whose creativity, mutual drive to change the world for the better, and entrepreneurial spirits are responsible for Noom's existence and continued growth. Thanks to Dr. Andreas Michaelides for elevating the scientific foundation of this book with his wise psychological insights and innate ability to understand the needs of Noomers. And a very special thanks to our Noom coaches, who work tirelessly one-on-one and in our groups to help our Noomers succeed, and whose compassion and skills have been integral to this book.

Many others on the Noom team have contributed their time, sweat, and tears—especially Jackson Tilley, who was, undoubtedly, the linchpin for this entire book project. He acted as connector, enforcer, decider, and mediator. Without his vision, dedication, and diplomacy, this book could not have happened. Thanks to Brittany Barry, who joined up to have Jackson's back and did the legwork necessary to bring this book across the finish line. Thanks to Emma Frane for being the greatest advocate for projects like this that propel the Noom brand forward, and a massive thanks to Kayla Reynolds for building Noom's curriculum into what it is today. Thank you as well to Noom's Brand and Creative Teams, especially Lella Rafferty, Zaid Al-Asady, Will Burroughs, Able Parris, Adrienne Ross, Rose Niermeijer, Anne Cassard, and Charlotte Duerden.

ACKNOWLEDGMENTS

Thanks are due to the entire Noom Research, Marketing, and Comms Teams—especially Melissa Rubenstein, Amelia Orlando, Sarah Lipman, Annabell Ho, Kelly Blessing, Meaghan McCallum, and Christine May—as well as Noom's Legal Team, Michal Rosen, Jamie Raghu, and Eric Cheng, and the folks at Frankfurt Kurnit Klein & Selz, especially Mark Merriman.

Thanks to Eve Adamson, whose knack for hearing and translating Noom's voice gave this book its flavor and structure, for being so quick and easy to work with. We also must thank everyone at Simon Element, especially Leah Miller, our benevolent leader who guided us through a publishing process that we knew nothing about, calmly keeping us informed about what was and wasn't possible and never panicking (at least not on the outside). Also thanks to publisher extraordinaire Richard Rhorer and associate publisher Suzanne Donahue, as well as Nicole Bond, Jessie McNeil, Patrick Sullivan for the fabulous cover, and Laura Levatino for the beautiful interior design. Thanks also to Brand Creative for their marketing genius and to the entire team at CAA, especially Cindy Uh, for brilliantly connecting all the working parts, and Jamie Stockton, for all the legal guidance along the way.

And finally, thanks to *you*. Whether you've been with us for a while or are just joining us, you, and your journey, are Noom's reason for being.

END NOTES

Chapter 1:
You Rule

1. Edward L. Deci and Richard M. Ryan, "The 'What' and 'Why' of Goal Pursuits: Human Needs and the Self-Determination of Behavior," Psychological Inquiry 11, no. 4 (2000): 227–68, DOI: 10.1207/S15327965PLI1104_01.

2. Nikos Ntoumanis et al., "When the Going Gets Tough: The 'Why' of Goal Striving Matters," *Journal of Personality* 82, no. 3 (June 2014): 225–36, https://psycnet.apa.org/doi/10.1111/jopy.12047.

3. "Noom Is Grounded in Science," Noom.com, https://web.noom.com/research/.

4. Gregory N. Ruegsegger and Frank W. Booth, "Health Benefits of Exercise," *Cold Spring Harbor Perspectives in Medicine* 8, no. 7 (July 2018), https://dx.doi.org/10.1101%2Fcshperspect.a029694.

5. Laurie R. Santos and Alexandra G. Rosati, "The Evolutionary Roots of Human Decision Making," *Annual Review of Psychology* 66 (January 2015): 321–74, https://doi.org/10.1146/annurev-psych-010814-015310.

6. B. H. Edell et al., "Self-Efficacy and Self-Motivation as Predictors of Weight Loss," *Addictive Behaviors* 12, no. 1 (1987): 63–66, DOI: 10.1016/0306-4603(87)90009-8.

7. This quiz is loosely based on the Stanford SPARQ Tools measure of self-efficacy: "New General Self-Efficacy Scale," SPARQtools, Stanford University, https://sparqtools.org/mobility-measure/new-general-self-efficacy-scale/#all-survey-questions.

8. E. T. Berkman, "The Neuroscience of Goals and Behavior Change," *Consulting Psychology Journal: Practice and Research* 70, no. 1 (2018): 28–44, https://doi.apa.org/doi/10.1037/cpb0000094.

9. Ryan R. Bailey, "Goal Setting and Action Planning for Health Behavior Change," *American Journal of Lifestyle Medicine* 13, no. 6 (November 2019): 615–18, https://doi.org/10.1177%2F1559827617729634.

10. Ronnie Dotson, "Goal Setting to Increase Student Academic Performance," *Journal of School Administration Research and Development* 1, no. 1 (Summer 2016): 44–46, https://files.eric.ed.gov/fulltext/EJ1158116.pdf.

11. David Scott Yeager and Carol S. Dweck, "Mindsets That Promote Resilience: When Students Believe That Personal Characteristics Can Be Developed," *Educational Psychologist* 47, no. 4 (2012): 302–14, http://dx.doi.org/10.1080/00461520.2012.722805.

12. Carol S. Dweck, *Mindset: The New Psychology of Success* (New York: Ballantine Books, 2007).

13. Tashana Samuel and Jared Warner, "'I Can Math!': Reducing Math Anxiety and Increasing Math Self-Efficacy Using a Mindfulness and Growth Mindset–Based Intervention in First-Year Students," *Community College Journal of Research and Practice* 45, no. 7 (September 2019): 1–18; and Peter A. Heslin, Jeni L. Burnette, and Nam Gyu Ryu, "Does a Growth Mindset Enable Successful Aging?" *Work, Aging and Retirement* 7, no. 2 (April 2021): 79–89.

14. David S. Lee and Oscar Ybarra, "Cultivating Effective Social Support through Abstraction: Reframing Social Support Promotes Goal-Pursuit," *Personality and Social Psychology Bulletin* 43, no. 4 (April 2017): 453–64, DOI: 10.1177/0146167216688205.

15. James Clear, *Atomic Habits: An Easy & Proven Way to Build Good Habits & Break Bad Ones* (New York: Avery, 2018).

16. Whitney S. Orth et al., "Support Group Meeting Attendance Is Associated with Better Weight Loss," *Obesity Surgery* 18 (2008): 391–94, https://doi.org/10.1007/s11695-008-9444-8.

17. Patrice Voss et al., "Dynamic Brains and the Changing Rules of Neuroplasticity: Implications for Learning and Recovery," *Frontiers in Psychology* 8 (2017), https://www.frontiersin.org/articles/10.3389/fpsyg.2017.01657/full.

18. Simon C. Dyall, "Long-Chain Omega-3 Fatty Acids and the Brain: A Review of the Independent and Shared Effects of EPA, DPA, and DHA," *Frontiers in Aging Neuroscience* 7 (2015), https://dx.doi.org/10.3389%2Ffnagi.2015.00052.

19. David Vauzour, "Dietary Polyphenols as Modulators of Brain Functions: Biological Actions and Molecular Mechanisms Underpinning Their Beneficial Effects," *Oxidative Medicine and Cellular Longevity* 2012 (2012), https://dx.doi.org/10.1155%2F2012%2F914273.

20. Sama F. Sleiman et al., "Exercise Promotes the Expression of Brain-Derived Neurotrophic Factor (BDNF) through the Action of the Ketone Body ß-Hydroxybutyrate," *eLife* 5 (2016): e15092 2016, https://dx.doi.org/10.7554%2FeLife.15092.

21. Kuljeet Singh Anand and Vikas Dhikav, "Hippocampus in Health and Disease: An Overview," *Annals of Indian Academy of Neurology* 15, no. 4 (October–December 2012): 239–46, https://dx.doi.org/10.4103%2F0972-2327.104323.

22. Nadia Aalling Jessen et al., "The Glymphatic System: A Beginner's Guide," *Neurochemical Research* 40 (2015): 2583–99, https://dx.doi.org/10.1007%2Fs11064-015-1581-6.

23. Chai M. Tyng et al., "The Influences of Emotion on Learning and Memory," *Frontiers in Psychology* 8 (2017), https://doi.org/10.3389/fpsyg.2017.01454.

24. Harvey S. Levin, "Neuroplasticity Following Non-Penetrating Traumatic Brain Injury," *Brain Injury* 17, no. 8 (2003): 665–74, https://doi.org/10.1080/0269905031000107151; YouRong Sophie Su, Anand Veeravagu, and Gerald Grant, "Neuroplasticity after Traumatic Brain Injury," in *Translational*

Research in Traumatic Brain Injury (Boca Raton, FL: CRC Press/Taylor and Francis Group, 2016); and Karen Caeyenberghs et al., "Evidence for Training-Dependent Structural Neuro-plasticity in Brain-Injured Patients: A Critical Review," *Neurorehabilitation and Neural Repair* 32, no. 2 February 2018): 99–114, https://www.ncbi.nlm.nih.gov/books/NBK326735/.

25. Adrian Meule, "The Psychology of Food Cravings: The Role of Food Deprivation," *Current Nutrition Reports* 9 (2020): 251–57, https://doi.org/10.1007/s13668-020-00326-0.

26. K. Richard Ridderinkhof and Marcel Brass, "How Kinesthetic Motor Imagery Works: A Predictive-Processing Theory of Visualization in Sports and Motor Expertise," *Journal of Physiology—Paris* 109, nos. 1–3 (February–June 2015): 53–63, https://doi.org/10.1016/j.jphysparis.2015.02.003; and Richard M. Suinn, "Visualization in Sports," in Anees A. Sheikh and Errol R. Korn, eds., *Imagery in Sports and Physical Performance* (New York: Baywood Publishing Company, 1994), 23–39.

27. Margaret Cocks, PhD, et al., "What Surgeons Can Learn from Athletes: Mental Practice in Sports and Surgery," *Journal of Surgical Education* 71, no. 2 (March–April 2014): 262–69, https://doi.org/10.1016/j.jsurg.2013.07.002.

28. E. K. Andersson and T. P. Moss, "Imagery and Implementation Intention: A Randomised Controlled Trial of Interventions to Increase Exercise Behaviour in the General Population," *Psychology of Sport and Exercise* 12, no. 2 (March 2011): 63–70, https://www.sciencedirect.com/science/article/abs/pii/S1469029210000932.

29. Leon Skottnik and David E. J. Linden, "Mental Imagery and Brain Regulation—New Links between Psychotherapy and Neuroscience," *Frontiers in Psychiatry* 10 (2019): 779, https://www.ncbi.nlm.nih.gov/pmc/articles/PMC6831624/.

30. Phillippa Lally et al., "How Are Habits Formed: Modelling Habit Formation in the Real World," *European Journal of Social Psychology* 40 (2010): 998–1009, http://repositorio.ispa.pt/bitstream/10400.12/3364/1/IJSP_998-1009.pdf.

Chapter 2:
Setting Goals and YBP (Your Big Picture)

1. Bettina Höchli, Adrian Brügger, and Claude Messner, "How Focusing on Superordinate Goals Motivates Broad, Long-Term Goal Pursuit: A Theoretical Perspective," *Frontiers in Psychology* 9 (2018), https://www.frontiersin.org/articles/10.3389/fpsyg .2018.01879/full.

2. Fred C. Lunenburg, "Goal-Setting Theory of Motivation," *International Journal of Management, Business, and Administration* 15, no. 1 (2011), http://www.nationalforum.com /Electronic%20Journal%20Volumes/Lunenburg,%20Fred%20 C.%20Goal-Setting%20Theoryof%20Motivation%20IJMBA%20 V15%20N1%202011.pdf.

3. E. Serra Yurtkoru et al., "Application of Goal Setting Theory," *PressAcademia Procedia* 3 (2017): 796–801, http://dx.doi.org /10.17261/Pressacademia.2017.660.

4. Hal E. Hershfield, "Future Self-Continuity: How Conceptions of the Future Self Transform Intertemporal Choice," *Decision Making Over the Life Span* 1235, no. 1 (October 2011): 30–43, https://dx.doi.org/10.1111%2Fj.1749-6632.2011.06201.x.

5. Johan Y. Y. Ng et al., "Self-Determination Theory Applied to Health Contexts: A Meta-Analysis," *Perspectives on Psychological Science* 7, no. 4 (July 2012): 325–40, https://doi .org/10.1177%2F1745691612447309.

6. Edwin A. Locke and Gary P. Latham, "Building a Practically Useful Theory of Goal Setting and Task Motivation: A 35-Year Odyssey," *American Psychologist* 57, no. 9 (2002): 705–17, https://psycnet.apa.org/doi/10.1037/0003-066X.57.9.705.

7. E. T. Berkman, "The Neuroscience of Goals and Behavior Change," *Consulting Psychology Journal: Practice and Research* 70, no. 1 (2018): 28–44, https://dx.doi.org /10.1037%2Fcpb0000094.

8. Edwin A. Locke and Gary P. Latham, eds., *New Developments in Goal Setting and Task Performance* (New York: Routledge, 2012).

9. Osahon Ogbeiwi, "Why Written Objectives Need to Be Really SMART," *British Journal of Healthcare Management* 23, no. 7 (July 2017), http://dx.doi.org/10.12968/bjhc.2017.23.7.324; and K. Blaine Lawlor, "Smart Goals: How the Application of Smart Goals Can Contribute to Achievement of Student Learning Outcomes," *Developments in Business Simulation and Experiential Learning* 39 (2012): 259–67, https://journals.tdl.org/absel/index.php/absel/article/view/90.

10. Locke and Latham, "Building a Practically Useful Theory of Goal Setting and Task Motivation."

11. Heather Behr et al., "How Do Emotions during Goal Pursuit in Weight Change over Time? Retrospective Computational Text Analysis of Goal Setting and Striving Conversations with a Coach during a Mobile Weight Loss Program," *International Journal of Environmental Research and Public Health* 18, no. 12 (2021): 6600, https://www.mdpi.com/1660-4601/18/12/6600.

12. Michaéla C. Schippers et al., "Writing about Personal Goals and Plans Regardless of Goal Type Boosts Academic Performance," *Contemporary Educational Psychology* 60 (January 2020), https://doi.org/10.1016/j.cedpsych.2019.101823.

13. Karishma Chhabria et al., "The Assessment of Supportive Accountability in Adults Seeking Obesity Treatment: Psychometric Validation Study," *Journal of Medical Internet Research* 22, no. 7 (July 2020): e17967, https://dx.doi.org/10.2196%2F17967.

14. Elizabeth A. Seeley and Wendi L. Gardner, "Succeeding at Self-Control through a Focus on Others: The Roles of Social Practice and Accountability in Self-Regulation," in K. D. Vohs and E. J. Finkel, eds., *Self and Relationships: Connecting Intrapersonal and Interpersonal Processes* (New York: Guilford Press, 2006), 407–25, https://psycnet.apa.org/record/2006-04109-020.

15. Aline D. Masuda et al., "The Role of a Vivid and Challenging Personal Vision in Goal Hierarchies," *Journal of Psychology: Interdisciplinary and Applied* 144, no. 3 (2010): 221–42, https://doi.org/10.1080/00223980903472235.

16. Tobias Kalenscher and Cyriel M. A. Pennartz, "Is a Bird in the Hand Worth Two in the Future? The Neuroeconomics of Intertemporal Decision-Making," *Progress in Neurobiology* 84, no. 3 (March 2008): 284–315, https://doi.org/10.1016/j.pneurobio.2007.11.004.

17. Berkman, "The Neuroscience of Goals and Behavior Change."

18. K. Fujita et al., "Construal Levels and Self-Control," *Journal of Personality and Social Psychology* 90, no. 3 (2006): 351–67, https://dx.doi.org/10.1037%2F0022-3514.90.3.351.

Chapter 3:
Habit Formation and Habit Change

1. Roel C. J. Hermans et al., "Mimicry of Food Intake: The Dynamic Interplay between Eating Companions," *PLOS ONE* 7, no. 2 (February 2012): e31027, https://doi.org/10.1371/journal.pone.0031027; and Suzanne Higgs and Jason Thomas, "Social Influences on Eating," *Current Opinion in Behavioral Sciences* 9 (June 2016): 1–6, https://doi.org/10.1016/j.cobeha.2015.10.005.

2. Tanya L. Chartrand and John A. Bargh, "The Chameleon Effect: The Perception-Behavior Link and Social Interaction," *Journal of Personality and Social Psychology* 76, no. 6 (1999): 893–910, https://faculty.fuqua.duke.edu/~tlc10/bio/TLC_articles/1999/Chartrand_Bargh_1999.pdf.

3. Oliver Genschow et al., "Mimicking and Anticipating Others' Actions Is Linked to Social Information Processing," *PLOS ONE* 13, no. 3 (March 2018): e0193743, https://dx.doi.org/10.1371%2Fjournal.pone.0193743.

4. Morten L. Kringelbach and Kent C. Berridge, "The Neuroscience of Happiness and Pleasure," *Social Research (New York)* 77, no. 2 (Summer 2010): 659–78, https://www.ncbi.nlm.nih.gov/pmc/articles/PMC3008658/.

5. R. An and J. McCaffrey, "Plain Water Consumption in Relation to Energy Intake and Diet Quality among US Adults, 2005–2012," *Journal of Human Nutrition and Dietetics* 29, no. 5 (October 2016): 624–32, https://doi.org/10.1111/jhn.12368.

Chapter 4:
Face-to-Face with Food

1. Michael Pollan, *In Defense of Food: An Eater's Manifesto* (New York: Penguin Books, 2009).

2. Daniela Martini et al., "Ultra-Processed Foods and Nutritional Dietary Profile: A Meta-Analysis of Nationally Representative Samples," *Nutrients* 13, no. 10 (2021), https://dx.doi.org/10.3390%2Fnu13103390; and Bernard Srour et al., "Ultra-Processed Food Intake and Risk of Cardiovascular Disease: Prospective Cohort Study," *British Medical Journal* 365 (2019): l1451, https://www.bmj.com/content/365/bmj.l1451.

3. Michael Via, "The Malnutrition of Obesity: Micronutrient Deficiencies That Promote Diabetes," *International Scholarly Research Notices* 2012 (2012), https://dx.doi.org/10.5402%2F2012%2F103472.

4. Noom, "Calorie Goals at Noom: Always a Work in Progress," Noom.com blog, March 2, 2022, https://web.noom.com/blog/in-the-news/calorie-goals-at-noom/; and Rhiannon Berry, Aikaterini Kassavou, and Stephen Sutton, "Does Self-Monitoring Diet and Physical Activity Behaviors Using Digital Technology Support Adults with Obesity or Overweight to Lose Weight? A Systematic Literature Review with Meta-Analysis," *Obesity Reviews* 22, no. 10 (October 2021): e13306, https://doi.org/10.1111/obr.13306.

5. Scott Howell and Richard Kones, "'Calories in, Calories out' and Macronutrient Intake: The Hope, Hype, and Science of Calories," *American Journal of Physiology—Endocrinology and Metabolism* 313 (2017): e608–12, https://journals.physiology.org/doi/pdf/10.1152/ajpendo.00156.2017.

6. "Lettuce, Iceberg (Includes Crisphead Types), Raw," US Department of Agriculture, Agricultural Research Service, April 1, 2019, https://fdc.nal.usda.gov/fdc-app.html#/food -details/169248/nutrients; and "Kale, Raw," US Department of Agriculture, Agricultural Research Service, April 1, 2019, https://fdc.nal.usda.gov/fdc-app.html#/food-details/323505 /nutrients.

7. Fiona McKiernan, Jenny A. Houchins, and Richard D. Mattes, "Relationships between Human Thirst, Hunger, Drinking, and Feeding," *Physiology & Behavior* 94, no. 5 (August 2008): 700–708, https://dx.doi.org/10.1016%2Fj.physbeh.2008.04.007.

8. Barry M. Popkin, Kristen E. D'Anci, and Irwin H. Rosenberg, "Water, Hydration, and Health," *Nutrition Reviews* 68, no. 8 (August 2010): 439–58, https://dx.doi.org/10.1111%2Fj.1753- 4887.2010.00304.x; and DeAnn Liska et al., "Narrative Review of Hydration and Selected Health Outcomes in the General Population," *Nutrients* 11, no. 1 (2019): 70, https://dx.doi .org/10.3390%2Fnu11010070.

9. Nita G. Forouhi et al., "Dietary Fat and Cardiometabolic Health: Evidence, Controversies, and Consensus for Guidance," *British Medical Journal* 361 (2018), https://dx.doi.org/10.1136%2Fbmj .k2139.

10. J. A. Nettleton et al., "Saturated Fat Consumption and Risk of Coronary Heart Disease and Ischemic Stroke: A Science Update," *Annals of Nutrition and Metabolism* 70, no. 1 (April 2017): 26–33, https://dx.doi.org/10.1159%2F000455681.

11. Patty W. Siri-Tarino et al., "Meta-Analysis of Prospective Cohort Studies Evaluating the Association of Saturated Fat with Cardiovascular Disease," *American Journal of Clinical Nutrition* 91, no. 3 (March 2010): 535–46, https://doi.org/10.3945/ajcn .2009.27725.

12. William Raphael and Lorraine M. Sordillo, "Dietary Polyunsaturated Fatty Acids and Inflammation: The Role of Phospholipid Biosynthesis," *International Journal of Molecular Sciences* 14, no. 10 (2013): 21167–88, https://dx.doi.org/10.3390 %2Fijms141021167.

13. Mohammad Perwaiz Iqbal, "Trans Fatty Acids—A Risk Factor for Cardiovascular Disease," *Pakistan Journal of Medical Sciences* 30, no. 1 (January–February 2014): 194–97, https://www.ncbi.nlm.nih.gov/pmc/articles/PMC3955571/.

14. Yangbo Sun et al., "Association of Fried Food Consumption with All Cause, Cardiovascular, and Cancer Mortality: Prospective Cohort Study," *British Medical Journal* 364 (2019), https://dx.doi.org/10.1136%2Fbmj.k5420.

15. Ann G. Liu et al., "A Healthy Approach to Dietary Fats: Understanding the Science and Taking Action to Reduce Consumer Confusion," *Nutrition Journal* 16, no. 53 (2017), https://dx.doi.org/10.1186%2Fs12937-017-0271-4.

16. Patty W. Siri-Tarino et al., "Saturated Fatty Acids and Risk of Coronary Heart Disease: Modulation by Replacement Nutrients," *Current Atherosclerosis Reports* 12, no. 6 (2010): 384–90, https://www.ncbi.nlm.nih.gov/pmc/articles/PMC2943062/.

17. Hidekatsu Yanai et al., "An Improvement of Cardiovascular Risk Factors by Omega-3 Polyunsaturated Fatty Acids," *Journal of Clinical Medicine Research* 10, no. 4 (2018): 281–89, https://dx.doi.org/10.14740%2Fjocmr3362w.

18. Liu et al., "A Healthy Approach to Dietary Fats."

19. Arne Astrup, MD, DMSc, et al., "Saturated Fats and Health: A Reassessment and Proposal for Food-Based Recommendations: *JACC* State-of-the-Art Review," *Journal of the American College of Cardiology* 76, no. 7 (August 2020): 844–57, https://doi.org/10.1016/j.jacc.2020.05.077.

20. Kevin D. Hall et al., "Effect of a Plant-Based, Low-Fat Diet versus an Animal-Based, Ketogenic Diet on Ad Libitum Energy Intake," *Nature Medicine* 27 (2021): 344–53, https://doi.org/10.1038/s41591-020-01209-1; Tian Hu et al., "Effects of Low-Carbohydrate Diets versus Low-Fat Diets on Metabolic Risk Factors: A Meta-Analysis of Randomized Controlled Clinical Trials," *American Journal of Epidemiology* 176, supplement 7 (October 2012): s44–s54, https://dx.doi.org/10.1093%2Faje%2Fkws264; and Nadia Mansoor et al., "Effects of Low-Carbohydrate Diets v. Low-Fat Diets on Body

Weight and Cardiovascular Risk Factors: A Meta-Analysis of Randomised Controlled Trials," *British Journal of Nutrition* 115, no. 3 (February 2016): 466–79, https://pubmed.ncbi.nlm.nih.gov/26768850/.

21.   Charu Gupta and Dhan Prakash, "Phytonutrients as Therapeutic Agents," *Journal of Complementary and Integrative Medicine* 11, no. 3 (2014), https://doi.org/10.1515/jcim-2013-0021.

22.   Christopher D. Gardner, PhD, et al., "Effect of Low-Fat vs. Low-Carbohydrate Diet on 12-Month Weight Loss in Overweight Adults and the Association with Genotype Pattern or Insulin Secretion: The DIETFITS Randomized Clinical Trial," *Journal of the American Medical Association* 319, no. 7 (2018): 667–79, https://doi.org/10.1001/jama.2018.0245; Kelly A. Meckling, Caitriona O'Sullivan, and Dayna Saari, "Comparison of a Low-Fat Diet to a Low-Carbohydrate Diet on Weight Loss, Body Composition, and Risk Factors for Diabetes and Cardiovascular Disease in Free-Living, Overweight Men and Women," *Journal of Clinical Endocrinology & Metabolism* 89, no. 6 (June 2004): 2717–23, https://doi.org/10.1210/jc.2003-031606; and Hall et al., "Effect of a Plant-Based, Low-Fat Diet versus an Animal-Based, Ketogenic Diet on Ad Libitum Energy Intake."

23.   Douglas Paddon-Jones et al., "Protein, Weight Management, and Satiety," *American Journal of Clinical Nutrition* 87, no. 5 (May 2008): 1558s–61s, https://doi.org/10.1093/ajcn/87.5.1558S.

24.   Róbert Agócs, Dániel Sugár, and Attila J. Szabó, "Is Too Much Salt Harmful? Yes," *Pediatric Nephrology* 35 (2020): 1777–85, https://dx.doi.org/10.1007%2Fs00467-019-04387-4.

25.   Jingxuan Quek et al., "The Association of Plant-Based Diet with Cardiovascular Disease and Mortality: A Meta-Analysis and Systematic Review of Prospect Cohort Studies," *Frontiers in Cardiovascular Medicine* 8 (2021), https://doi.org/10.3389/fcvm.2021.756810.

26.   Yessenia Tantamango-Bartley et al., "Vegetarian Diets and the Incidence of Cancer in a Low-Risk Population," *Cancer Epidemiology, Biomarkers & Prevention* 22, no. 2 (February 2013): 286–94, https://dx.doi.org/10.1158%2F1055-9965.EPI-12-1060; and Somaye Rigi et al., "The Association between

Plant-Based Dietary Patterns and Risk of Breast Cancer: A Case-Control Study," *Scientific Reports* 11, no. 3391 (2021), https://www.nature.com/articles/s41598-021-82659-6.

27. Anna Roszkowska et al., "Non-Celiac Gluten Sensitivity: A Review," *Medicina* 55, no. 6 (2019): 222, https://dx.doi.org/10.3390%2Fmedicina55060222.

28. "Best Diets Overall 2022," *U.S. News & World Report*, 2022, https://health.usnews.com/best-diet/best-diets-overall.

29. Hu et al., "Effects of Low-Carbohydrate Diets versus Low-Fat Diets on Metabolic Risk Factors."

30. Frederick F. Samaha, MD, et al., "A Low-Carbohydrate as Compared with a Low-Fat Diet in Severe Obesity," *New England Journal of Medicine* 348 (2003): 2074–81, https://doi.org/10.1056/nejmoa022637.

31. Nassib Bezerra Bueno et al., "Very-Low-Carbohydrate Ketogenic Diet *v.* Low-Fat Diet for Long-Term Weight Loss: A Meta-Analysis of Randomised Controlled Trials," *British Journal of Nutrition* 110, no. 7 (2013), https://doi.org/10.1017/s0007114513000548.

32. Antonio Paoli, "Ketogenic Diet for Obesity: Friend or Foe?" *International Journal of Environmental Research and Public Health* 11, no. 2 (2014): 2092–107, https://dx.doi.org/10.3390%2Fijerph110202092.

33. Ruth E. Patterson, PhD, et al., "Intermittent Fasting and Human Metabolic Health," *Journal of the Academy of Nutrition and Dietetics* 115, no. 8 (August 2015): 1203–12, https://dx.doi.org/10.1016%2Fj.jand.2015.02.018.

Chapter 5:

The Psychology of Eating

1. J. H. Flavell and H. M. Wellman, "Metamemory," in Robert V. Kail and John W. Hagen, eds., *Perspectives on the Development*

of Memory and Cognition (Hillsdale, NJ: L. Erlbaum Associates, 1977), 3–34; and Elisabeth Norman et al., "Metacognition in Psychology," *Review of General Psychology* 23, no. 4 (October 2019): 403–24, https://journals.sagepub.com/doi/abs/10.1177/1089268019883821?journalCode=rgpa.

2. Lucia Tecuta et al., "Do Metacognitions Mediate the Relationship between Irrational Beliefs, Eating Disorder Symptoms and Cognitive Reappraisal?" *Psychotherapy Research* 31, no. 4 (2021): 1–10, https://www.tandfonline.com/doi/abs/10.1080/10503307.2020.1831098?journalCode=tpsr20.

3. Jamie Hartmann-Boyce et al., "Experiences of Reframing during Self-Directed Weight Loss and Weight Loss Maintenance: Systematic Review of Qualitative Studies," *Applied Psychology: Health and Well-Being* 10, no. 2 (July 2018): 309–29, https://pubmed.ncbi.nlm.nih.gov/29856139/; and Eli Natvik et al., "An Experientially Derived Model of Flexible and Intentional Actions for Weight Loss Maintenance after Severe Obesity," *Frontiers in Psychology* 10 (2019): 2503, https://www.ncbi.nlm.nih.gov/pmc/articles/PMC6863797/.

4. Deborah R. Wahl et al., "Healthy Food Choices Are Happy Food Choices: Evidence from a Real-Life Sample Using Smartphone-Based Assessments," *Scientific Reports* 7, no. 17069 (2017), https://www.nature.com/articles/s41598-017-17262-9.

5. Anton J. M. Dijker, "Moderate Eating with Pleasure and without Effort: Toward Understanding the Underlying Psychological Mechanisms," *Health Psychology Open* 6, no. 2 (July 2019), https://dx.doi.org/10.1177%2F2055102919889883.

6. Vanessa Juth et al., "Understanding the Utility of Emotional Approach Coping: Evidence from a Laboratory Stressor and Daily Life," *Anxiety, Stress & Coping* 28, no. 1 (2015): 50–70, https://doi.org/10.1080/10615806.2014.921912.

7. Hasida Ben-Zur, "Emotion-Focused Coping," in Virgil Zeigler-Hill and Todd K. Shackelford, eds., *Encyclopedia of Personality and Individual Differences* (Springer, 2020), 1343–45, https://doi.org/10.1007/978-3-319-24612-3_512.

8. Stanislava Popov, Jelena Sokić, and Dušan Stupar, "Activity Matters: Physical Exercise and Stress Coping during the 2020

COVID-19 State of Emergency," *Psihologija* (2021), DOI: 10.2298/PSI200804002P.

9. Michael J. Morris, Elisa S. Na, and Alan Kim Johnson, "Salt Craving: The Psychobiology of Pathogenic Sodium Intake," *Physiology & Behavior* 94, no. 5 (August 2008): 709–21, https://dx.doi.org/10.1016%2Fj.physbeh.2008.04.008.

10. Nicole M. Avena, Pedro Rada, and Bartley G. Hoebel, "Evidence for Sugar Addiction: Behavioral and Neurochemical Effects of Intermittent, Excessive Sugar Intake," *Neuroscience & Biobehavioral Reviews* 32, no. 1 (2008): 20–39, https://dx.doi.org/10.1016%2Fj.neubiorev.2007.04.019.

11. Meule, "The Psychology of Food Cravings."

12. Amy Taetzsch et al., "Food Cravings: Associations with Dietary Intake and Metabolic Health," *Appetite* 152 (September 2020): 104711, https://doi.org/10.1016/j.appet.2020.104711.

13. L. Christensen and L. Pettijohn, "Mood and Carbohydrate Cravings," *Appetite* 36, no. 2 (April 2001): 137–45, https://doi.org/10.1006/appe.2001.0390.

14. Dylan D. Wagner et al., "Inducing Negative Affect Increases the Reward Value of Appetizing Foods in Dieters," *Journal of Cognitive Neuroscience* 24, no. 7 (July 2012): 1625–33, https://dx.doi.org/10.1162%2Fjocn_a_00238.

15. Alyssa Lundahl and Timothy D. Nelson, "Sleep and Food Intake: A Multisystem Review of Mechanisms in Children and Adults," *Journal of Health Psychology* 20, no. 6 (2015): 794–805, https://journals.sagepub.com/doi/abs/10.1177/1359105315573427.

16. Chia-Lun Yang, Jerry Schnepp, and Robin M. Tucker, "Increased Hunger, Food Cravings, Food Reward, and Portion Size Selection after Sleep Curtailment in Women without Obesity," *Nutrients* 11, no. 3 (2019): 663, https://dx.doi.org/10.3390%2Fnu11030663.

17. Popov, Sokić, and Stupar, "Activity Matters."

18. Jessica Bullins et al., "Drive for Consumption, Craving, and Connectivity in the Visual Cortex during the Imagery of Desired

Food," *Frontiers in Aging Neuroscience* 5 (2013), https://doi
.org/10.3389/fnagi.2013.00077.

19. I. Wolz et al., "Subjective Craving and Event-Related Brain
    Response to Olfactory and Visual Chocolate Cues in Binge-Eating
    and Healthy Individuals," *Scientific Reports* 7, no. 41736 (2017),
    https://www.nature.com/articles/srep41736.

20. Marcia Levin Pelchat et al., "Images of Desire: Food-Craving
    Activation during fMRI," *NeuroImage* 23, no. 4 (December 2004):
    1486–93, https://doi.org/10.1016/j.neuroimage.2004.08.023.

21. Rebecca G. Boswell and Hedy Kober, "Food Cue Reactivity
    and Craving Predict Eating and Weight Gain: A Meta-Analytic
    Review," *Obesity Reviews* 17, no. 2 (February 2016): 159–77,
    https://pubmed.ncbi.nlm.nih.gov/26644270/.

22. Ibid.

23. Mike Keesman et al., "Mindfulness Reduces Reactivity to Food
    Cues: Underlying Mechanisms and Applications in Daily Life,"
    Current Addiction Reports 4 (2017): 151–57, https://dx.doi.org
    /10.1007%2Fs40429-017-0134-2.

24. Julien Lacaille et al., "The Effects of Three Mindfulness Skills on
    Chocolate Cravings," *Appetite* 76 (May 2014): 101–12, https://
    doi.org/10.1016/j.appet.2014.01.072.

25. Clear, *Atomic Habits*.

26. Tracy Epton et al., "The Impact of Self-Affirmation on Health-
    Behavior Change: A Meta-Analysis," *Health Psychology* 34,
    no. 3 (March 2015): 187–96, https://pubmed.ncbi.nlm.nih.gov
    /25133846/.

27. John W. Apolzan et al., "Frequency of Consuming Foods Predicts
    Changes in Cravings for Those Foods during Weight Loss: The
    POUNDS Lost Study," *Obesity* 25, no. 8 (August 2017): 1343–48,
    https://dx.doi.org/10.1002%2Foby.21895.

28. The Noom Satiety Scale was inspired by the Magnitude
    Scale of Perceived Satiety; see Armand V. Cardello et al.,
    "Development and Testing of a Labeled Magnitude Scale of

Perceived Satiety," *Appetite* 44, no. 1 (February 2005): 1–13, https://doi.org/10.1016/j.appet.2004.05.007.

29. Kirsi-Marja Zitting et al., "Human Resting Energy Expenditure Varies with Circadian Phase," *Current Biology* 28, no. 22 (November 2018): 3685–90, https://doi.org/10.1016/j.cub .2018.10.005; and Katharina Kessler et al., "The Effect of Diurnal Distribution of Carbohydrates and Fat on Glycaemic Control in Humans: A Randomized Controlled Trial," *Scientific Reports* 7, no. 44170 (2017), https://doi.org/10.1038/srep44170.

30. Masaki Takahashi et al., "Effects of Meal Timing on Postprandial Glucose Metabolism and Blood Metabolites in Healthy Adults," *Nutrients* 10, no. 11 (2018): 1763, https://dx.doi.org/10.3390 %2Fnu10111763.

31. Amber W. Kinsey and Michael J. Ormsbee, "The Health Impact of Nighttime Eating: Old and New Perspectives," *Nutrients* 7, no. 4 (2015): 2648–62, https://dx.doi.org/10.3390%2Fnu7042648.

32. Samuel L. Buckner, Paul D. Loprinzi, and Jeremy P. Loenneke, "Why Don't More People Eat Breakfast? A Biological Perspective," *American Journal of Clinical Nutrition* 103, no. 6 (June 2016): 1555–56, https://doi.org/10.3945/ajcn.116.132837.

33. M. D. Klok, S. Jakobsdottir, and M. L. Drent, "The Role of Leptin and Ghrelin in the Regulation of Food Intake and Body Weight in Humans: A Review," *Obesity Reviews* 8, no. 1 (January 2007): 21–34, https://doi.org/10.1111/j.1467-789X.2006.00270.x.

34. M. Sakurai et al., "Skipping Breakfast and 5-Year Changes in Body Mass Index and Waist Circumference in Japanese Men and Women," *Obesity Science and Practice* 3, no. 2 (June 2017): 162–70, https://dx.doi.org/10.1002%2Fosp4.106; and Leila Azadbakht, PhD, et al., "Breakfast Eating Pattern and Its Association with Dietary Quality Indices and Anthropometric Measurements in Young Women in Isfahan," *Nutrition* 29, no. 2 (February 2013): 420–25, https://doi.org/10.1016 /j.nut.2012.07.008.

35. S. Fanelli, C. Walls, and C. Taylor, "Skipping Breakfast Is Associated with Nutrient Gaps and Poorer Diet Quality among Adults in the United States," *Proceedings of the Nutrition*

Society 80, no. OCE1 (April 2021), https://doi.org/10.1017 /S0029665121000495.

36. Ibid.

37. James A. Betts et al., "The Causal Role of Breakfast in Energy Balance and Health: A Randomized Controlled Trial in Lean Adults," *American Journal of Clinical Nutrition* 100, no. 2 (August 2014): 539–47, https://doi.org/10.3945/ajcn.114.083402.

38. Daniela Jakubowicz et al., "Meal Timing and Composition Influence Ghrelin Levels, Appetite Scores and Weight Loss Maintenance in Overweight and Obese Adults," *Steroids* 77, no. 4 (March 2012): 323–31, https://doi.org/10.1016 /j.steroids.2011.12.006.

39. Juliane Richter et al., "Twice as High Diet-Induced Thermogenesis after Breakfast vs. Dinner on High-Calorie as Well as Low-Calorie Meals," *Journal of Clinical Endocrinology & Metabolism* 105, no. 3 (March 2020): e211–21, https://doi.org/10.1210/clinem/dgz311.

40. Klaas R. Westerterp, "Diet Induced Thermogenesis," *Nutrition & Metabolism* 1, no. 5 (2004), https://dx.doi.org/10.1186 %2F1743-7075-1-5.

41. Antonio Paoli et al., "The Influence of Meal Frequency and Timing on Health in Humans: The Role of Fasting," *Nutrients* 11, no. 4 (2019): 719, https://dx.doi.org/10.3390%2Fnu11040719.

42. Barbara J. Rolls, "What Is the Role of Portion Control in Weight Management?" *International Journal of Obesity* 38 (2014): s1– s8, https://dx.doi.org/10.1038%2Fijo.2014.82.

43. Julia A. Ello-Martin, Jenny H. Ledikwe, and Barbara J. Rolls, "The Influence of Food Portion Size and Energy Density on Energy Intake: Implications for Weight Management," *American Journal of Clinical Nutrition* 82, no. 1 (July 2005): 236s–41s, https://doi.org/10.1093/ajcn/82.1.236s.

44. M. Peng, "How Does Plate Size Affect Estimated Satiation and Intake for Individuals in Normal-Weight and Overweight Groups?" *Obesity Science and Practice* 3, no. 3 (September 2017): 282–88, https://dx.doi.org/10.1002%2Fosp4.119.

45. Ibid.

46. Noa Zitron-Emanuel and Tzvi Ganel, "Food Deprivation Reduces the Susceptibility to Size-Contrast Illusions," *Appetite* 128 (September 2018): 138–44, https://doi.org/10.1016/j.appet.2018.06.006.

47. Zhiping Yu, Claudia Sealey-Potts, and Judith Rodriguez, "Dietary Self-Monitoring in Weight Management: Current Evidence on Efficacy and Adherence," *Journal of the Academy of Nutrition and Dietetics* 115, no. 12 (December 2015): 1934–38, https://www.jandonline.org/article/S2212-2672(15)00449-9/pdf.

48. Jack F. Hollis et al., "Weight Loss during the Intensive Intervention Phase of the Weight-Loss Maintenance Trial," *American Journal of Preventive Medicine* 35, no. 2 (August 2008): 118–26, https://doi.org/10.1016/j.amepre.2008.04.013.

49. Michele L. Patel et al., "Comparing Self-Monitoring Strategies for Weight Loss in a Smartphone App: Randomized Controlled Trial," *JMIR Mhealth Uhealth* 7, no. 2 (2019): e12209, https://doi.org/10.2196/12209.

50. Sang Ouk Chin et al., "Successful Weight Reduction and Maintenance by Using a Smartphone Application in Those with Overweight and Obesity," *Scientific Reports* 6, no. 34563 (2016), https://doi.org/10.1038/srep34563.

51. Andreas Michaelides et al., "Weight Loss Efficacy of a Novel Mobile Diabetes Prevention Program Delivery Platform with Human Coaching," *BMJ Open Diabetes Research & Care* 4, no. 1 (2016), https://doi.org/10.1136/bmjdrc-2016-000264.

52. Philip J. Tuso et al., "Nutritional Update for Physicians: Plant-Based Diets," *Permanente Journal* 17, no. 2 (Spring 2013): 61–66, https://pubmed.ncbi.nlm.nih.gov/23704846/.

53. C. Hauck and T. Ellrott, "Food Addiction: Addictive-Like Eating Behavior: The Current State of Research with the Yale Food Addiction Scale," *Ernaehrungs Umschau* 64, no. 6 (2017): 102–10.

54. Jae-Ho Yang and Bo-Kyeong Kim, "Guilt and the Consumption of Products with an Unhealthy Image," *Sustainability* 13, no. 21 (2021): 11953, https://www.mdpi.com/2071-1050/13/21/11953.

55. Vasanti S. Malik, Matthais B. Schulze, and Frank B. Hu, "Intake of Sugar-Sweetened Beverages and Weight Gain: A Systematic Review," *American Journal of Clinical Nutrition* 84, no. 2 (August 2006): 274–88, https://dx.doi.org/10.1093%2Fajcn%2F84.1.274.

56. Qing Yang, "Gain Weight by 'Going Diet'? Artificial Sweeteners and the Neurobiology of Sugar Cravings," *Yale Journal of Biology and Medicine* 83, no. 2 (June 2010): 101–8, https://www.ncbi.nlm.nih.gov/pmc/articles/PMC2892765/.

57. Ibid.

58. Katie C. Hootman et al., "Erythritol Is a Pentose-Phosphate Pathway Metabolite and Associated with Adiposity Gain in Young Adults," *Proceedings of the National Academy of Sciences of the United States of America* 114, no. 21 (May 2017): E4233–40, https://www.pnas.org/doi/10.1073/pnas.1620079114.

59. Michelle Pearlman, Jon Obert, and Lisa Casey, "The Association between Artificial Sweeteners and Obesity," *Current Gastroenterology Reports* 19, no. 64 (2017), https://link.springer.com/article/10.1007%2Fs11894-017-0602-9.

60. Janet M. Warren, Nicola Smith, and Margaret Ashwell, "A Structured Literature Review on the Role of Mindfulness, Mindful Eating and Intuitive Eating in Changing Eating Behaviours: Effectiveness and Associated Potential Mechanisms," *Nutrition Research Reviews* 30, no. 2 (December 2017): 272–83, https://pubmed.ncbi.nlm.nih.gov/28718396/.

Chapter 6:
Beyond Food

1. Robert Plomin et al., "Top 10 Replicated Findings from Behavioral Genetics," *Perspectives on Psychological Science* 11, no. 1 (January 2016): 3–23, https://dx.doi.org/10.1177%2F1745691615617439.

2. Stephen M. Rappaport, "Genetic Factors Are Not the Major Causes of Chronic Diseases," *PLOS ONE* 11, no. 4 (2016): e0154387, https://dx.doi.org/10.1371%2Fjournal.pone.0154387.

3. Dariush D. Farhud, "Impact of Lifestyle on Health," *Iranian Journal of Public Health* 44, no. 11 (November 2015): 1442–44, https://www.ncbi.nlm.nih.gov/pmc/articles/PMC4703222/.

4. Andrew B. Shreiner, John Y. Kao, and Vincent B. Young, "The Gut Microbiome in Health and in Disease," *Current Opinion in Gastroenterology* 31, no. 1 (January 2015): 69–75, https://dx.doi.org/10.1097%2FMOG.0000000000000139.

5. Saskia Heijnen et al., "Neuromodulation of Aerobic Exercise—A Review," *Frontiers in Psychology* 6 (2016), https://doi.org/10.3389/fpsyg.2015.01890.

6. E. E. Hill et al., "Exercise and Circulating Cortisol Levels: The Intensity Threshold Effect," *Journal of Endocrinological Investigation* 31 (2008): 587–91, https://doi.org/10.1007/bf03345606.

7. Hilla Sharon-David and Gershon Tenenbaum, "The Effectiveness of Exercise Interventions on Coping with Stress: Research Synthesis," *Studies in Sport Humanities* 22 (2017): 19–29, http://dx.doi.org/10.5604/01.3001.0012.6520.

8. Emma Childs and Harriet de Wit, "Regular Exercise Is Associated with Emotional Resilience to Acute Stress in Healthy Adults," *Frontiers in Physiology* 5 (2014), https://dx.doi.org/10.3389%2Ffphys.2014.00161.

9. Brett A. Dolezal et al., "Interrelationship between Sleep and Exercise: A Systematic Review," *Advances in Preventive Medicine* 2017 (2017), https://dx.doi.org/10.1155%2F2017%2F1364387.

10. Darren E. R. Warburton, Crystal Whitney Nicol, and Shannon S. D. Bredin, "Health Benefits of Physical Activity: The Evidence," *Canadian Medical Association Journal* 174, no. 6 (March 2006): 801–9, https://dx.doi.org/10.1503%2Fcmaj.051351.

11. Kristine Beaulieu et al., "Exercise Training Reduces Reward for High-Fat Food in Adults with Overweight/Obesity," *Medicine & Science in Sports & Exercise* 52, no. 4 (April 2020): 900–908, https://doi.org/10.1249/mss.0000000000002205.

12. Karen E. Foster-Schubert et al., "Effect of Diet and Exercise, Alone or Combined, on Weight and Body Composition in Overweight-to-

Obese Postmenopausal Women," *Obesity* 20, no. 8 (August 2012): 1628–38, https://dx.doi.org/10.1038%2Foby.2011.76.

13. Hadi Daneshmandi et al., "Adverse Effects of Prolonged Sitting Behavior on the General Health of Office Workers," *Journal of Lifestyle Medicine* 7 (2017): 69–75, https://dx.doi .org/10.15280%2Fjlm.2017.7.2.69.

14. Jaehyun Joo et al., "The Influence of 15-Week Exercise Training on Dietary Patterns among Young Adults," *International Journal of Obesity* 43 (2019): 1681–90, https://www.nature.com/articles /s41366-018-0299-3.

15. Rania A. Mekary et al., "Weight Training, Aerobic Physical Activities, and Long-Term Waist Circumference Change in Men," *Obesity* 23, no. 2 (February 2015): 461–67, https:// doi.org/10.1002/oby.20949; and Kathryn H. Schmitz et al., "Strength Training and Adiposity in Premenopausal Women: Strong, Healthy, and Empowered Study," *American Journal of Clinical Nutrition* 86, no. 3 (September 2007), https://doi .org/10.1093/ajcn/86.3.566.

16. Wayne L. Westcott, "Resistance Training Is Medicine: Effects of Strength Training on Health," *Current Sports Medicine Reports* 11, no. 4 (July/August 2012): 209–16, https://doi.org/10.1249 /jsr.0b013e31825dabb8.

17. Ibid.

18. Rebecca A. Seguin et al., "Strength Training Improves Body Image and Physical Activity Behaviors among Midlife and Older Rural Women," *Journal of Extension* 51, no. 4 (August 2013): 4FEA2, https://www.ncbi.nlm.nih.gov/pmc/articles /PMC4354895/.

19. M. Jay Polsgrove, Brandon M. Eggleston, and Roch J. Lockyer, "Impact of 10 Weeks of Yoga Practice on Flexibility and Balance of College Athletes," *International Journal of Yoga* 9, no. 1 (2016): 27–34, https://dx.doi.org/10.4103%2F0973-6131.171710.

20. M. Javnbakht, R. Hejazi Kenari, and M. Ghasemi, "Effects of Yoga on Depression and Anxiety of Women," *Complementary Therapies in Clinical Practice* 15, no. 2 (May 2009): 102–4,

https://doi.org/10.1016/j.ctcp.2009.01.003; Karen Pilkington et al., "Yoga for Depression: The Research Evidence," *Journal of Affective Disorders* 89, nos. 1–3 (December 2005): 13–24, https://doi.org/10.1016/j.jad.2005.08.013; Sat Bir S. Khalsa, "Treatment of Chronic Insomnia with Yoga: A Preliminary Study with Sleep-Wake Diaries," *Applied Psychophysiology and Biofeedback* 29 (2004): 269–78, https://doi.org/10.1007/s10484-004-0387-0; and Catherine Woodyard, "Exploring the Therapeutic Effects of Yoga and Its Ability to Increase Quality of Life," *International Journal of Yoga* 4, no. 2 (2011): 49–54, https://dx.doi.org/10.4103%2F0973-6131.85485.

21.　Phil Page, "Current Concepts in Muscle Stretching for Exercise and Rehabilitation," *International Journal of Sports Physical Therapy* 7, no. 1 (February 2012): 109–19, https://www.ncbi.nlm.nih.gov/pmc/articles/PMC3273886/#B1.

22.　Shigenori Ito, "High-Intensity Interval Training for Health Benefits and Care of Cardiac Diseases: The Key to an Efficient Exercise Protocol," *World Journal of Cardiology* 11, no. 7 (July 2019): 171–88, https://dx.doi.org/10.4330%2Fwjc.v11.i7.171.

23.　Romeo B. Batacan Jr. et al., "Effects of High-Intensity Interval Training on Cardiometabolic Health: A Systematic Review and Meta-Analysis of Intervention Studies," *British Journal of Sports Medicine* 51, no. 6 (2017), http://dx.doi.org/10.1136/bjsports-2015-095841.

24.　Karine Spiegel, PhD, et al., "Brief Communication: Sleep Curtailment in Healthy Young Men Is Associated with Decreased Leptin Levels, Elevated Ghrelin Levels, and Increased Hunger and Appetite," *Annals of Internal Medicine* (December 2004), https://doi.org/10.7326/0003-4819-141-11-200412070-00008.

25.　Stephanie M. Greer, Andrea N. Goldstein, and Matthew P. Walker, "The Impact of Sleep Deprivation on Food Desire in the Human Brain," *Nature Communications* 4, no. 2259 (2013), https://doi.org/10.1038/ncomms3259.

26.　Pleunie S. Hogenkamp et al., "Acute Sleep Deprivation Increases Portion Size and Affects Food Choice in Young Men," *Psychoneuroendocrinology* 38, no. 9 (September 2013): 1668–74, https://doi.org/10.1016/j.psyneuen.2013.01.012.

27. Olivia E. Knowles et al., "Inadequate Sleep and Muscle Strength: Implications for Resistance Training," *Journal of Science and Medicine in Sport* 21, no. 9 (September 2018): 959–68, https://doi.org/10.1016/j.jsams.2018.01.012.

28. Jonathon P. R. Scott, Lars R. McNaughton, and Remco C. J. Polman, "Effects of Sleep Deprivation and Exercise on Cognitive, Motor Performance and Mood," *Physiology & Behavior* 87, no. 2 (February 2006): 396–408, https://doi.org/10.1016/j.physbeh.2005.11.009.

29. Mindy Engle-Friedman, "The Effects of Sleep Loss on Capacity and Effort," *Sleep Science* 7, no. 4 (December 2014): 213–24, https://doi.org/10.1016/j.slsci.2014.11.001.

30. James A. Levine, MD, "Non-Exercise Activity Thermogenesis (NEAT)," *Best Practice & Research Clinical Endocrinology & Metabolism* 16, no. 4 (December 2002): 679–702, https://doi.org/10.1053/beem.2002.0227.

31. Jose Morales et al., "Stress and Autonomic Response to Sleep Deprivation in Medical Residents: A Comparative Cross-Sectional Study," *PLOS ONE* 14, no. 4 (2019): e0214858, https://dx.doi.org/10.1371%2Fjournal.pone.0214858.

32. Kazue Okamoto-Mizuno and Koh Mizuno, "Effects of Thermal Environment on Sleep and Circadian Rhythm," *Journal of Physiological Anthropology* 31, no. 14 (2012), https://dx.doi.org/10.1186%2F1880-6805-31-14.

33. Fredrik Valham, MD, et al., "Ambient Temperature and Obstructive Sleep Apnea: Effects on Sleep, Sleep Apnea, and Morning Alertness," *Sleep* 35, no. 4 (April 2012): 513–17, https://doi.org/10.5665/sleep.1736.

34. Leena Tähkämö, Timo Partonen, and Anu-Katriina Pesonen, "Systematic Review of Light Exposure Impact on Human Circadian Rhythm," *Journal of Biological and Medical Rhythm Research* 36, no. 2 (2019), https://doi.org/10.1080/07420528.2018.1527773.

35. Brianna Chu et al., "Physiology, Stress Reaction," *StatPearls* (2021), https://www.ncbi.nlm.nih.gov/books/NBK541120/.

36. Tarani Chandola, Eric Brunner, and Michael Marmot, "Chronic Stress at Work and the Metabolic Syndrome: Prospective Study," *British Medical Journal* 332 (2006), https://dx.doi.org/10.1136%2Fbmj.38693.435301.80.

37. Maayan Yitshak-Sade et al., "The Association between an Increase in Glucose Levels and Armed Conflict-Related Stress: A Population-Based Study," *Scientific Reports* 10, no. 1710 (2020), https://www.nature.com/articles/s41598-020-58679-z.

38. Chu et al., "Physiology, Stress Reaction"; and Agnese Mariotti, "The Effects of Chronic Stress on Health: New Insights into the Molecular Mechanisms of Brain-Body Communication," *Future Science* 1, no. 3 (2015), https://dx.doi.org/10.4155%2Ffso.15.21.

39. Janice K. Kiecolt-Glaser et al., "Daily Stressors, Past Depression, and Metabolic Responses to High-Fat Meals: A Novel Path to Obesity," *Biological Psychiatry* 77, no. 7 (April 2015): 653–60, https://doi.org/10.1016/j.biopsych.2014.05.018.

40. Ariana Chao et al., "Food Cravings Mediate the Relationship between Chronic Stress and Body Mass Index," *Journal of Health Psychology* 20, no. 6 (2015): 721–29, https://dx.doi.org/10.1177%2F1359105315573448.

41. Diane L. Rosenbaum and Kamila S. White, "The Role of Anxiety in Binge Eating Behavior: A Critical Examination of Theory and Empirical Literature," *Health Psychology Research* 1, no. 2 (2013), https://dx.doi.org/10.4081%2Fhpr.2013.e19.

42. Jared D. Martin et al., "Functionally Distinct Smiles Elicit Different Physiological Responses in an Evaluative Context," *Scientific Reports* 8, no. 3558 (2018), https://doi.org/10.1038/s41598-018-21536-1.

43. Kevin P. Madore, PhD, and Anthony D. Wagner, PhD, "Multicosts of Multitasking," *Cerebrum* 2019 (March–April 2019), https://www.ncbi.nlm.nih.gov/pmc/articles/PMC7075496/.

44. Joshua S. Rubinstein, David E. Meyer, and Jeffrey E. Evans, "Executive Control of Cognitive Processes in Task Switching," *Journal of Experimental Psychology: Human Perception and*

Performance 27, no. 4 (2001): 763–97, https://www.apa.org
/pubs/journals/releases/xhp274763.pdf.

45. Qingyi Huang et al., Linking What We Eat to Our Mood: A Review
of Diet, Dietary Antioxidants, and Depression," *Antioxidants*
8, no. 9 (2019), https://dx.doi.org/10.3390%2Fantiox8090376;
Janice K. Kiecolt-Glaser et al., "Omega-3 Supplementation
Lowers Inflammation and Anxiety in Medical Students: A
Randomized Controlled Trial," *Brain, Behavior, and Immunity*
25, no. 8 (November 2011): 1725–34, https://doi.org/10.1016/j
.bbi.2011.07.229; and Matthew R. Hilimire, Jordan E. DeVylder,
and Catherine A. Forestell, "Fermented Foods, Neuroticism,
and Social Anxiety: An Interaction Model," *Psychiatry Research*
228, no. 2 (August 2015): 203–8, https://doi.org/10.1016/j
.psychres.2015.04.023.

Chapter 7:

Mastering Motivation

1. Stefano I. Di Domenico and Richard M. Ryan, "The Emerging
Neuroscience of Intrinsic Motivation: A New Frontier in Self-
Determination Research," *Frontiers in Human Neuroscience* 11
(2017), https://dx.doi.org/10.3389%2Ffnhum.2017.00145.

2. James O. Prochaska and Wayne F. Velicer, "The Transtheoretical
Model of Health Behavior Change," *American Journal of Health
Promotion* 12, no. 1 (September 1997): 38–48, https://doi.org
/10.4278/0890-1171-12.1.38.

3. P. M. Gollwitzer, "Implementation Intentions: Strong Effects of
Simple Plans," *American Psychologist* 54, no. 7 (1999): 493–503,
http://dx.doi.org/10.1037/0003-066X.54.7.493.

4. Judy Cameron, Katherine M. Banko, and W. David Pierce,
"Pervasive Negative Effects of Rewards on Intrinsic Motivation:
The Myth Continues," *Behavior Analyst* 24 (2001): 1–44,
https://link.springer.com/article/10.1007%2FBF03392017.

5. Ibid.

6. Gerard H. Seijts, Gary P. Latham, and Meredith Woodwark, "Learning Goals: A Qualitative and Quantitative Review," in Edwin A. Locke and Gary P. Latham, eds., *New Developments in Goal Setting and Task Performance* (New York: Routledge, 2012).

7. Edwin A. Locke and Gary P. Latham, "The Development of Goal Setting Theory: A Half Century Retrospective," *Motivation Science* 5, no. 2 (2019): 93–105, https://www.decisionskills .com/uploads/5/1/6/0/5160560/locke_latham_2019_the _development_of_goal_setting_theory_50_years.pdf.

8. Dori M. Steinberg, PhD, RD, et al., "Weighing Every Day Matters: Daily Weighing Improves Weight Loss and Adoption of Weight Control Behaviors," *Journal of the Academy of Nutrition and Dietetics* 115, no. 4 (April 2015): 511–18, https://dx.doi .org/10.1016%2Fj.jand.2014.12.011; Jeffrey J. VanWormer et al., "The Impact of Regular Self-Weighing on Weight Management: A Systematic Literature Review," *International Journal of Behavioral Nutrition and Physical Activity* 5, no. 54 (2008), https://ijbnpa .biomedcentral.com/articles/10.1186/1479-5868-5-54; and Alberto Hernández-Reyes et al., "Effects of Self-Weighing during Weight Loss Treatment: A 6-Month Randomized Controlled Trial," *Frontiers in Psychology* 11 (2020), https://doi.org/10.3389 /fpsyg.2020.00397.

9. Kirk Plangger et al., "Little Rewards, Big Changes: Using Exercise Analytics to Motivate Sustainable Changes in Physical Activity," *Information & Management* 59, no. 5 (July 2022): 103216, http://dx.doi.org/10.1016/j.im.2019.103216.

10. Daniel Johnson et al., "Gamification for Health and Well-Being: A Systematic Review of the Literature," *Internet Interventions* 6 (November 2016): 89–106, https://doi.org/10.1016/j .invent.2016.10.002.

11. Dexter Louie, Karolina Brook, and Elizabeth Frates, "The Laughter Prescription: A Tool for Lifestyle Medicine," *American Journal of Lifestyle Medicine* 10, no. 4 (2014): 262–67, https:// dx.doi.org/10.1177%2F1559827614550279.

12. A. H. Maslow, "A Theory of Human Motivation," *Psychological Review* 50, no. 4 (1943): 370–96, https://doi.org/10.1037 %2Fh0054346.

13. Abraham H. Maslow, *Motivation and Personality* (New York: Harper & Row, 1970).

14. Douglas T. Kenrick et al., "Renovating the Pyramid of Needs: Contemporary Extensions Built upon Ancient Foundations," *Perspectives on Psychological Science* 5, no. 3 (2010): 292–314, https://dx.doi.org/10.1177%2F1745691610369469.

15. Kelly J. Bouxsein, Henry S. Roane, and Tara Harper, "Evaluating the Separate and Combined Effects of Positive and Negative Reinforcement on Task Compliance," *Journal of Applied Behavior Analysis* 44, no. 1 (Spring 2011): 175–79, https://dx.doi.org/10.1901%2Fjaba.2011.44-175.

16. Tiffany Kodak et al., "Further Examination of Factors That Influence Preference for Positive versus Negative Reinforcement," *Journal of Applied Behavior Analysis* 40, no. 1 (Spring 2007): 25–44, https://doi.org/10.1901/jaba.2007.151-05; and S. B. Cho et al., "Positive and Negative Reinforcement Are Differentially Associated with Alcohol Consumption as a Function of Alcohol Dependence," *Psychology of Addictive Behaviors* 33, no. 1 (2019): 58–68, https://psycnet.apa.org/doi/10.1037/adb0000436.

17. Michail Mantzios and Helen H. Egan, "On the Role of Self-Compassion and Self-Kindness in Weight Regulation and Health Behavior Change," *Frontiers in Psychology* 8 (2017), https://doi.org/10.3389/fpsyg.2017.00229.

18. Garriy Shteynberg and Adam D. Galinsky, "Implicit Coordination: Sharing Goals with Similar Others Intensifies Goal Pursuit," *Journal of Experimental Social Psychology* 47, no. 6 (November 2011): 1291–94, https://doi.org/10.1016/j.jesp.2011.04.012.

Chapter 8:
Thought Distortions

1. A. Vaish, T. Grossmann, and A. Woodward, "Not All Emotions Are Created Equal: The Negativity Bias in Social-Emotional

Development," *Psychological Bulletin* 134, no. 3 (2008): 383–403, https://dx.doi.org/10.1037%2F0033-2909.134.3.383.

2. Katerina Rnic, David J. A. Dozois, and Rod A. Martin, "Cognitive Distortions, Humor Styles, and Depression," *Europe's Journal of Psychology* 12, no. 3 (August 2016), https://dx.doi.org/10.5964 %2Fejop.v12i3.1118.

3. Ciro Conversano et al., "Optimism and Its Impact on Mental and Physical Well-Being," *Clinical Practice & Epidemiology in Mental Health* 6 (2010): 25–29, https://dx.doi.org/10.2174 %2F1745017901006010025.

4. Denise M. Matel-Anderson, Abir K. Bekhet, and Mauricio Garnier-Villarreal, "Mediating Effects of Positive Thinking and Social Support on Suicide Resilience," *Western Journal of Nursing Research* 41, no. 1 (January 2019): 25–41, https://do .org/10.1177%2F0193945918757988.

5. Matthew D. Lieberman et al., "Putting Feelings into Words: Affect Labeling Disrupts Amygdala Activity in Response to Affective Stimuli," *Psychological Science* 18, no. 5 (2006): 421–28, https://www.scn.ucla.edu/pdf/AL(2007).pdf.

6. Ellen Sinclair, Rona Hart, and Tim Lomas, "Can Positivity Be Counterproductive when Suffering Domestic Abuse? A Narrative Review," *International Journal of Wellbeing* 10, no. 1 (2020): 26–53, https://www.internationaljournalofwellbeing.org/index .php/ijow/article/view/754/843.

7. Allison S. Troy, Amanda J. Shallcross, and Iris B. Mauss, "A Person-by-Situation Approach to Emotion Regulation: Cognitive Reappraisal Can Either Help or Hurt, Depending on the Context," *Psychological Science* 24, no. 12 (December 2013): 2505–14, https://doi.org/10.1177/0956797613496434.

8. Susan Nolen-Hoeksema, Blair E. Wisco, and Sonja Lyubomirsky, "Rethinking Rumination," *Perspectives on Psychological Science* 3, no. 5 (September 2008): 400–424, https://doi.org/10.1111 %2Fj.1745-6924.2008.00088.x.

9. Dawn Querstret and Mark Cropley, "Assessing Treatments Used to Reduce Rumination and/or Worry: A Systematic Review,"

Clinical Psychology Review 33, no. 8 (December 2013): 996–1009, http://dx.doi.org/10.1016/j.cpr.2013.08.004.

10. Candace M. Raio et al., "Reappraisal—but Not Suppression—Tendencies Determine Negativity Bias after Laboratory and Real-World Stress Exposure," *Affective Science* 2 (2021): 455–67, https://dx.doi.org/10.1007%2Fs42761-021-00059-5.

11. Nora Görg et al., "Trauma-Related Emotions and Radical Acceptance in Dialectical Behavior Therapy for Posttraumatic Stress Disorder after Childhood Sexual Abuse," *Borderline Personality Disorder and Emotion Dysregulation* 4, no. 15 (2017), https://dx.doi.org/10.1186%2Fs40479-017-0065-5.

Chapter 9:
Miraculous Mindfulness

1. Shian-Ling Keng, Moria J. Smoski, and Clive J. Robins, "Effects of Mindfulness on Psychological Health: A Review of Empirical Studies," *Clinical Psychology Review* 31, no. 6 (August 2011): 1041–56, https://dx.doi.org/10.1016%2Fj.cpr.2011.04.006.

2. Antonio Crego et al., "Relationships between Mindfulness, Purpose in Life, Happiness, Anxiety, and Depression: Testing a Mediation Model in a Sample of Women," *International Journal of Environmental Research and Public Health* 18, no. 3 (2021): 925, https://dx.doi.org/10.3390%2Fijerph18030925.

3. Kandhasamy Sowndhararajan and Songmun Kim, "Influence of Fragrances on Human Psychophysiological Activity: With Special Reference to Human Electroencephalographic Response," *Scientia Pharmaceutica* 84, no. 4 (2016): 724–51, https://dx.doi.org/10.3390%2Fscipharm84040724.

4. Warren, Smith, and Ashwell, "A Structured Literature Review on the Role of Mindfulness, Mindful Eating, and Intuitive Eating in Changing Eating Behaviors."

5. Ibid.

6. Christine E. Cherpak, "Mindful Eating: A Review of How the Stress-Digestion-Mindfulness Triad May Modulate and Improve

Gastrointestinal and Digestive Function," *Integrative Medicine: A Clinician's Journal* 18, no. 4 (August 2019): 48–53, https://www.ncbi.nlm.nih.gov/pmc/articles/PMC7219460/.

7. Yong Zhu, PhD, and James H. Hollis, PhD, "Increasing the Number of Chews before Swallowing Reduces Meal Size in Normal-Weight, Overweight, and Obese Adults," *Journal of the Academy of Nutrition and Dietetics* 114, no. 6 (June 2014): 926–31, https://doi.org/10.1016/j.jand.2013.08.020.

8. Desleigh Gilbert and Jennifer Waltz, "Mindfulness and Health Behaviors," *Mindfulness* 1 (2010): 227–34, https://link.springer.com/article/10.1007%2Fs12671-010-0032-3.

9. Serhiy Y. Chumachenko et al., "Keeping Weight Off: Mindfulness-Based Stress Reduction Alters Amygdala Functional Connectivity during Weight Loss Maintenance in a Randomized Control Trial," *PLOS ONE* 16, no. 1 (2021): e0244847, https://doi.org/10.1371/journal.pone.0244847.

10. Sara W. Lazar et al., "Meditation Experience Is Associated with Increased Cortical Thickness," *Neuroreport* 16, no. 17 (November 2005): 1893–97, https://www.ncbi.nlm.nih.gov/pmc/articles/PMC1361002/.

11. Katherine L. Narr et al., "Relationships between IQ and Regional Cortical Gray Matter Thickness in Healthy Adults," *Cerebral Cortex* 17, no. 9 (September 2007): 2163–71, https://doi.org/10.1093/cercor/bhl125.

12. David R. Vago and David A. Silbersweig, "Self-Awareness, Self-Regulation, and Self-Transcendence (S-ART): A Framework for Understanding the Neurobiological Mechanisms of Mindfulness," *Frontiers in Human Neuroscience* 6 (2012), https://doi.org/10.3389/fnhum.2012.00296.

13. Kimberly C. Roberts and Sharon Danoff-Burg, "Mindfulness and Health Behaviors: Is Paying Attention Good for You?" *Journal of American College Health* 59, no. 3 (2010): 165–73, https://doi.org/10.1080/07448481.2010.484452.

Chapter 10:
What's Next?

1. John Spencer Ingels et al., "The Effect of Adherence to Dietary Tracking on Weight Loss: Using HLM to Model Weight Loss over Time," *Journal of Diabetes Research* 2017 (2017), https://dx.doi.org/10.1155%2F2017%2F6951495; VanWormer et al., "The Impact of Regular Self-Weighing on Weight Management"; Rena R. Wing and Suzanne Phelan, "Long-Term Weight Loss Maintenance," *American Journal of Clinical Nutrition* 82, no. 1 (July 2005): 222s–25s, https://doi.org/10.1093/ajcn/82.1.222S; Anna-Leena Vuorinen et al., "Frequency of Self-Weighing and Weight Change: Cohort Study with 10,000 Smart Scale Users," *Journal of Medical Internet Research* 23, no. 6 (June 2021): e25529, https://www.jmir.org/2021/6/e25529; and Yaguang Zheng et al., "Self-Weighing in Weight Management: A Systematic Literature Review," *Obesity* 23, no. 2 (February 2015): 256–65, https://doi.org/10.1002/oby.20946.

2. Troels Krarup Hansen et al., "Weight Loss Increases Circulating Levels of Ghrelin in Human Obesity," *Clinical Endocrinology* 56, no. 2 (February 2002): 203–6, https://doi.org/10.1046/j.0300-0664.2001.01456.x.

3. Rexford S. Ahima, "Revisiting Leptin's Role in Obesity and Weight Loss," *Journal of Clinical Investigation* 118, no. 7 (July 2008): 2380–83, https://dx.doi.org/10.1172%2FJCI36284.

4. "The National Weight Control Registry," National Weight Control Registry, http://www.nwcr.ws/.

5. Siao Mei Shick et al., "Persons Successful at Long-Term Weight Loss and Maintenance Continue to Consume a Low-Energy, Low-Fat Diet," *Journal of the Academy of Nutrition and Dietetics* 98, no. 4 (April 1998): 408–13, https://doi.org/10.1016/s0002-8223(98)00093-5.

6. Rene Dailey et al., "The Buddy Benefit: Increasing the Effectiveness of an Employee-Targeted Weight-Loss Program," *Journal of Health Communication* 23, no. 3 (2018), https://doi.org/10.1080/10810730.2018.1436622.

INDEX

ABOUT THE AUTHOR

NOOM is a consumer-first digital health platform that empowers its users to achieve holistic health outcomes through behavior change. Noom was founded in 2008 with a mission to help people everywhere lead healthier lives. Fueled by a powerful combination of technology, psychology, and human coaching, Noom is backed by more than a decade of user research and product development. Today, Noom's platform includes two core programs: Noom Weight for weight management and Noom Mood for stress management. Learn more by visiting noom.com.